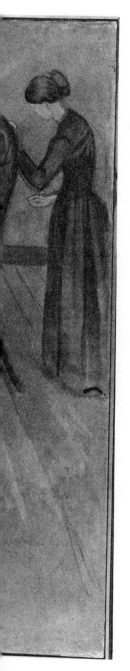

Fragments

on the

Deathwatch

Beacon Press

Boston

Louise Harmon

Beacon Press

25 Beacon Street

Boston, Massachusetts 02108-2892

www.beacon.org

Beacon Press books are published under the auspices of
the Unitarian Universalist Association of Congregations.

03 02 01 00 99 98   8 7 6 5 4 3 2 1

The text of this book was set in 12.5/14.5 Perpetua
with the commentary set in 9.5/14.5 Hoffmann Light.
The display typefaces are Beach Savage and Hoffmann Book.
Book design by Margaret McCutcheon Wagner.
Composition by Wilsted & Taylor Publishing Services.

Library of Congress Cataloging-in-Publication Data

Harmon, Louise.

Fragments on the deathwatch / Louise Harmon.

p. cm.

Includes bibliographical references and index.

ISBN 0-8070-4118-1 (cloth)

1. Death—Social aspects.   2. Death—Psychological aspects.

3. Right to die.   4. Terminal care.   1. Title.

HQ1073.H37 1998

306.9—dc21   97-36018

This book is dedicated to my father,

John E. Harmon, Jr.

—to his soul and to the trillium in the ravine

Contents

Fragments

on the

Deathwatch

1

Deathwatches

THE other night I saw a documentary on television about some elephants in Botswana. The herd was in trouble. Water was scarce, and the elephants were on the move, following the ancient paths of their ancestors. Seismic shifts and severe drought had drained the Savuti Channel, forcing thousands of buffalo, zebra, and elephants to trudge seventy miles north through the dust and searing heat to the banks of the Linyanti River.[1]

An elderly cow staggered behind the others, weakened from starvation, dehydration, and advanced age. Suddenly she slipped in the sand. The wind blew so fiercely across the hot, dry land that when she fell only a muffled cry could be heard over the white howl of air in motion. It was like watching a silent movie. Her legs sprawled and dangled; her parched body almost rolled over, propelled by her weight and the speed of her fall. Her head arched back; her trunk curled; her mouth opened wide in a protest of pain. But the sound of her body as it hit the ground could not be heard over the unrelenting wind. At least I could not hear it as I drank a cup of coffee and watched her die from my cozy kitchen on Long Island.

As she lay there panting on the ground, the narrator commented in his neutral male voice, the voice of science and reason, "They wait, clearly reluctant to leave her. In the blazing sun, she became dehydrated. Because the survival of the herd is more important than the life of an individual, the old cow is left to die—alone."[2]

Then, because the medium of film forces us to see the world through the eyes of another, I too, like the elephants, had to move on, following the herd as it crossed the wheat-colored land in search of food and water. And I too, like the elephants, wanted to stay with her. I did not want her to die alone.

Elephants attend the births and deaths of members of their species. When an elephant calf is born, some of the herd will encircle the mother, acting as midwives and sentries. When the calf is delivered, the attendants will trumpet loudly, swaying their bodies and flapping their ears. Then they will fondle and caress the dark, damp baby and help it to stand. After the celebration is over, a hush will descend upon the herd.[3] Perhaps the elephants fall silent out of respect for the new family; perhaps out of fatigue; perhaps out of wonder, if there is such a thing as elephant wonder. I see no reason why there should not be.

Certainly there is elephant grief, particularly when an elephant calf dies. Sometimes the mother cannot let go. There is an account of an African cow who carried her dead baby around for several days, putting the lifeless calf down to eat or drink, then picking it up again when she moved on.[4] In captivity, elephants have also been known to mourn the death of their mates. Lakshmi, an elderly circus cow, was inconsolable after the death of her longtime mate. She continued to walk about the empty post of her dead companion and stopped eating altogether. Within two weeks, Lakshmi was dead, presumably of a broken heart.[5]

At the end of life, an elephant rarely dies alone. The same research team that filmed the fallen cow in Botswana also documented the death of an old bull. After the elephant had fallen, the other members of the herd huddled around him. Four hours later, when he died, they approached his body in two and threes, "sweeping their trunks slowly over him, not touching him for the most part but maintaining an inch of distance between his skin and the moist tips of their trunks. The ritual was more impressive for its silence. Not a rumble was uttered, and no scraping of skin or sand broke the afternoon stillness."[6] There is beauty in their gestures, in their shared silence, in the very fact that they attend.

WHEN I first learned about the complex social behavior of whales and dolphins, it occurred to me that, in many ways, these cetaceans were just like wet elephants.[7] Elephants, whales, and dolphins all exhibit what animal behaviorists call "epimeletic" behavior, the succorant behavior of the adult members of a group toward another adult that is in distress or dying.[8]

There are many documented instances of elephants helping a member of the herd who is in distress. In one account, an elephant bull, wounded by a gunshot, fell to the ground. Three adult male companions "closed in on him one on either side and one behind, and they just boosted him on to his feet and, in that formation, supporting him on either side, set off, wheeling gradually round to the left and back to the forest."[9]

Cetaceans engage in similar kinds of epimeletic behavior. One is called "standing by," although the old whalers used more nautical terms such as "heaving to" or "bringing to." When a cetacean companion is distressed or wounded, the entire school remains close, or "stands by," even at the risk of danger.[10] In another kind of epimeletic behavior, called "excitement," the succorants approach the distressed animal and make a display of extreme agitation, sometimes even attempting a rescue. Sperm whales, for example, have been known to attack whale boats that have harpooned a member of their school, or to push an injured animal away from a source of danger.[11]

Another kind of cetacean epimeletic behavior is called "supporting behavior." Cetaceans exhibit supporting behavior when a weakened animal is unable to break surface; members of the group will push him towards the light and air so that he can breathe. Supporting a distressed adult companion may imitate maternal behavior toward a newborn calf. As soon as a calf is born, the mother pushes it to the surface to draw its first breath. Her adult companions, typically females known as "aunts," will often assist. Much like elephants, the group seems to take an active interest in its newly minted member.[12]

What motivates cetaceans to care for one another? Animal behaviorists do not agree. Some argue that epimeletic behavior is nothing more than an instinctive reaction—a matter of ancient chemistry.[13] Others believe that whales and dolphins are capable of altruism,[14] but differ on the conditions for its occurrence. Some argue that epimeletic behavior may be attributable to kin selection; others counter that the cetaceans' fluid social structure does not allow for the formation of stable schools of related individuals.[15] Some believe that expectations of reciprocity underlie epimeletic behavior—the aquatic version of Hobbes's explanation of our motivation for being kind to others.ᶜ Others worry about whether cetaceans can recognize each other, a necessary condition of reciprocity.[16] All theorists, regardless of their point of view, warn of the dangers of anthropomorphism.

I am not certain that I understand the sin of anthropomorphism.ᶜᶜ Am I supposed not to argue that whales and dolphins are like human beings, or am I supposed not to argue that human beings are like

---

ᶜ Alasdair MacIntyre relates a famous story about Thomas Hobbes:

Aubrey has a story of how, outside St. Paul's Cathedral, an Anglican clergyman who had seen Hobbes give alms to a poor man tried to improve the occasion by asking of Hobbes (who was reputedly impious and atheistic) if he would have given the alms, had not Christ commanded it. Hobbes' reply was that he gave the alms because not only did it please the poor man, but it pleased him to see the poor man pleased. Thus Hobbes tries to exhibit his own behavior as consistent with his theory of motives, namely that human desires are such that they are all self-interested.[1]

ᶜᶜ Margaret C. Tavolga gives a typical warning:

One of the most deceptive, and therefore one of the most dangerous, pitfalls awaiting the observer of dolphins is reliance on anthropomorphism.... The observer is led to describe the behavior of the animal in human terms, and ascribe to the animal motives that he cannot be sure are actually there, as he is incapable of seeing inside the mind of the animal to determine its purposes. Some descriptions of dolphin behavior abound in statements of purpose that can properly be ascribed only to humans. It is sincerely to be hoped that such accounts, most of which are misleading and probably inaccurate, will not gain credence in the literature to the extent that they are believed implicitly by other workers in the field.[2]

whales and dolphins? Or is it just that I am not to confuse their intelligences, cetacean, and human, to take one for the other?

I am also not certain that it matters. Since I am not an animal behaviorist, I do not fall under the jurisdiction of their gods: I can probably commit the sin of anthropomorphism with impunity. Of course, I might be wrong about this. By virtue of my tenuous membership in the academy, I may be bound by a version of intellectual comity.[17] I have crossed the boundaries of my own competence, and when venturing into a foreign land I may have to submit to the authority of foreign deities.⟨⟨⟨

So perhaps I do sin, but the fact is I recognize the behavior of those elephants as they gather around a dying bull, sweeping their trunks over his parched body and facing his death with reverence. I recognize the behavior of those whales and dolphins as they nudge a floundering member of their school towards the air. It does not matter to me if you call the behavior human or if you call the behavior elephantine or cetacean. What matters to me is that I have seen the behavior before. I see something there that has meaning for me.

My father died last year.

HE was ninety-two pounds when he died. During those last few months, my mother was with him every day, to sit beside him, to read to him, to tune the radio to his favorite station, to dress his bed-

---

⟨⟨⟨ I am undoubtedly guilty of taking an anthropocentric approach to the study of animal behavior. Harry F. Harlow, a scholar of animal psychology, is unabashed about his commission of this variant of the sin of anthropomorphism:

> Throughout my entire academic life I had never suffered for research ideas, since I simply stole the research ideas from human studies or human problems. I always believed that I should never do anything with monkeys that would not have significance with man.... I firmly believe that one should never study problems in monkeys that cannot be solved in man. What direction my research might have taken had this not been true, I have no idea.[3]

sores, to remind the nurses to turn him over from side to side. He could not talk or see, but she thought he might be able to hear the music, the books, the words of love and affection.❮

I was far away. Inside the body they had both given me, another struggle was going on. As he was painfully pulling away, his granddaughter, curled up tightly inside of me, was moving onto shore. Because I was her vessel, I could not move. The seas were too turbulent. And so we were both bedbound, my father and I—each of us intent on an act of creation, a moment of definition, one at the beginning and the other at the end.

My father managed his mission before I could bring her to him. I am sorry he did not get to see those dark brown eyes, or to feel the cool alabaster of her skin. I love her all the more for the tentative way in which she arrived, but I will always regret that she kept me in my bed. That I was not able to sit beside him, read to him, tune the radio to his favorite station, or turn his fragile body from side to side.

I belonged there, inside that green curtain in the nursing home, with my mother, my brother, and my sister. I wanted to attend.

IN many ways, a dying human being is like any other dying animal: an organism in extremis. The body's task is winnowed down to the bare essentials: heartbeat and breath, heartbeat and breath. Maintaining homeostasis is all that matters. The mind—the thinking, ex-

---

❮ John LaPuma's research demonstrates the tenacity of our sense of hearing: "Extensive research on the auditory brain-stem function of comatose patients shows that the majority have normal brain-stem auditory evoked responses (BAERs), a recording of afferent nerve impulses, regardless of the level of coma."

Normal BAERs suggest that many comatose patients can actually hear. There are many anecdotal accounts of comatose patients who have recovered and can remember words of encouragement from doctors and family members.

pressive, remembering part of the human being—often withdraws, sacrificed on the crumbling altar of survival. There is a turning in toward the self, a curvature of the spine that directs the remaining life force towards the center. The knees of a dying human being are tucked up under the body. The arms are folded like a praying mantis, a caricature of mute supplication—and the petition is for safety. After the mind has gone, a primitive defensive reflex persists, instinctively protecting the body. It is more than just a metaphor: we literally do curl up and die.

This does not happen in isolation. A human being usually dies in the presence of others. Someone keeps vigil on his going out, a vigil known as the deathwatch. Originally the term "deathwatch" referred to a small beetle that makes a ticking sound that supposedly presaged death, but by the 1890s it had come to mean either the "guard set over a criminal before his execution," or, more universally, "a vigil kept over the dead or dying."[18] Depending upon the time and place, the deathwatch had a distinct mise-en-scène.

Dying was a public affair.❝ As soon as serious illness made its pres-

---

❝ One source of Jewish law, concerning visitation of the sick, death, and mourning is the Shulhan Arukh, compiled in the sixteenth century by Rabbi Joseph Karo of Safed. Rabbi Moses Isserles of Kracow composed the glosses that accompany almost every paragraph of the work and added traditions from the Ashkenazic community to Karo's compilation, which derived primarily from the Sephardic tradition.

Chapter 335 of the Shulhan Arukh covers visitations of the sick: "It is a religious duty to visit the sick. Relatives and close friends should enter at once, others after three days. If the illness is serious, both groups can visit him at once."

Specific rules govern seating ("One who visits the sick ... should sit in front of the patient, for the Divine Presence rests above a sick person"); when to visit ("One should not visit the sick during the first three hours of the day ... and not during the last three hours of the day"); what language to pray in ("if in the presence of the sick person, in any language, if not in his presence, in Hebrew"); whom to visit ("Refrain from visiting those who suffer from diseases that might

ence known, the windows and doors were closed, the candles were lit, and the sickroom filled with people.⟨ Everyone came: family, friends, neighbors, fellow workers, the faithful, sometimes even strangers.⟨⟨ When Emma Bovary ate arsenic, her doctor considered bringing his two sons to witness her death, "in order to accustom them to great occasions; that this might be a lesson, an example, a

---

be too embarassing or uncomfortable to withstand a visit"); and how the sick person should look after his debts and outstanding credits.

Chapter 339 covers how to treat someone who is dying:

One who is dying is considered a living being in all respects. We may not tie up his jaws, nor remove the pillow from under him, nor place him on sand, nor summon the town on his behalf, nor close his eyes before his soul departs. And whoever closes his eyes before death, is regarded as a murderer. One may not rend garments nor make a lamentation for him nor bring a coffin into the house for him before he dies.... When a person is about to die one should not leave him so that he does not depart this life alone. Gloss: It is a *mitzvah* to stand by a person during the departure of his soul.[5]

⟨ Franz Kafka describes a deathwatch in the early twentieth century:

The bed was set up in the middle of the room, the candlesticks were borrowed from friends and relatives.... Some forty men stood around his bed all day to receive inspiration from the death of a pious man. He was conscious until the end and at the right moment, his hand on his breast, he began to repeat the death prayers. During his suffering and after his death the grandmother, who was with the women gathered in the next room, wept incessantly, but while he was dying she was completely calm because it is a commandment to ease the death of the dying man as much as one can. "With his own prayers he passed away." He was much envied for this death that followed so pious a life.[6]

⟨⟨ Saint-Simon describes a dying woman in the early eighteenth century:

She lay in bed with all her bed-curtains open, candles all around the room, and women keeping vigil around her.... She summoned all her servants, down to the lowest one, asked their forgiveness, confessed her sins, and presided ... over ... her own death.[7]

solemn picture, that should remain in their heads later on."[19] ««« Only a maternal veto kept them away. ««««

There were different roles to play in the deathwatch. Depending upon the circumstances of the patient—social, economic, and medical—a doctor would be called. ««««« The doctor's role at the death-

---

««« Phillipe Aries argues that Flaubert's vivid and medically detailed description of Emma Bovary's hideous and agonizing death by suicide foreshadowed the modern notion of the "dirty death." Aries contrasts the early nineteenth century, in which death was seen as beautiful, to the second half of the nineteenth century, when death was "sometimes even depicted as disgusting."[8]

As further evidence of the view that death was dirty and indecent, Aries also discusses Leo Tolstoy's *The Death of Ivan Ilyich*, an unsentimental and relentlessly realistic portrayal of the dying process. The protagonist, a former judge, dies a painful, protracted death. Tolstoy details the pain, odors, discomfort, denial, isolation, and anger that terminal illness and impending death can bring. In the death scene of the last chapter, the doctor, priest, and members of the family were called. Ilyich, however, took three terrible days to die. He screamed incessantly and "struggled in that black sack into which he was being thrust by an invisible, resistless force. Finally, when the gasping and rattling in his throat became inaudible, he heard someone say, 'It is finished!' He repeated to himself, 'Death is finished.... it is no more!' He drew in a breath, stopped in the midst of a sigh, stretched out, and died."[9] It is a horrible scene, a deathwatch to remember.

««« One literary critic, Eric Rhode, claims that the Victorians in particular used deathbed scenes to encourage piety: "It allowed for a moral lesson. It strengthened social and religious values by rallying the faithful and troubling the doubters."[10]

««««« I use the term "doctor" generically. Different places and different historical periods have seen a variety of practitioners and healers. Individuals who did not consider themselves to be doctors (and whom others did not consider to be doctors) would also provide medical care: midwives, apothecaries, and bone-setters, to name only a few.[11]

watch was usually that of referee.﹤ He presided over the body's decline, calling the shots and keeping score.﹤﹤ The doctor would declare death the winner, closing the eyelids as a sign the game was over.﹤﹤﹤ There was little he could do. Although a doctor could try to make his patient comfortable, medical science had a limited arsenal to forestall or reverse the process. There was little anyone could do but watch and wait.﹤﹤﹤﹤

George Rosen notes that in this country as late as 1864 practitioners of medicine included "allopaths of every class in allopathy; homeopaths of high and low dilutions; hydropaths mild and heroic; chronothermalists; Thomsonians, Mesmerists, herbalists, Indian doctors, clairvoyants, spiritualists with healing gifts, and I know not what besides."[12]

﹤ A more disturbing description of a deathwatch occurs in "A Country Doctor," a short story by Kafka. In this story, the family and village elders strip a doctor who has failed to save a boy with a worm-ridden wound. As they strip him, a school choir sings, "Strip his clothes off, then he'll heal us; / If he doesn't, kill him dead? / Only a doctor, only a doctor."[13]

Surely the story is an account of a doctor's nightmare.

﹤﹤ Nor were this country's physicians a monolithic group in terms of training, social standing, or methods of practice. In the early nineteenth century, a handful of successful urban practitioners—such as Henry James's character, Dr. Austin Sloper, father of Catherine Sloper, the remarkable heroine of *Washington Square*—comprised the top of the hierarchy. They enjoyed formal medical training, often with hospital experience and education in Edinburgh or London, and competed for the wealthiest and most socially prominent patients. Most of the nation's physicians, however, trained under the apprentice system and may never have attended formal lectures or seen the inside of a hospital. Many apprentice-trained physicians competed directly with the other assorted practitioners.[14]

﹤﹤﹤ Closing the eyes of the dead appears to be a very old custom, common to most cultures.

And God spoke to Israel in visions of the night, and said, "Jacob, Jacob." And he said, "Here am I." Then he said, "I am God, the God of thy father: do not be afraid to go down to Egypt; for I will there make of you a great nation: I will go down with you to Egypt; and I will also bring you up again: and Joseph's hand shall close your eyes." (Genesis 46:2–4, *The New Oxford Annotated Bible*).

The practice of closing the eyes of the dead developed from the fear that some sort of danger or curse would threaten a living person seen by the corpse's eye. A common belief, according to Webb Garrison, was that anyone "who came within the field of vision of a dead person was thereby doomed to follow soon that person to the grave. It was not always easy to keep the eyes closed before rigor mortis set in: often the eyelids had to be weighted. Coins sometimes served this purpose. They also provided the dead person with "the toll exacted for crossing into the next world."[15]

$\mathfrak{C}\mathfrak{C}\mathfrak{C}$ Probably the most famous deathwatch in Western civilization occurred during Jesus' crucifixion, "a Roman penalty reserved for slaves and selected criminals, with the condemned person usually dying from a combination of exhaustion and exposure."[16] John tells us that in attendance at the crucifixion, standing by the cross of Jesus, were his mother, his mother's sister, Mary, the wife of Clopas, and Mary Magdalene (John 19:25, *The New Oxford Annotated Bible*).

Another famous deathwatch in Western civilization is recorded in Plato's account of the death of Socrates. *The Phaedo* relates the conversation between Socrates and one of his students, Crito, after Socrates decided to submit to his death sentence. As his students entered, Socrates was bidding farewell to his family. This deathwatch was a time for philosophic exploration, embracing such subjects as the relationship of soul to body, the crime of suicide, the soul's immortality, and the nature of knowledge. When Socrates finally stopped the dialogue and took the poison, his students began to weep; he asked them not to, because "a man should die in peace." Finally, when he was on the very edge of death, Socrates uncovered his face (he had covered himself up) and reminded Crito, "I owe a cock to Asclepius; will you remember to pay the debt?" And then Socrates died.[17]

The epic of Gilgamesh also contains a famous death scene. Gilgamesh, who reigned in the Mesopotamian city of Uruk during the third millennium, was

Indeed, the medical profession was often fatalistic and frank about its inability to cure certain diseases, accepting the inevitability of some deathwatches.◖ In 1836, Jacob Bigelow wrote about the naive young medical student who "goes forth into the world believing that if he does not cure disease it is his own fault. Yet, when a score or two of years have passed over his head, he will come at length to the conviction that some diseases are controlled by nature alone."[20] Bigelow goes on to describe the role of the doctor at a deathwatch. A doctor should not "frustrate the intentions of nature, when they are salutary, or embitter the approach of death when it is inevitable. . . . [W]e may do much good by a palliative and preventive course, by alleviating pain, procuring sleep, guarding the diet, regulating the alimentary canal—in fine, by obviating such sufferings as admit of mitigation. . . . The longer and more philosophically we contemplate this subject, the more obvious it will appear that the physician is but the minister and servant of nature."[21]

While the doctor tried to obviate suffering, a spiritual leader would also be called to play a role in the deathwatch. In the Christian

---

said to be two parts god and one part man. The epic portrays his friendship with Enkidu, "a child of the mountain" who grew up with wild animals. Gilgamesh and Enkidu embarked on a journey to make a name for themselves, during which they offended the goddess Ishtar, who placed a curse on Enkidu. Gilgamesh attended Enkidu at his sickbed for over twelve days and, upon Enkidu's death, addressed the counselors of Uruk in one of the most beautiful laments in all literature.[18]

◖ In the early nineteenth centry, Jacob Bigelow defined a "self-limited" disease: A self-limited disease is one ... which receives limits from its own nature and not from foreign influences; one which, after it has obtained foothold in the system, cannot, in the present state of our knowledge, be eradicated or abridged by art, but to which there is due a certain succession of processes to be completed in a certain time; which time and processes may vary with the constitution of the patient, and may tend to death or to recovery, but are not known to be shortened or greatly changed by medical treatment.[19]

tradition, at a sign from the doctor that the end was near, the priest or minister would be sent for. He would say prayers and perform rituals on the body in preparation for the transition from life to death. Catholics who were seriously ill, for example, received the sacrament of Extreme Unction from a priest.⫶ The rite involved anointing the organs of the external senses with consecrated oil and praying at each unction while mentioning the corresponding sense.[22] Protestants rejected the anointing of the sick as a Sacrament, but there were other special prayers for the dying. The presence of the spiritual leader was not only for the benefit of the dying person; he was also there for the participants of the deathwatch. It was a religious occasion and required the authority of a holy man.

But the most important role in the deathwatch was played by the dying person. The spotlight fell on him. It was his day to die, and he had certain obligations. Before lapsing into silence, he was expected to bid farewell to those he loved, to make gifts, to extract promises, to make amends for ancient wounds, and to make preparations for his departure. During his own deathwatch, the dying person knew just what to say; he was relieved of the burden of originality. The script was written for him.

Sometimes the deathwatch would be recorded for posterity.⫶⫶ If

---

⫶ The recipient of the sacrament of the Anointing of the Sick must be baptized and "have attained the use of reason," reflecting the theological tradition that "this Sacrament is a complement of the Sacrament of Penance. To receive the Sacrament, an adult possessing the use of reason must have an intention to receive it."[20] That intention need never have been expressly formulated; it may be implied, even if the subject is now unconscious, from his or her desire to live and die as a Catholic. Today, theologians do not wait until the subject is in the last moments of life, believing that the sacrament's maximum benefit can be derived as soon as the subject is in danger of death from sickness or old age. Thus, it may be received as many times as the subject succumbs to serious illness.[21]

⫶⫶ There is also a Hasidic tradition of recording the dying words of famous teachers and leaders of the community, in the belief that, since how a man

the dying person were a famous man, it became customary to publish his final utterances, presumably for purposes of instruction and inspiration. One suspects at times there may have been rehearsals of the scene—or at least some judicious wordsmithing in anticipation. Martin Luther's dying words, for example, do not bear the hallmark of spontaneity: "Father in heaven, though this body is breaking away from me, and I am departing this life, yet I know that I shall be forever with thee, for no one can pluck me out of thy hand."[23] Thomas Jefferson too seems to have chosen his last words with care: "I resign my soul to God, and my daughter to my country."[24]

Others were less prepared for their performance. Goethe's last utterance was a simple request to open the shutters in the bedroom and let in more light.[25] A stern housekeeper attended Carl Jung in his final illness, and his last words were spoken to his son as she left the room: "Quick, help me out of bed before she comes back or she will stop me. I want to look at the sunset."[26] Others commented on the experience of dying itself. Cotton Mather allegedly cried in exultation, "Is this dying? Is this all? Is this what I feared when I prayed against a hard death? Oh, I can bear this. I can bear it!"[27] Thomas Edison's words are particularly moving. In his final moments of consciousness, he whispered, "It's very beautiful . . . over there."[28]

The deathbed scene was more than a convention of art and literature.« It was played over and over again, in cities and in small towns, in isolated farmhouses. Just as family and friends convened at the

---

meets his death is a reflection of how he has led his life, one might capture a whole life's philosophy in how a man chooses to die. Thus, recording the last moments of the masters became a sacred task. One such collection is the *Histalkut Hanefesh*, edited by Benjamin Mintz in 1930. Each description contains a deathwatch. For example, on the last evening of Baal Shem Tov's life, "his intimates were gathered around him and he preached to them about the giving of the Torah." When death came to Rabbi Elimelekh, he "placed his hands upon the foreheads of his four disciples and gave them each a portion of his soul."[22]

birth of a baby,[29] so they reconvened at his death. With the passage of time, of course, the constituency of the deathwatch would change; different faces attended the entrance and the exit.⟪ But every human being was more or less assured that his birth and death would be

⟪ One of the funniest death scenes in literature is in Lewis Carroll's *Through the Looking-Glass and What Alice Found There*. The Walrus and the Carpenter lured the Oysters out for a walk and then ate them, but not without much carrying on by the Walrus.

> "I weep for you," the Walrus said:
> "I deeply sympathize."
> With sobs and tears he sorted out
> Those of the largest size,
> Holding his pocket-handkerchief
> Before his streaming eyes.
> "O Oysters," said the Carpenter,
> "You've had a pleasant run!
> Shall we be trotting home again?"
> But answer came there none—
> And this was scarcely odd, because
> They'd eaten every one.[23]

Here was an unsentimental Victorian death scene.

⟪ Emily Dickinson wrote a poem about a deathwatch from the point of view of a dying person who is aware of those gathered around her bed, waiting for death to come:

> I heard a Fly buzz—when I died—
> The Stillness in the Room
> Was like the Stillness in the Air—
> Between the Heaves of Storm—
> The Eyes around—had wrung them dry—
> And Breaths were gathering firm
> For that last Onset—when the King

witnessed. Ultimately, our coming in and going out might have been lonely, but at least we were not alone;⟨ the community gathered around to attend, to keep vigil, to create a warm space to envelop us. That warm space was called "home." ⟨⟨

WE no longer die at home. Starting in the 1930s, the locus of our dying moved from the home to the hospital or some other health-care facility.⟨⟨⟨ On the surface, it seemed like the logical thing to do. After all, sick people went to the hospital because all those things that sick people needed were there: doctors, nurses, laboratories,

---

Be witnessed—in the Room—
I willed my Keepsake—Signed away
What portion of me be
Assignable—and then it was
There interposed a Fly—
With Blue—uncertain stumbling Buzz—
Between the light—and me—
And then the Windows failed—and then
I could not see to see—[24]

⟨ In my presentation of the deathwatch, I assume that the members of the deathwatch are themselves alive. Katherine Anne Porter made me question this assumption. In her story "Pale Horse, Pale Rider," Miranda, a twenty-four-year-old journalist, almost died of influenza at the very end of the First World War. As she fell ill, she thought that she ought to go home, since "it's a respectable old custom to inflict your death on the family if you can manage it."[25] She chose to stay in her room, however, and was eventually taken to the hospital, presumably to die.

Miranda "sank easily through deeps under deeps of darkness until she lay like a stone at the farthest bottom of life." Pulled toward a "hard unwinking angry point of light," she reached "a deep clear landscape of sea and sand, of soft meadow and sky," where "[m]oving toward her leisurely as clouds through the shimmering air came a great company of human beings ... all the living she had known. Their faces were transfigured, each in its own beauty, beyond what she remembered of them."[26] They encircled Miranda "smoothly on silent feet" and she moved easily among them. Medical intervention brought her back to life, but she felt a stranger to her own body. She mourned for what she had so briefly won, "but did not let onto her friends who visited her the next day."

Miranda's experience made me think that there may be a parallel to the deathwatch on the other side, a mirror image of our gathering at her bedside, in which others move toward her on silent feet. The ritual may have two parts, a farewell and a greeting.

❮❮ Morris Adler writes about the symbolic significance of prayer in the home:
Thus does a community symbolically and actually share in the sorrow of one of its members. The grief of the individual reechoes in the life of the group.... The religious service of this little group, representing the larger community, takes place in the home. It is a tribute to the central position of the home. Where a family lives and loves and fashions the most intimate bonds to link persons one to the other, there you have a sanctuary no less than the synagogue. Its holiness is of no lesser kind than that with which the formal house of prayer of the entire community is invested. The poignancy and sanctity of grief are best expressed in the intimate sanctuary of the home.[28]

❮❮❮ Society's migration from the country to urban centers may also have affected our attitudes towards death. In a radio interview, writer Grace Paley read one of her poems, "Fear":

I am afraid of nature
because of nature   I am mortal
my children and my grandchildren
are also mortal
I lived in the city for forty years
In this way   I escaped fear.[29]

After reading the poem, she remarked:
I really meant what I said. I was simply thinking of the movement of life and death, in the fields and in the mountains, and in the animals around me, which

new diagnostic and therapeutic technologies. Because all of those things had been so wildly successful in the recent past, we had a new expectation of survival: Dying people came to be viewed as sick people. And sick people went to the hospital.〔

What does it mean to be dying? In a sense, we are all dying from the moment of birth, but that is not how we use the word. We use it predictively, as an expression of the "likelihood of death within some temporal perspective."[30] Some argue that "dying" is a state in which a person suffers from an irreversible disease known to produce death.[31] I use the term "dying" to refer to someone who is expected to die within a relatively short period of time. The definition is not precise, but it will suffice. Precision is often overrated—and the fact

---

are very close to you, much more close to you. You know, we think about the cities as being so dangerous, and full of guns and so forth, but in a very strange way, you are really closer to birth and life and death in the countryside.[30]

〔 Philippe Aries argues that the dying person's bedroom has moved from home to hospital due to both our change in attitudes and "technical medical reasons." In the hospital, death can remain hidden: "The hospital is the only place where death is sure of escaping a visibility—or what remains of it—that is hereafter regarded as unsuitable and morbid. The hospital has become the place of the solitary death."[31]

Aries sees a relationship between our change in attitudes toward death and the replacement of the home with the hospital as the place where death takes place. He argues that attitudes toward death changed in the second half of the nineteenth century; death came to be seen as improper, unseemly, and "dirty."

It is indecent to let someone die in public. It is no longer acceptable for strangers to come into a room that smells of urine, sweat, and gangrene, and where the sheets are soiled. Access to this room must be forbidden, except to a few intimates capable of overcoming their disgust, or to those indispensable persons who provide certain services. A new image of death is forming, a hidden death, hidden because it is ugly and dirty.[32]

is, you don't need it at all to understand the twentieth-century death-watch. Sick people usually get better; dying ones do not.

That simple move from dying person to sick person, from the home to the hospital, had hidden, undreamed of consequences. When we left our homes, we lost power over our own deaths, and over the deaths of those we love.⁣«‹ Once inside the hospital walls, dying became the sole province of medicine, and this has had a profound effect on the deathwatch.⁣«‹‹ The deathwatch has almost disappeared.[32]

«‹ In *Quartet in Autumn*, Barbara Pym describes a hospital deathwatch cut short by the arbitrary imposition of a no-visitation rule. The novel concerns four single elderly people who worked in the same office. After her retirement, one of the women collapsed and was taken to the hospital to die. When her friends came to see her, the nurse always refused to let them visit the dying woman, saying that "Miss Ivory was quite comfortable." The nurse explained that the patient must be "kept very quiet, no excitement." Consequently, Miss Ivory died alone. As one of her survivors put it, "If they said, 'No Visitors,' then we can't very well barge in."[33]

«‹‹ The death scene in John Gunther's *Death Be Not Proud* is one of the earliest descriptions of a hospital deathwatch and the powerlessness that family members can feel when a loved one dies in that setting. When Johnny Gunther took a sudden turn for the worse because of a cerebral hemorrhage, his parents had him immediately moved to the hospital. Everything about the move was a disaster. The emergency door at the hospital was locked. The switchboard had gone to pieces. The nurse did not know what to do. An attendant downstairs was hysterical. The cab driver who drove them back was drunk. When the end was near, someone rang an emergency bell, and after "all those months of doctors and doctors and doctors, it happened that no doctor was there at that precise moment." The last few lines about the hospital deathwatch are for me deeply moving: "Johnny died at 11:02 p.m. Frances reached for him through the ugly, transparent, raincoat-like curtain of the oxygen machine."[34]

In the late twentieth century, most of the people who would have once gathered around the bed in Munch's painting have been excluded. Even those who remain have a small role to play, a role defined not by social custom or religious tradition, but by what is deemed medically necessary. It is true: we may not die alone. If we are lucky, someone will be in the room, but that someone may be a medical professional, someone whose job it is to be in the room.

Hospital rules may curtail the deathwatch altogether. Restrictions on visitors are strict in hospitals organized by wards, such as in large, urban charity institutions⁣ᶜ or in many hospitals in Great Britain. Visitors create increased demands on the nurses—demands that often cannot be met with a large patient population and a barely adequate staff. Their presence in a dying patient's room means that a "more constant vigilance over the patient's condition must be maintained, this requiring, in effect, the removal of a nurse from other activities to spend her time exclusively at the bedside,"[33] though the nurses may rationalize discouraging visitors as "shielding" them from the "unpleasantness of seeing someone die."[34] The handling of death can only be kept routine if the ward is kept free of outsiders—outsiders who make demands, outsiders who scrutinize.

Depending on social and economic status, that well-guarded patient may not even die in the presence of the hospital staff. The disappearance of the deathwatch is all but complete among the hospital-

---

ᶜ David Sudnow describes the visiting facilities of a large, urban, West Coast charity hospital:

> There are no visitors' waiting rooms on the ward itself; the only place a visitor can await the beginning of visiting hours is in the general hospital lobby, at the front of the building, which, with its long benches, resembles a train station. If, during a visit with a patient, a relative is asked to leave the room, he must stand in the ward corridor. None of the doors to the individual rooms is closed … so that a visitior can witness nearly everything that goes on in neighboring rooms.… During visiting hours, as one walks down the hall to a patient's room, he is quite likely to see several patients' bodies exposed as bed clothes are changed or examinations conducted.[35]

ized poor from whom the hospital staff may even take flight. Several years ago, my eighty-eight-year-old great-aunt was a Medicaid patient on a ward in a public hospital, and in the middle of the night, a woman patient was rolled into the bed next to her, hooked up to oxygen, and deserted. The nurse's final act was to pull the curtains around the bed—curtains that were so close to my great-aunt that she brushed up against them trying to get help. The patient seemed to be in respiratory distress; she was breathing in a heavy, labored way. My great-aunt tried to call the nurses for help. No one came, and eventually the gasping and the rasping stopped. My great-aunt sat up all night, waiting for someone to come. Finally someone did come—someone from Dietary with the breakfast tray—and when she threw open the curtain, there lay the woman on her back in the bed, stone cold and blue, her mouth wide open like a fish. She had died all alone in the middle of the night.

During the late 1960s, deaths on medical and surgical wards in charity hospitals in Great Britain occurred "more often than not . . . with no staff members present."[35] Frequently, nosy roomates, like my great-aunt, would notice the impending death before members of the staff. To avoid this, hospitals would transfer patients who were expected to "terminate" to private parts of the hospital, pulling curtains around them, creating a setting "much less conducive to social interaction and the consequent dangers of discovery that a history of friendliness between patients and an interest in the happenings of one's roommates would entail."[36]

Even in middle-class, private hospitals, it can be difficult to gain access to a dying patient's room. A dying patient means more work, and, once again, visitors get in the way. To the nursing staffs of medical and surgical units, the term "deathwatch" has a more specific meaning: "guarding a dying person in anticipation of his death."[37] During the nursing deathwatch, the "patient is treated as in a transitory state, the relevant facts about him being the gradual decline of clinical life signs"; as the patient gets close to death, "his status as a body becomes more evident," and the nurses' attention shifts from trying to alleviate his discomfort and administering medical treatments to the "sheer activity of 'timing' his biological events."[38] The deathwatch of family and friends cannot compete with this medical deathwatch, and they are often excluded from the room, or only permitted access for short periods of time.

If that room is an intensive care unit (ICU), the deathwatch is only a shadow of its former self, a sketch from memory, a vestigial impression laid down in the sand.⟨ Just as dying moved from the house to the hospital, within those walls dying moved from the wards and the units to the inner sanctum of the ICU. There death has become mechanized; the struggle for heartbeat and breath has been taken over by machines.

For the sick, these machines buy valuable time; they temporarily perform vital functions until the body is ready to work again. Overall, the survival statistics of ICU patients are rather heartening: 70 to 80 percent leave the unit alive. The condition of the patient's body

---

⟨ Underlying the creation of a special care unit is the principle that patients with similar medical problems can be treated more efficiently if they are gathered together in one location. The first special care unit, established in 1923, was a postoperative recovery room. Specially trained nurses could easily detect and correct common postoperative problems, such as airway blockage or bleeding. Over the past fifty years, hospitals have developed increasingly specialized units: "preoperative, postoperative, neonatal, coronary, burn, and trauma centers."[36]

In 1942, a Boston area hospital set aside a ward to treat thirty-nine burn victims of the Coconut Grove nightclub fire. This burn unit served as the model for the modern ICU. During World War II and the Korean and Vietnam wars, the organization of special care units improved. As cardiac surgery progressed in the late 1950s, hospitals set up coronary care units to accommodate the intensive nursing and complicated monitoring devices required for postoperative patients. Other medical specialties, such as respiratory and physical therapy, also contributed to the development of the ICU. In the early 1960s, only 10 to 20 percent of hospitals in the United States had ICUs. Now most of the nation's six thousand hospitals have them. A smaller hospital located in a rural area may have only a two-bed ICU, primarily for cardiac monitoring. A major acute-care hospital in an urban area, however, may have several ICUs with large populations of patients and postoperative complications.[37]

upon admission to the ICU largely determines his chances of survival. Postoperative patients who are relatively healthy to start with fare well. Trauma victims also tend to survive. Predictably, the old, the frail, the critically ill are most at risk. The patient with multiple life-threatening conditions has a much greater chance of dying. Of those patients with renal failure and respiratory failure, 80 to 90 percent die. Ninety percent of patients with cardiac arrest do not come out of the ICU alive.[39]

While life-sustaining equipment may prolong the process, the longer a patient remains in the ICU, the less likely he is to leave alive. Typically patients suffering from acute organ system failure (OSF) are transferred to the ICU. For all medical and most surgical admissions, a single OSF lasting more than one day results in a mortality rate approaching 40 percent. The death rate among patients who have had two OSFs for more than a day increases to 60 percent. Advanced age increases both the probability of organ system failure occurring and of dying after an incident of OSF. Mortality among patients with three or more OSFs who lived after three days is 99 percent.[40]

But those are just numbers: data collected by a diligent researcher from a ream of hospital charts. When a patient enters the ICU, there is no plastic bracelet around his wrist indicating what side of the percent sign his fate resides on. The sick and the dying are indistinguishable, and intensive care is lavished upon every patient without discrimination.

There is very little beauty in the ICU. It pulsates with the rhythmic hum of life-support machines. It is aggressively clean. The smells of sickness and death have been washed away with a fluid the color of aquamarine. Day and night, night and day, fluorescent lights cast their purple-yellow glow on the scene, making the healthy look like the sick, the sick look like the dying, and the dying look already gone. ⟨⟨

⟨⟨ In *Love and Other Infectious Diseases: A Memoir,* Molly Haskell describes her first ICU visit when her husband had fallen ill from some mysterious infec-

The deathwatches that take place there are sparsely attended. Visiting is only permitted for small groups of close family members, since an ICU is a labor-intensive operation, designed to facilitate nursing, not visitation. In the ICU, there is usually one nurse assigned to each patient to perform a job that consists primarily of manipulating machines. The machines are large, three-dimensional objects that take up lots of room; so are people. There is no space in the room for a large deathwatch, and the absence of chairs sends the message that no one is expected. Visitors have to stand.

What is it like to participate in a deathwatch in such a place? It may be a struggle just to get there. Since the hospital is often located miles away, each visit may be preceded by a long solitary drive, with time to spare for dreadful anticipation. Once the car is finally parked, there is that terrible journey through the hospital corridors to reach the ICU—through waiting rooms, banks of elevators that never arrive, and a maze of hallways.ᶜ And then there is the prob-

---

tion. She, too, was struck by the bizarre physical environment of the ICU, its isolation from the rest of the hospital, and the predominance of machines:

> The ICU was itself an otherworldly experience. I was the only visitor—they'd agreed to let me in for a few minutes before regular hours. It was an antiseptic enclosure cut off from the rest of the hospital and the flow of life by its restricted visiting hours (11:00 to 11:45 in the morning, 5:00 to 5:45 in the evening). It was like an airship, suspended in space, sterile because there were none of the ordinary signs or sounds of life, only the whirring and clicking of machines surrounding mummylike patients, each click signaling that death had been forestalled by another moment.[38]

ᶜ One of the most disturbing aspects of being in a hospital is the disorientation one feels in the maze of hallways, waiting rooms, elevator banks, and patients' rooms. One study has focused on the prerequisites for "wayfinding" through a complex and unfamiliar environment. Behavioral scientists seem to agree that the degree of sameness or variation of interior spaces will affect one's ability to recognize and use a landmark. Similarly, being able to see one part of the building from another makes it easier to maintain a point of reference. The overall com-

lem of the eyes—the eyes in your head that do not obey the order to stare straight ahead, but instead dart in and out of rooms, left and right, drawn by the undeniable attraction of someone else's darkest night. Once at the ICU, a "security" guard yields up a laminated piece of cardboard, bearing the number of the bed that holds the dying person. Visiting hours are strictly limited. An ICU deathwatch is therefore episodic. It is sliced into thin slivers of time, and the attendance of such a death becomes a series of black-and-white stills. Upon each successive visit, a new image of a body frozen in time is created and added to the pile of memories.« It is never clear which image will be the last until someone announces that the series is over.

So for brief intervals, day after day, night after night, sometimes for twenty minutes, sometimes for half an hour, segments of the deathwatch take place. Several feet away, one set of outlets over, there lies another person, sick or dying, dying or sick, and perhaps another deathwatch. At best, members of the nursing staff move silently in and out of the cubicle, monitoring machines. At worst, they make cheerful, brittle remarks about "our night," or "our day."

---

plexity of the layout naturally will affect the comprehensibility of the environment. Various design techniques can facilitate wayfinding, however, such as appropriate signage, the use of a main artery, and the use of landmarks to serve as points of reference.[39]

A deathwatch seems like a poor time to be taxing one's cognitive processes by engaging in spatial problem-solving.

« Molly Haskell describes the inhuman appearance of the patients in the ICU:
I walked along the small passageway, between two glass panes, where the patients, four on the right, two on the left, were lined up side by side, with tubes of the most expensive lifesaving machinery in the world reaching like tentacles into every orifice, and with their faces, peering out from oxygen masks, unrecognizable as to sex and age. They weren't humans, but cyborgs, half man-half machine, new arrivals on display from the planet of near-death.[40]

It is difficult to talk at all, and even more impossible to exchange words of intimacy. It is not a good place for prayer or resolution, or even idle chatter.« It is not a good place at all.

SOMETIMES the common law reminds me of Columbus, Ohio, where I grew up. In this country, new ideas, fashions, and expressions all tend to start on either edge of the continent and slowly roll inward, like a billiard ball on a slightly elevated field of green felt. Contrary to the parochial opinions of those who have lived their entire lives on the East or West Coast, new ideas, fashions, and expressions eventually do make their way to Columbus, Ohio, provided they were important enough at their point of origin. They just get there later, sometimes by several years.

It is the same with the law. If some new problem is generated from a dramatic change in social reality, that new problem will slowly roll towards the appellate courts. Just as it may take a new idea several years to reach Columbus, Ohio, it may take a new problem several years to reach judicial attention. Arrival at both destinations, however, is ensured by the force of gravity.

Thus it was inevitable that the horrors of the late-twentieth-century deathwatch would eventually land in the pocket of an appellate court. Karen Quinlan was twenty-one years old when, for unknown reasons, she suffered two fifteen-minute periods of inter-

---

« The Catholic chaplain in one large urban charity hospital in the late 1960s made rounds every morning and administered Extreme Unction to all Catholic patients appearing on the "critical patients' [sic] list." After completing his rounds, he stamped an index card with a rubber stamp which read:

Last Rites Administered
Date: Clergyman:

Every day he consulted the files to see if new patients had been admitted to the wards and/or put on the critical list. The stamp prevented him from performing the rite twice on the same patient.[41]

rupted respiration that resulted in irreversible brain damage.[41] She was not brain dead, however, according to the definition promulgated by the Ad Hoc Committee of Harvard Medical School, but was instead described as being in a "persistent vegetative state."[42] She could not maintain her vital processes, or so it was believed at the time, without the assistance of a respirator.[43]

After a long period of time, when it had become apparent that her condition was irreversible, her family and parish priest agreed that she should be removed from the respirator. After her family requested that Dr. Morse, Karen Quinlan's treating physician, disconnect the respirator, Dr. Morse "felt he could not and would not agree to the cessation of the respirator assistance," concluding that "to terminate the respirator would be a substantial deviation from medical tradition, that it involved ascertaining 'quality of life,' and that he would not do so."[44]

When her doctor refused, despite the family's offer to release him from liability, her father, Joseph Quinlan, petitioned the court to appoint him as guardian of the person and property of his daughter. He also proposed that the letters of guardianship, if granted, contain the express power to authorize the discontinuation of all extraordinary medical procedures.[45] The jurisdiction was New Jersey; the case was *In the Matter of Karen Quinlan, an Alleged Incompetent.*

What an odd expression: "In the matter of." In many ways, the case of Karen Quinlan was about the matter of Karen Quinlan. Perhaps because it was the first such case to reach an appellate court, there are pages and pages of medical details about her body, its functions, its posture, and its ghastly dependence on machines.[46] Interestingly enough, the graphic word picture was the only image to which Judge Muir, author of the lower court opinion, would permit himself access. Karen Quinlan's attorney, Paul Armstrong, urged Judge Muir to "personally witness and appreciate Karen's condition" in the hospital ICU, but Judge Muir did not feel that was appropriate, "recognizing that emotion is an aspect that I cannot decide a case on."[47] Not only the court was fascinated by her body; the media too was morbidly obsessed. Towards the end of her ordeal, armed deputies had to guard Karen Quinlan's room in the nursing home twenty-four hours a day. The main reason for the tight security was the media's repeated efforts to take a photograph of her. Members of the press offered the Quinlans as much as $100,000 for a photograph of their daughter, and that was only a "starting figure."[48] No photographs of Karen Quinlan in her semi-vegetative state were ever published, however, and the lower court confined itself to this graphic word picture:

> In the decorticate posturing the upper arms are drawn into the side of the body. The forearms are drawn in against the chest with the hands generally at right angles to the forearms, pointing towards the waist. The legs are drawn up against the body, knees are up, feet are in near the buttocks and extended in ballet-type pose.[49]

Who was this ballerina? Why were we so hypnotized by her curling in,[c] by the merger of her body with machines? What were we afraid of? Some unnameable malevolence often associated with other forms of the living dead?[cc] Of a human being who has turned into a machine? Or were we just afraid of ourselves in a similar position,[ccc] spinning our own futures from a web of dreadful possibilities?

---

[c] Once the cognitive function of the brain is gone, the central nervous system acts in a more primitive fashion. In an individual in whom only the brainstem is active, certain bodily reactions, such as grasping and sucking, are still present.[42]

[cc] I am surprised that no science-fiction writer has chosen the permanently unconscious patients in an ICU as suitable subjects for possession by evil spirits (at least no science-fiction writer that I know of). A person in a semi-vegetative state has all the indicia of having experienced a "false death," or having the look of the living dead.

Maya Deren describes how the death rituals of the Haitian Voudoun are intended to prevent both a false death and a false life:

> The initial act of the survivor is to determine that the death is real or a false death brought on by magic. For, if the regular rituals that dissociate the soul from the body should be performed in ignorance of the fact that the death is

false, the body would remain as a live but emptied vessel, subject to the direction of any alien force (usually the malevolent one which engineered the magic precisely for such a purpose). The dread *zombie*, the major figure of terror, is precisely this: the body without a soul, matter without morality.... A zombie is nothing more than a body deprived of its conscious powers of cerebration.[43]

To be possessed by the Haitian god, the *loa*, Deren explains, the "self must leave.... The serviteur must be induced to surrender his ego." The fear that the zombie generates may be the same fear that a human being in a semi-vegetative state generates. In both, consciousness has ceased, but the body's existence continues. A human being in a semi-vegetative state has already permanently lost the self. This would make the permanently unconscious patient in an ICU extremely vulnerable to possession, or so it seems to me.

(((Paul Schilder writes about the "deep community between the postural models" of human beings:

The postural model of our own body is connected with the postural model of the bodies of others. There are connections between the postural models of fellow human beings. We experience the body images of others. Experience of our body-image and experience of the bodies of others are closely interwoven with each other.[44]

The postural model of Karen Quinlan's body may threaten us because we identify with it and experience it as potentially our own.

Psychologist Seymour Fisher theorizes that the degree to which seeing the disablement of another person provokes anxiety depends upon how definite we feel about our own body boundaries. The sight of someone's mutilated or deformed body is threatening because it suggests that the same thing could happen to us. Thus, the less definite one's body boundaries are, the more disturbing it will be to see a maimed or disabled person.[45]

A fear of deformation is apparently not confined to the human species. Jane Goodall observed the reaction of a troop of chimpanzees to an adult male member who had been stricken by polio. When he shuffled up to the feeding area, dragging a useless arm behind him, "the group of chimps already in camp stared for a moment and then, with wide grins of fear, rushed for reassurance to embrace and pat each other while staring at the unfortunate cripple."[46]

Those are questions I cannot answer, and questions the law does not ask. Instead the cases purport to be about Karen Quinlan and her right of privacy and self-determination. And in a sense, that is indeed what they are about. At least they are about the Karen Quinlan who used to be.

The trial court heard testimony on whether Karen Quinlan would elect, if competent, to disconnect the respirator.[50] She had made several statements to family members and friends about various friends and relatives who were themselves trapped in interminable death-watches, including an aunt and a close family friend who had died from cancer. Karen Quinlan seemed to have been consistent in her belief that she "would not want to be kept alive that way."[51] Her mother, Julia, testified that Karen Quinlan not only made such statements in talking about terminally ill relatives or friends, but also in "just general conversation. We had discussed the fact of being kept alive by extraordinary means, not referring—not making references to any individual."[52]

The Attorney General cross-appealed, challenging on hearsay grounds the trial court's admission of Karen Quinlan's prior statements about her distaste for continuance of life-support systems in circumstances not unlike her own.[53] Both the lower court and the Supreme Court of New Jersey agreed that Karen Quinlan's statements were "remote and impersonal, lack(ing) significant weight,"[54] rendering their admission into evidence insignificant. Her thoughts —about her own death and the sorrow of living in suspended animation—had not made a sufficiently deep impression. The tide had too easily and quickly washed away her words of worry and concern. She was, after all, only twenty-one years old when she had stopped talking.

But the court cases were not only about Karen Quinlan, that tragic ballerina; they were also about the horrors of the late-twentieth-century deathwatch. Her family asked the court: Who is the choreographer here? Why is our daughter still dancing? The music has stopped, and still we stand silently at her bedside, forced to witness her agony, day after day, night after night, and still nothing happens. Karen has no more story to move through, no more reason to cross the stage. Why doesn't the curtain come down, for God's sake? For Karen's sake? For our sake? Has time stopped? Are we trapped in her deathwatch for an eternity?

When Joseph Quinlan filed a petition in Chancery Division, he sought not only guardianship over the matter of his daughter, but power over her death. What the Quinlans really wanted was spiritual release for Karen and permission to return to the nineteenth century deathwatch of Munch's painting. They wanted to gather around her bed as a family and let nature take its course. Then, "if it is God's will to take her, she can go on to life after death."[55] They wanted the doctor to give up his fight and retire into the corner to assume his former role of referee. They wanted their parish priest to come forward, anoint their daughter, and prepare her for the journey home. They wanted her deathwatch to come to an end, to move her from that lonely threshold, and to give themselves the freedom and the right to grieve.

The Quinlans' struggle over Karen's deathwatch captured the public's imagination. Later, many others would become silent stars in similar constellations,[56] but Karen Quinlan's deathwatch was the first, the prototype. Although her story was deeply embedded in the soil of New Jersey, it transcended the boundaries of fact and became a twentieth-century tragedy.

Over ten years later, another young woman lay in a Missouri state hospital in a "persistent vegetative state,"[57] that same physical and spiritual limbo which had held Karen Quinlan captive for so long.◖

◖ Dr. Fred Plum coined the phrase "persistent vegetative state," referring to a body which is functioning entirely in terms of its internal controls. It maintains temperature. It maintains heart beat and pulmonary ventilation. It maintains digestive activity. It maintains reflex activity of muscles and nerves for low-level conditioned responses. But there is no behavioral evidence of either self-awareness or awareness of the surroundings in a learned manner.[47]

Why the term "vegetative" has never been stated. My sister-in-law, Joyce Clark Harmon, R.N., M.S., worked for over ten years in an ICU, and in a liquid conversation one evening, she told me of the terminology that ICU nurses and

The victim of a car accident at twenty-five, a gastrostomy feeding and hydration tube had kept Nancy Cruzan alive without cognitive function for over five years, and "medical experts testified she could live another thirty years."[58] With such oppressive longevity, the parents of Nancy Cruzan were not likely even to survive their daughter's deathwatch. She might outlive them all and die alone, attended only by some indifferent state employee in the first quarter of the twenty-first century.

Like the members of Karen Quinlan's deathwatch, Nancy Cruzan's parents brought their lament to the judicial system, first to the state courts, and finally to the United States Supreme Court.[59] The Cruzans wanted much the same thing: relief for Nancy and for themselves; power over their daughter's death; permission to bring her deathwatch to an end. As Joseph Cruzan put it, "It just consumes me trying to figure out what to do. I feel as Nancy's father, I've let her down. . . . It's like having a death in the family, and the state says, 'I'm sorry, but you can't bury that person.'"[60]

Even if the state is not an active player in the conflict,[61] and we merely feel its presence in the wings, the state is always there in some sort of directorial capacity. By providing a judicial forum, the state constructs the theatre in which these conflicts are resolved. It then lines up the players, deciding who may address the audience and who may not; at the same time, the state decides whose interests matter and whose do not. And when the families of Karen Quinlan and Nancy Cruzan petitioned the courts, the state decided to focus on the rights of the silent daughters who lay curled up in those hospital

---

doctors use. There were private names for certain kinds of patients, names that were cautiously revealed as if they were a source of shame. Someone in a coma was "gorked out." An indigent patient with poor hygiene was a "dirtball." The badly burned were "crispy critters," and those with only lower brain functions were "veggies, rutabagas, or squash." (Humor appears to be insulation from the stress of working with the critically ill.) I am struck, however, by the repetition of the vegetable metaphor even in the formal medical terminology.

beds, waiting for some way, some day, to die. The members of the deathwatch were pushed to one side.

True, they were needed procedurally: someone had to file the petition and ask for relief. The law provides a mechanism for invoking the rights of those who cannot speak for themselves, but once that mechanism is activated, the law ignores the petitioner, and focuses instead upon the silent party.❲ The guardian may be procedurally expedient, but once the lawsuit is launched, he can be left on the shore. Substantively, he is dispensable, and that is the way it is supposed to be.

But in these deathwatch cases, the petitioners are more than nominal, procedural plaintiffs, triggering a piece of litigation that could not have started in any other way. The petitioners are substantive plaintiffs as well, not just hollow masks through which resound the

---

❲ In *Vacco v. Quill*, in which the Supreme Court held that New York's prohibition on assisting suicide did not violate the Equal Protection Clause, some of the petitioners were silent for reasons other than incompetency—they were already dead.[48] The same was true of some of the formerly "gravely ill" plaintiffs in *Washington v. Glucksberg*, the companion opinion which held that Washington's prohibition against "caus[ing] or aid[ing] a suicide did not violate the Due Process clause."[49] They too were dead by the time the Supreme Court rendered its opinion. However, on the day the petitions were filled, these plaintiffs had been competent adults, complaining directly to the federal courts about their prolonged and painful terminal illnesses. Even though their pain was in the past tense, it was never fictional or indirect. As Justice Stevens pointed out in his concurrence to *Vacco v. Quill*, "The now-deceased plaintiffs in this action may in fact have had a liberty interest even stronger than Nancy Cruzan's because, not only were they terminally ill, they were suffering constant and severe pain."[50] The pain of the other petitioners in these cases, physicians who were deterred from prescribing lethal medication to mentally competent, terminally ill patients, was more akin to derivative pain—the pain of watching someone else in pain. But the physicians had their own particular kind of direct pain as well: the burden of caring for patients who could not be cared for.

pain of another. They too are aggrieved; they too are in pain. It may be derivative pain, the pain of watching a loved one linger on in misery, but that does not rob it of its authenticity.

IT went on for months and months, and because we live so far apart, my family had to keep vigil on the telephone. Over the years, this is how we have come to share our lives. We call each other often and talk the private language of our family. Distance does not have to defeat intimacy.

With my mother, the interval of silence between calls is about two weeks long. If more time goes by, I do not feel right in my skin, always imagining the worst: maybe she has been devoured by the San Andreas fault; maybe she is ill, or depressed. When we finally do talk, it is a relief. At first, we cover the intervening weeks with broad, bold strokes of generality. Later, after assurances of reasonably good health, happiness, and terrestrial stability, we exchange bursts of fabulous details about what was said and what was worn and what was said and what was eaten. We say nothing of consequence. Rather, the words exchanged form a crazy quilt of velvet and cotton, of flower prints and moiré satin, joined together by metallic threads and rickrack, by the unfinished sentences of mother and daughter, and by their shared assumptions and history.

But when my father was sick, there was a new and horrible dimension to our conversations. I had to ask, and she had to answer, "How is Daddy?" There were only two responses: "Just the same," or "Worse." Then there were the words of elaboration.

They were not words about my father. They were not words about the man who gave his children a sense of belonging in the world, a love of music, travel, and history. They were words about my father's body. About his broken, infected skin. About his bladder and his bowels. About what came out and what went in. About how his hands had frozen into the shape of a garden trowel. About how he moaned all the time like some miserable animal, beyond names, beyond faces, beyond recognition.

And yet, not beyond pain.

I hated those conversations, and I hated having to repeat them to my brother and sister on the telephone. They left all of us somber and silent. But as much as I hated those conversations, I knew that we had to have them. The three of us needed to know what was going on and, more important, our mother needed to tell us. Just as my father was wrapped in his own chrysallis of pain, separated from her by the gauze of disease and debilitation, so too was my mother in pain as she watched him die. It was not a pain to be borne alone.

I T is the pain of those elephants in Botswana who were reluctantly forced to desert the old dying cow in their search for food and water. It is the pain of agitated cetaceans who surround a distressed companion, or support his failing body at the surface of the water so that he may breathe. It is the pain of members of human deathwatches, those who gathered around the dying person's bed in Munch's painting, those who gather around the interminably ill person's bed in twentieth-century hospitals. It was the Quinlans's pain, and the Cruzans's pain. It was my mother's pain as she turned my father's body from side to side, over and over again. It was my pain, and the pain of my brother and sister.

But it is not a pain that the law is willing to recognize. Although the anguish of the members of the deathwatch may echo in the courthouse halls, we do not allow that anguish to penetrate the courtroom walls. That we do not hear it is a fiction held tightly in place by the mortar of another fiction. We pretend that we are listening to the voices of the silent, curled-up daughters; we make decisions to terminate the life-sustaining treatment in the name of their autonomy.[62] Through the doctrine of substituted judgment, the court makes the decision that the incompetent patient would have made were she competent.[63] It is a subjective test, seeking not to determine what most people would do under similar circumstances, but what this particular patient—this Karen Quinlan or this Nancy Cruzan— would have done. The doctrine enables the court to extend the common law and constitutional rights of self-determination to incompetent patients,[64] but in order to make the substituted judgment, we must pay fictional attention to the words of someone who is no longer there. And that pretense ensures another pretense: that we do not hear the voices of those who are there, the members of the deathwatch. Their pain may exist as a matter of human psychology, but it does not find expression in pleadings, depositions, transcripts, briefs, or appellate decisions. And as far as the law is concerned, if their pain does not find expression on the right pieces of paper, it does not exist at all.

2

Paintiffs, Procedure, and the Limits of Law Wishes

In my first year of law school, I had a recurring problem. When I briefed cases, I could not remember who was the plaintiff and who was the defendant. The shorthand versions of pi and delta were unfamiliar and did not help; they only added to my confusion. I was too embarrassed to reveal this rather fundamental deficiency to anyone, although now that I read answers to law school exams, instead of write them, I realize that my problem was not unique. At least once during each period of bluebook blues, I encounter a student who zealously analyzes an entire baroque fact pattern, confusing the plaintiff and the defendant.

In order to get straight who the plaintiff was, I used to remove the "l" from the word to create a new word: "paintiff." Paintiffs were people who came to the courthouse in pain.ᶜ They had been hurt or

---

ᶜ "Pain" originally meant "suffering or loss inflicted for a crime or offense; punishment; penalty; a fine." It came from the Latin, "paena," which meant penalty or punishment. If I had known my word derivations better, I would have picked the word "complain" as my heuristic device, since its original meaning evokes the appropriate imagery. To "complain" meant to "give expression to sorrow or suffering." It also came from the Latin, "com" plus "plangere," meaning to lament or bewail, and originally meaning to strike or beat the breast or head in

injured somehow and were seeking a remedy. It was easy to find them in a tort case, with all that blood and torn tissue. In a property case, it was more difficult, probably because I did not own much at the time. Finding the paintiff in an easement case, for example, was hard for me. I had to mentally move into somebody's house and start walking all over the neighbor's yard, or else be walked all over. In Civil Procedure, I never did find the paintiff, which undoubtedly accounted for my poor performance in the course.《

I have carried the heuristic device with me over the years, asking of each case that I read: Who is the paintiff? Who is in pain? What is the nature of that pain? What caused that pain? What can or should the law do about that pain? Do I care about that pain?

My answer to the last question determines the degree of attention I will pay to a judicial decision. Fortunately, I am not a judge, but a curious reader of curious cases. I read them because I want to, not because I have to. A judge does not have that luxury. He cannot put down a pleading because he is uninterested in the plaintiff's pain; he must take every complaint seriously.《《

---

sign of grief. Circa 1450, "complain" also came to mean a "formal statement of a grievance to or before a competent authority; to lodge a complaint, bring a charge."[1]

《 Once I had mastered the task of finding the plaintiff, my next intellectual hurdle was to find the referents for the players in an appellate decision: the appellant and the appellee. (Just as torts were not filled with strawberries, there were no apples in judicial decisions.) In a sense, the appellant was a meta-plaintiff, someone who came into the appellate court in pain from the decision of the court below.

《《 In Owen Fiss's words, the judge has an obligation to engage in a "dialogue." Our law of civil procedure, as well as the law of evidence, determines what claims the judge must adjudicate, and what witnesses the judge must listen to in order to render his decision:

It is a dialogue with very special qualities: (a) Judges are not in control of their

Nor does the judge have the luxury of caring about the pain of peripheral players in a lawsuit.««« The constraints that the rules of procedure and evidence impose do not permit the judge's empathy to graze in any pasture. He is confined by the artificial boundaries of the grievance, by the way in which the pain was packaged and presented.

The judge is fenced in by words, but I am not.

WHO are the paintiffs in a case like *Quinlan* or *Cruzan?* It might be the silent, curled-up daughters, but I doubt it. The question of whether a person in a semi-vegetative state feels pain has been debated in medical journals. The question arises in other clinical contexts: Does the human neonate and fetus perceive pain, for example,

agenda, but are compelled to confront grievances or claims they would otherwise prefer to ignore. (b) Judges do not have full control over whom they must listen to. They are bound by rules requiring them to listen to a broad range of persons or spokesmen. (c) Judges are compelled to speak back, to respond to the grievance or the claim, and to assume individual responsibility for that response. (d) Judges must also justify their decisions.[2]

««« Sometimes a judge is permitted to consider, however, through a utilitarian analysis, the potential pain to the defendant if he had exercised more care. Nuisance law provides an example. The *Restatement (Second) of Torts* suggests that to determine whether "[a]n intentional invasion of another's interest in the use and enjoyment of land is unreasonable," a judge may consider whether "the gravity of the harm outweighs the utility of the actor's conduct." In determining the utility of the defendant's conduct, one factor that a judge may consider, apart from the social value of that conduct and its "suitability ... to the character of the locality," is "the impracticability of preventing or avoiding the invasion." Thus, the judge may consider how painful it would have been to the defendant to take the measures needed to avoid the harm, or how painful it would be to require him to "carry on his activity with more skill or care or in a different manner or at a different time and thereby avoid a substantial part of the harm."[3]

or is a patient under general anesthesia or in a coma aware of painful physical touches or unpleasant sensations? Dr. Michael McQuillan concludes that "the pathways sufficient for the perception and modulation of pain need not rise nor descend to levels generally thought necessary for consciousness. Pain may be expressed not only in language, but also in autonomic and motor behavior that can be shown to correlate in a linear fashion with subjective pain sensation."[1] Thus, according to McQuillan, we cannot rule out the possibility that an unconscious person, or one in a persistent vegetative state, might perceive pain. Other physicians disagree, arguing that such patients cannot perceive the pain that attends starvation or dehydration.[2] We simply do not know—and cannot know—how or even whether Karen Quinlan or Nancy Cruzan suffered.[c] We are at an epistemological disadvantage.

Of course, we are always at an epistemological disadvantage with respect to each other. Sometimes this philosophical problem is referred to as "knowledge solipsism." It differs from the more familiar form of solipsism, the metaphysical claim that only the self exists. Knowledge solipsism is a much less radical claim—that the self is the origin of the knowledge of existence. It does not assert that there is only one source of knowledge; rather, it rules out the possibility that one could have direct knowledge of the sensations of others.[3] We can only know our own sensations; our "knowledge" of the feelings of others must be indirect, based on probability or analogy.[4] With respect to pain, we can only truly know our own pain and must infer

---

[c] Dr. McQuillan distinguishes "between pain as a particular kind of sensation and the affective response to pain that is called suffering." I should perhaps acknowledge here a certain crudeness in my use of the term "pain" with respect to the members of the deathwatch. In McQuillan's terms, I am actually referring more to their suffering—presumably psychic, emotional, and spiritual—although certainly that pain could manifest itself in physical sensations. The pain that the members of the deathwatch witness is the particular kind of physical sensation that is experienced by the dying person, whatever that sensation may be.[4]

the pain of others based on trust. We trust that when others wince, or cry, or say they are in pain, they are experiencing sensations akin to our own in similar circumstances. And the truth is: most of us do not let these philosophical quandaries get in the way of feeling the pain of others. We let empathy do the job that philosophy cannot handle.

Empathy fails us, however, when we try to imagine the pain of Karen Quinlan or Nancy Cruzan. The nature of their suffering is alien to us because it registered on a body that was no longer familiar. The analogy crumbles. We cannot crawl into their minds and feel at home there, the way we might crawl into the mind of someone who is conscious and alert and inhabits a nervous system much like our own. If Karen Quinlan and Nancy Cruzan felt pain, it was not a pain that I can claim to understand. I can only respond on the level of abstraction: If they felt pain, whatever that might have meant to them, I too would have wanted the pain to come to an end. If they were in fact paintiffs, their petitions should have been granted.««

But it does not take much imagination to feel the pain of the members of Karen Quinlan's deathwatch, or of Nancy Cruzan's, or to appreciate how they were paintiffs in their respective cases. Perhaps it would help to have lived through a similar deathwatch, to have turned one's own father's body from side to side, over and over again.

«« The trial court heard in *Quinlan* heard evidence that Karen Quinlan herself understood the pain of the members of the deathwatch, at least before she lost her cognitive function. Karen Quinlan's sister, Mary Ellen, testified regarding Karen's feelings about the deaths of two people who were well-known to her:

> Karen was talking about Mr. Birch dying, and her girlfriend's father dying. But when she talked to me, she was saying, in so many words, that she wouldn't want to be kept alive because she watched part of the family die, too. Not just the person who died legally. And she was saying that, like she was very good friends with this girl, and she watched what this girl went through and that was what she was referring to, to me, when she said she wouldn't want to be kept alive.[5]

Perhaps, but it hardly seems a requisite to feeling empathy that we should have to wear the same shoes to understand the pressure of the leather—only that we should have the same kind of feet.

ONE day last spring, I was at the beach with my friend. Actually, we were having lunch in the front seat of her car, a ferocious March wind having blown away our plan of eating with our feet in the sand. The sky was full of luminous, silver clouds; the water was choppy, slate gray.

I had been telling her about my concern for the families of Karen Quinlan and Nancy Cruzan, for the members of the deathwatch. "They are the ones in pain in those cases, not the patients. As far as anyone can tell, the patients are not even aware of their situations."

She knew what I was talking about, having gone through her mother's prolonged deathwatch last year. "In some ways, what you say is right, of course," she said. "Look at my mother. Her dying almost killed my sister and me. Even though she was virtually gone, we still felt we had to go see her every night. Night after night, week after week, through those endless yellow halls, into that dark little room. It looked out onto a parking lot." She rested her sandwich on her lap and stared out at the Long Island Sound through the car window. "And there she was, skin and bones, her mouth open, her eyes staring blankly at the wall." She picked up her sandwich and took a bite. "I don't know why we went at all," she mumbled. "She didn't even know we were there."

I did not respond, but left her in silence with her dredged up pain. Then, after a while, I said, "You see what I mean, then. The pain in that situation didn't really belong to your mother, even though that is what the law pretends. If she had been on life-support systems, year after year, and you and your sister didn't feel that you could stand it any more, witnessing her slow disintegration, you would have to petition a court to withdraw the medical treatment. But you wouldn't petition in your own name. You'd have to bring the lawsuit in her name. Then the court would use a legal fiction called 'substituted judgment' to make the lawsuit sound as if your mother were doing the asking, even though the pain really belonged to you and your sister—to the members of the deathwatch.⟨ The law doesn't directly confront your pain." I paused for a moment, coming up for air. "I hate that kind of pretense in the law."

She did not respond at first to my spate of words, but unwrapped a baggie of quartered apples. Then, because she is who she is, she sought refuge in the comforting impersonality of legal discourse, in the sanctuary of words that do not self-refer.

"You don't mean to suggest, do you, that we grant the members of the deathwatch some sort of legal recourse?"

I knew that her question was coming. There is a wonderful sameness to our friendship, to the patterns of what we say and what we do not say to one another. I start off by worrying about something. I keep it to myself. It lives inside me for a long time, slowly building pressure against the walls of my body, but never crossing the somatic boundary. Then, in the pale hours of one sleepless morning, it begins to pour out of my mouth and my nose and my ears like ectoplasm, like cool, white steam, and I try to hold it in my hand, to make it palpable, to give it a shape, to find it a name.

Within a day or so, I bring my worry to her, crudely formed in new sentences, tentative and conditional, and it always sounds clumsy when it hits the air.⟨⟨ What does she do with it, my tender,

---

⟨ The doctrine of substituted judgment appeared, in the context of medical decision-making, in the lower court decision in *Quinlan*.[6] The court states: "The assertion that Karen would elect, if competent, to terminate the respirator requires careful examination." The need to use the legal fiction that Karen Quinlan was making the decision herself, that the court was merely placing itself in her place and acting as she would have acted in similar circumstances, stems from her incompetency and the court's desire to "afford to that [incompetent] person the same panoply of rights and choices it recognizes in competent persons."[7]

⟨⟨ Something always happens to my ideas when they move from the inside of my mind to the ears of another human being. I found a description of the same

fledgling expression of concern? She tries to cram it into "some sort of legal recourse."

It is her way of dealing with the unknown. It may also be a way of justifying her own existence as a teacher of law. She needs the apparent neutrality and abstraction of legal rhetoric to create the illusion that law consists of a body of secret knowledge—secret knowledge that she has mastered and now is charged with the sacred duty of transmitting. The language of the law may also relieve her of her memories—mother memories too heavy to bear at lunch, in the light, in the presence of a friend.

"Legal recourse." I hid my annoyance. "I don't know. I've just started thinking about it."

"Well, what sort of lawsuit do you think it would be? I mean, there has to be some sort of right that's being infringed upon." She was sputtering in that ineffable way that only those who teach law can sputter. "What kind of right do you want to give to the members of the deathwatch? And what kind of remedy are you going to grant them if someone infringes on that right?"

Socratic Sputter . . . Pedagogical Sputter . . . Critical Sputter. I was searching for the right kind of sputter.

"It's all well and good to talk about hating the legal fiction and having the law be honest and confront the real pain directly," she

---

phenomenon while reading *The House at Pooh Corner.* Eeyore had been bounced into the river, and Pooh had suggested that he throw a large stone into the water so that Eeyore would be washed to the shore. The plan backfired. Eeyore claimed that he had to dive underwater to avoid being hit by the stone and was critical of Pooh's idea. Piglet tried to comfort Pooh:

"It's just Eeyore," said Piglet. "I thought your Idea was a very good Idea." Pooh began to feel a little more comfortable, because when you are a Bear of Very Little Brain, and you Think of Things, you find sometimes that a Thing which seemed very Thingish inside you is quite different when it gets out into the open and has other people looking at it.[8]

My problem, I suspect, has something to do with being a Bear of Very Little Brain.

continued. "But you really have to give the lawsuit more structure than that. Define the harm done to the members of the deathwatch —your paintiffs, as you call them—and decide what you want done about it."

Structural sputter.

My friend is a great believer in the natural order of things. She needs to know that the plaintiff has a substantive right, and that for infringements of that right there is an ideal remedy. *Ubi jus, ibi remedium*: Where there is a right, there is a remedy.[5] I hear her humming over the breakfast dishes, carefully putting the plates on the dish drainer in descending order, the forks and spoons all facing the same way in the cutlery basket. Closely related to the dichotomy of right and remedy is the dichotomy of substance and procedure. It holds that procedure is distinct from substance. We use procedure as a means of fashioning the remedy, and the remedy, in turn, as a means of protecting against the infringement of the substantive right. Her beliefs are motivated by a deep need for symmetry and logical progression, by the sense of control that she derives from those little numbered boxes into which she puts her ideas. From a dish drainer properly used.

I drive her crazy with my messy mind, by the way I move unpredictably, and often irresponsibly, from thought to thought, making unconscious connections between wildly disparate things. Not only do I throw plates on top of knots of forks and spoons, but often I do not wash the dishes at all.

It is odd that we are such good friends, but we need each other. I need her—to return to her predictable model of social reality, legal order, and to the comfort of her certitude. She needs me to disturb. She would never admit it, of course. She does not even like me to ask philosophical questions, as if my ruminations somehow put her at risk.

Perhaps her need to suppress my worries derives from sororal angst. Few people remember what happened to Alice's sister in the end of *Alice's Adventures in Wonderland*. In the beginning of the story, this sensible, older sister was educating Alice from a book with no pictures or conversations in it. Alice fell asleep, and when she woke, she told her sister all about her adventures in her "curious dream." Alice then runs off, and her sister "sat still just as she had left her, leaning her head on her hand, watching the setting sun, and thinking of little Alice and all her wonderful Adventures, till she too began dreaming after a fashion." She dreamed of Alice looking up at her before the dream had started, "and still as she listened, or seemed to listen, the whole place around her became alive with the strange creatures of her little sister's dream." Suddenly, the sister's world became inhabited with a White Rabbit, a March Hare, the Queen of Hearts, a baby sneezing on a Duchess' knee, a shrieking Gryphon, a squeaking Lizard, a sobbing Mock Turtle, and "the choking of the suppressed guinea-pigs."[6]

My friend might be afraid that she is Alice's sister. By permitting me to dream promiscuously, she is in danger of disappearing into a hole. It is better, or so she believes, to keep us both above the ground, safely under the shade of a tree, reading books with no talk and no illustrations. Of course, she is wrong, both about herself, and about me. We are neither of us in danger from asking philosophical questions—the danger lies in not asking them. And at some level, one of roots and rock, she must know that. Otherwise, she would not let me bring my worries to her at all. Otherwise, we would not be such good friends.

FOR a while, I stopped talking to my friend about the members of the deathwatch and tried to answer some of her questions about the kind of lawsuit they might bring. In trying to answer the threshold question of who my paintiffs might be, I found myself all alone at one end of the spectrum. That solitude prompted this question: Is the deathwatch of necessity a two-part relation? Could I be the only member of my own deathwatch, all alone in the forest, under falling trees, keeping a solitary vigil over my dying body?[c]

In some sense, and for a while, it seemed to me that I could. After all, the role of a dying person would be no different from the other roles that I have played. Since the first time I leaned over and apprehended that chasm between self and other, I have watched myself perform: the role of child; the role of mother; the role of student; the role of teacher. They are all different persons. Indeed, our idea of persons comes not only from seventeenth-century notions of moral agency, but also from a more ancient source, the Greek theater. "An actor dons masks, literally *per sonae*, that through which the sound comes, for the many roles he acts."[7]

Some roles I chose to play, and others were forced upon me, but inside, at least the way I experience consciousness, there seems to be an inner self who sometimes takes part, and sometimes does not.[«] Pain and joy command her participation, but always she watches and listens. When I am alone, and playing no role, she is there with me,

---

[«] Berkeley's famous hypothetical is about a tree falling in an empty forest. If no one is there to hear it, does it make a sound? Berkeley (1685–1783) addressed this philosophical issue as he sought to refute a version of materialism, predominant in the seventeenth century, which held that immediate objects of perception exist independent of the mind. In the *Three Dialogues*, Berkeley claims that sounds "have no real being without the mind." Once we conceive of any "thing," we bring it into a relationship with the percipient—ourselves—and thus Berkeley concludes that nothing can exist independent of the mind.[9]

[««] George Herbert Mead observes that the self is a social construct:

> The self, as that which can be an object to itself, is essentially a social structure, and it arises in social experience. After a self has arisen, it in a certain sense provides for itself its social experiences, and so we can conceive of an absolutely solitary self. But it is impossible to conceive of a self arising outside of social experience. When it has arisen we can think of a person in solitary confinement for the rest of his life, but who still has himself as a companion, and is able to think and to converse with himself as he had communicated with others. That process to which I have just referred, of responding to one's self as another responds to it, taking part in one's own conversation with others, being aware of what one is saying and using that awareness of what one is saying to determine what one is going to say thereafter—that is a process with which we are all familiar.[10]

and we talk up a blue streak.⟨ She is my constant companion and the only witness to the various roles that I have come to play. Sometimes she writes under my name.⟨⟨

I am aware that my belief in an inner self is inconsistent with the tenets of postmodernism. The postmodern "self" is nothing more than a shattered, cultural construct—bits and pieces of mirror collaged and tenuously pasted together with the glue of illusion. But it is not one of my goals to be consistent with the tenets of postmodernism, and when there is a meltdown of the multiple roles that I play, there is still a hard core resistant to heat, someone who seems to be identified with me.

There is no doubt that she would attend at least the early stages of my deathwatch. But upon the disappearance of that inner self, the cessation of that private dialogue, someone else would have to see it through, to keep solitary vigil over my dying body. Otherwise, there would be no one to watch the death. I could die all alone in the forest, under falling trees, but I could not be the only member of my own deathwatch.

So I guess by definition the deathwatch must be a two-part relation. There will always be one who watches, and one who is watched: one vertical and the other horizontal.

⟨ A blue streak is "something moving very fast," or "continuous, rapid, or interminable speech": "to talk a blue streak." Its parallel in the British vernacular is "to talk the hind leg off a donkey," which describes the behavior of a victim of logorrhea or logomania. Logomania is "abnormal talkativeness," whereas logorrhea is "pathologically excessive and incoherent talkativeness."[11]

Patricia Williams writes eloquently about the cacophony of inner voices, suggesting that their competition may foster personal growth and the discovery of new ideas:

It is also wise, I know, to maintain some consciousness of where I am when I am other than the voice itself. If the other voice in my head is really me too, then it means that I have shifted positions, ever so slightly, and become a new being, a different one from her, over there. It gets confusing sometimes, so I leave markers of where I've been, particularly if it's not just a voice but a place that I want to come back to in time.[12]

   With respect to my own inner dialogue, we are definitely logomaniacal and, when worried, we suffer from logorrhea.

‟ I found my own thoughts echoing in a poem by Ray Bradbury:

I do not write—
The other me
Demands emergence constantly.
But if I turn to face him much too swiftly
Then
He sidles back to where and when
He was before
I unknowingly cracked the door
And let him out.
Sometimes a fire-shout beckons him,
He reckons that I need him,
So I do. His task
To tell me who I am behind this mask.
He Phantom is, and I facade
That hides the opera he writes with God,
While I, all blind,
Wait raptureless until his mind
Steals down my arm to wrist, to hand, to fingertips
And, stealing, find
Such truths as fall from tongues
And burn with sound,
And all of it from secret blood and secret soul on secret ground.

At the end of the poem, he asks:

Did R.B. write that poem, that line, that speech?
No, inner-ape, invisible, did teach.
His reach, clothed in my flesh, stays mystery;
Say not my name.
Praise other me.[13]

I HAD settled in my own mind that the deathwatch must be a two-part relation; at a minimum, there would always be one who watches, and one who is watched.ᶜ But that statement marked both the beginning and the end of certainty. Beyond the notion of a two-part relation, I had to deal with probability. How was I going to identify who the watchers and the watched might be?

More likely than not, the dying member of the deathwatch would be a single individual. Of course, there have been instances of corporate death throughout history, due to natural disasters or the cruelty of man.ᶜᶜ In our own century, the scale of slaughter during warfare

---

ᶜ Arnold Toynbee, too, notes that dying was a two-part relation: "This two-sidedness ... is a fundamental feature of death—not only of the premature death of the spirit, but of death at any age and in any form. There are always two parties to a death; the person who dies and the survivors who are bereaved." Those who strive to "deprive death of its sting" by holding that death is nothing more than an annihilation of the person who dies overlook the "crucial fact that, in a death, there are two parties to the event.... [M]an is a social creature; and a fact of capital importance about death's sting is that it is two-pronged."[14]

Dr. Cicely Saunders, founder of St. Christopher's Hospice in London, prefers to invoke the words spoken in the Garden of Gethsemane, "Watch with Me," to capture the needs of the dying. Her version of the deathwatch is more communal; the dying person and the members of the deathwatch are in collaboration, or at least witness the arrival of death together.

I have tried to sum up the demands of this work we are planning in the words "Watch with Me." Our most important foundation for St. Christopher's is the hope that in watching we should learn not only how to free patients from pain and distress, how to understand them and never let them down, but also how to be silent, how to listen and how just to be there.[15]

ᶜᶜ From the late seventeenth century through the beginning of the twentieth, Westerners abided by "relatively humanitarian" standards for the conduct of war. Those standards plummeted when the Germans invaded Belgium in August of

has grown to appalling proportions.⟫⟫⟫ And when the number of those dying increases substantially, the deathwatch becomes a social convention that must give way to utility. Contemporary accounts of the bubonic, pneumonic, and septicaemic plagues of fourteenth-century Western Europe and Asia, for example, often remarked upon the disappearance of the deathwatch. Defoe writes about the effect of the Great Plague of 1665 on the deathwatch; because of the risk of infection, no one wanted to participate in deathwatches, and sick people wandered into the countryside to die alone: "It was known to us all that abundance of poor despairing Creatures, who had the Distemper upon them, and were grown stupid or melancholy by their Misery, as many were, wandered away into the Fields, and Woods, and into secret uncouth Places, almost any where to creep

---

1914, as civilians were no longer spared the atrocities of war. In 1937, horror "swept across the Western world," in Toynbee's phrase, with the bombing of Guernica, Spain, which indiscriminately made victims of civilians of all ages. The bombings of the Second World War dwarfed those of the First World War and its aftermath. Yet, sadly, Toynbee writes, those bombings "caused less perturbation. For producing a shock, atrociousness, by itself, is not enough; there must also be novelty."[16]

⟫⟫⟫ There is an entire body of literature on the deathwatches of the Holocaust. One of the most painful pieces to read is Elie Wiesel's *The Death of My Father.* Wiesel, present at his father's death in Buchenwald, finds no solace in the circumstances of his father's death or the deathwatch imposed upon him as the survivor.

> His death did not even belong to him. I do not know to what cause to attribute it, in what book to inscribe it. No link between it and the life he had led. His death, lost among all the rest, had nothing to do with the person he had been. It could just as easily have brushed him in passing and spared him. It took him inadvertently, absentmindedly. By mistake. Without knowing that it was he; he was robbed of his death.[7]

into a Bush, or Hedge and Die."[8] In some instances, the deathwatch had to be legislated against, to impede the spread of disease.《

But while there have been many instances of corporate death throughout history, that is not the norm. Most of us will experience death on our own, and those are the deathwatches that I am interested in, with one individual lying down. As with our births, we tend to die seriatim.

More likely than not the other part of the relation, those who watch, will also consist of more than one person. It will probably be a group.《《 *Webster's* defines a group as a "number of individuals assembled together or having some unifying relationship." But beyond this

---

《 For example, an Italian statute mandated isolation of the dying and prohibited others from nursing them:

> Everyone sick of the plague is to be brought out of the town to the fields, there to die or recover. Those who have nursed plague patients are to remain secluded for ten days before having intercourse with anyone. The clergy are to examine the sick and report to the authorities on pain of being burnt at the stake and confiscation of their possessions. Those who introduce the plague shall forfeit all their goods to the State. Finally, with the exception of those set apart for the purpose, no one shall administer to those sick of the plague on pain of death and forfeiture of their possessions.[18]

《《 The term "group" may be used, in sociology and anthropology, in at least two ways. In one sense, it can "describe any collectivity whose members are alike in some way." In a more narrow sense, and in the sense that I am using the term, "group" refers to units that have "some distinctive interdependent social relationships with one another," i.e., organized groups. In an organized group, the individual members "make up a larger social whole with common aims, interdependent roles and a distinctive subculture." Presumably a deathwatch constitutes an organized group, in the sense that its members have a common aim, but it would be fleeting in duration and possess no formal governing structure.[19]

nebulous definition, how do we determine what individuals are in that number? What does it mean to assemble? **«««** What is the unifying relationship? Is there some organizing principle for their identification? And even if we could identify the members of the deathwatch, what would the law have to do with that entity?

««« Are public executions a form of deathwatch? Consider how many similarities to a private deathwatch there are in this description of a hanging:

Death by hanging, like most kinds of death in the eighteenth century, was public. Not isolated from the community or concealed as an embarrassment to it, the execution of the death sentence was made known to every part of the metropolis and the surrounding villages. On the morning of a hanging day the bells of the churches of London were rung buffeted. The cries of hawkers selling ballads and "Last Dying Speeches" filled the streets. The last preparations for death in the chapel at Newgate were open to those able to pay the gaoler his fee. The malefactor's chains were struck off in the press yard in front of friends and relations, the curious, the gaping and onlookers at the prison gate. The route of the hanging procession crossed the busiest axis of the town at Smithfield, passed through one of the most heavily populated districts in St. Gile's and St. Andrew's, Holborn, and followed the most-trafficked road, Tyburn Road, to the gallows. There the assembled people on foot, upon horseback, in coaches, crowding near-by houses, filling the adjoining roads, climbing ladders, sitting on the wall enclosing Hyde Park and standing in its contiguous cow pastures gathered to witness the hanging.[20]

In our own century, there is what might be called the media version of a deathwatch. Do all those who read or hear about an event in some sense "assemble" and become members of the deathwatch? In the early 1970s, for example, as the horrors of toxic poisoning were being discovered in the fishing and farming town of Minamata on the Japanese island of Kyushu, "parades of politicians and governmental environmentalists would move rapidly from home to home among a select few patients, bowing, listening, looking sad and moving on. All this was dutifully and 'objectively' recorded by reporters and cameramen."[21]

AT first, I decided that I could always rely upon the nuclear family as my organizing principle. It was an easy term to define: "The term nuclear family refers to a unit consisting of husband, wife, and dependent offspring."[9] At the deathwatch, I would get out a piece of yellow chalk and draw a circle on the floor around the spouse and children, or the mother and father and the dying person's siblings. All the other members of the deathwatch who might be gathered around the bed would be outside the circle, their toes covered with the yellow dust of exclusion. I would not let them sue because of their tenuous relationship with the dying person.

That sounded like a good rule to me, both for its apparent simplicity and accuracy. Simple because of the ease of application: To find the potential paintiffs, a court would only have to consult a roughly hewn family tree. Accurate because in *Quinlan* and *Cruzan*, the two most famous cases, the moving parties had been the parents of the dying person, even if the siblings had been left out. It seemed like a harmless expansion to include the brothers and sisters in such a lawsuit, and, if the dying person were married, it seemed appropriate to look to the spouse and children too.[10]

When I was learning to sew, my mother used to complain that I could complicate anything. Any time a single-stranded thread presented itself in a furrow of fabric, my fingers would mysteriously find a way to turn that single stranded thread into an octopus with snarled limbs.

Sartorially speaking, she was right. Later she used to accuse me of the same tendency in my everyday dealings with life. I could start out with a single-stranded choice of what to order for lunch, and my mind would mysteriously find a way to turn it into a tangled moral choice about eating meat.

Philosophically speaking, she was wrong. I did not create that knot of threads; it had been there long before I opened the menu. The difference was that I had seen the knot, and perhaps because the threads lay close together, she had seen only a single strand. What looked to her like filial alchemy was in fact just her misperception of the problem's simplicity.

So it was with the circle on the floor around the nuclear family.

The longer I lived with that organizing principle, the more the problem increased in complexity, and, as my fingers discovered the density of the knot, I came to appreciate the crudeness of the solution. What had seemed like a rule endowed with the virtues of simplicity and accuracy turned out to be an unyielding formal abstraction that flew in the face of reality.

By looking at the other deathwatch cases, the other cases in which pleadings were made to terminate life-support systems, I became convinced that my yellow chalk line was a useless convention. Some of those people who participated most intensely in deathwatches were not members of the dying person's nuclear family at all. One was an old friend and head of the patient's religious order.[11] Another was a nephew, and longtime fan and devotee of his now eighty-four-year-old, incompetent aunt; another a close friend who lived with the patient for several years; another a second cousin.[12] Sadly enough, some of the dying persons in the cases did not have any members of the nuclear family to gather around them.[13] At times it was difficult to find a family member who cared enough to come forward to serve the role of procedural plaintiff.[14] ᴄ And in other instances, there were bitter conflicts over who would be a member of the deathwatch and who would not: instances where members of the nuclear family sought to exclude others from the circle who could not claim consanguinity.

Not surprisingly, one of the cases concerned a gay couple.[15] Sharon Kowalski, a twenty-seven-year-old woman, had been living with her partner, Karen Thompson, and "had exchanged rings, and

---

ᴄ Patients who have been both mentally disabled and institutionalized for a long time are often not part of any social network. Their personal histories almost guarantee that no one will be present at their deathwatches.

In a beautiful essay, Kathryn Montgomery Hunter confronts the problem of decision-making for a homeless patient, William T., who having lost contact with his family "was lost to work and friends and a home before he was through adolescence." She suggests the image of a Greek chorus, consisting of all those in the hospital who have cared for him: the attending physicians, residents, nurses, and

named each other as beneficiary in their life insurance policies."[16] Sharon suffered brain damage in a terrible car accident, after which she demonstrated the mental capacity of a four-to-six-year-old child, and her ability to communicate was severely limited. Kowalski's parents were not aware of the nature of their daughter's relationship with Thompson; nor had Kowalski "admitted it prior to the accident."[17] Both Karen Thompson and Kowalski's father petitioned for guardianship, and the battle of who would care for Sharon was hotly contested in the Minnesota state courts. The probate court had appointed the father guardian but granted both parties equal visitation rights, access to financial and medical records, and the right to confer with Sharon's doctors. Eventually the relationship between her partner and her father deteriorated, and the trial court terminated Thompson's access to her records and doctors and gave the father the power to limit visitations. He immediately terminated Thompson's visitation rights.[18]

Thompson appealed, claiming that her confidential relationship with Sharon was essentially that of a spouse, warranting her appointment as guardian. After losing many rounds in the lower courts, the Minnesota Court of Appeals finally granted guardianship to Karen Thompson, the patient's partner, finding that, "Sharon has the capacity reliably to express a preference . . . and she has clearly chosen to return home with Thompson if possible. This choice is further supported by the fact that Thompson and Sharon are a family of affinity, which ought to be accorded respect."[19] The Kowalski case ended up

---

other personnel. In the absence of any family, this informal, ad hoc group would assemble to advise William T.'s attending physician.

William T.'s life intersects the lives of those who hoped to cure, who never meant to become gatekeepers to medical care or arbiters of death. Some of them believe their care was wasted on William; some believe it was their duty. Some believe both things at once. For their own well-being and the well-being of their profession, a ritual that takes note of these intersecting lives and crossed purposes is required. We cannot ask for one better than that which served Sophocles and his inescapably tragic view of human life.[22]

being a struggle over who could be the patient's guardian, instead of who could be present at her deathwatch, but the battle lines were drawn in the same place—between the patient's biological family and the family she had chosen, through the exercise of her will and of her heart.

So though at first glance *Quinlan* and *Cruzan* may have looked like the norm, upon closer scrutiny, there really was no norm, or what was passed off as the norm turned out to be someone's unarticulated aspiration. This does not mean there were no deathwatches with members of the nuclear family in close attendance. Most were.⟨ It

---

⟨ Deference to family decision-making reflects a *long* tradition of noninterference by the state in family matters. I italicize the term "long" because the view of the family as a sphere of privacy and autonomy is primarily a product of the nineteenth century. Notions of familial privacy and a tradition of noninterference in the family developed from a broader nineteenth-century tradition of liberal individualism, as embodied in John Stuart Mill's Harm Principle:

> [T]he principle requires liberty of tastes and pursuits; of framing the plan of our life to suit our own character; of doing as we like, subject to such consequences as may follow: without impediment from our fellow-creatures, so long as what we do does not harm them, even though they should think our conduct foolish, perverse, or wrong.... [T]he only freedom which deserves the name, is that of pursuing our own good in our own way, so long as we do not attempt to deprive others of theirs, or impede their efforts to obtain it. Each is the proper guardian of his own health, whether bodily, or mental and spiritual. Mankind are greater gainers by suffering each other to live as seems good to themselves, than by compelling each to live as seems good to the rest.[23]

Expanding Mill's principle from the individual to the family, however, has some inherent conceptual difficulties. In particular, the meaning of "harm to others" is unclear when, by definition, there are interpersonal relations. Any time the law deals with one person's relationship to another, there is the risk of harm to others. Carl Schneider argues that "not only are there many opportunities within families to harm other members; there are many incentives," including psychological and "financial interest[s] in a decision adverse to the interests of other family members."[24]

just means that the scene with the members of the nuclear family gathered around the dying person's bed was only the most common of the many kinds of deathwatches. And by drawing the chalk circle at those heels, and those heels only, the state would be implicitly sanctioning one pattern of family life and punishing all others.❝

I did not want any part of a project like that. Even though I came from a nuclear family much like the Quinlans and the Cruzans, I could see that there are many kinds of gardens to grow in, and that human love and intimacy can flourish in any kind of soil—or in no soil at all, like stubborn moss in the cracks of city sidewalks, or graceful epiphytes suspended in air. To exclude from the deathwatch those who have truly loved the dying person, just because their names cannot be painted on a family tree,❝❝ seemed not only arbi-

---

The constitutional right of privacy, discovered in the Fourteenth Amendment and the penumbrae of the Bill of Rights,[25] derives in part from legal principles relating to the family. The privacy doctrine has "some extension to activities relating to marriage ... procreation ... contraception ... child rearing and education."[26]

❝ Walter O. Weyrauch notes that "the concept of the family is culturally determined and subject to ethnic and cultural variations."

Legally, a family group may be based on consanguinity, or affinity by marriage alone; but there may be de facto relationships also, without blood relationship or marriage, and these may or may not be legally recognized.... [S]mall group classifications, regardless of whether they originate in psychology, sociology, or anthropology, do not necessarily coincide with legal classifications.... [L]egal classifications [of family] tend to be more narrow and rigid than group classifications.... [They are] "cerebral" ... [a]bstract and relatively removed from specific factual situations.[27]

❝❝ Some have argued that the ideal of the nuclear family is an anachronism as well. Colonial families were "extensions of the larger community" and also served as the primary unit of economic production, education, and socialization of the young.[28] The same was true of the preindustrial family in England. In the

trary, but cruel.⟪⟪⟪ There had to be some other organizing principle, some other way of determining who should be able to bring their pain to the court's attention, and who should not.

I was finding no answers in the law. Then one day while hiding in

mid-eighteenth century, "work, religion, recreation, and amusements were confined to a small, relatively undifferentiated community."[29]

The introduction of factory methods of production and the move from the country to the cities led the father, and later the mother, to work outside the home. This decline of domestic economic production meant that public authorities assumed increasing responsibility for the education and socialization of the young. Others have taken on most of the traditional functions of the family, and the ideal family of the eighteenth century has become little more than a romanticized social construction.[30]

People in the industrial West from traditional nuclear families often assume that this family structure is universal. Scholars, however, have debated that issue. George P. Murdock, for example, argues that the nuclear family is not only universal, but typically has four functions: sexual, economic, reproductive, and educational. Murdock defines the family as "a social group characterized by common residence, economic cooperation, and reproduction" that includes "adults of both sexes, at least two of whom maintain a socially approved sexual relationship, and one or more children, own or adopted, of the sexually cohabiting adults."[31] It sounds a great deal like *Leave It to Beaver.*

Anthropologist Melford Spiro's study of kibbutz life in Israel challenged Murdock's assumptions. Spiro initially concluded that, at least in a familial society like the kibbutz, the nuclear family could be eliminated.[32] Spiro later altered his interpretation of the data from the kibbutz study, concluding that the strong role of the nuclear family in the socialization of children required a reconsideration of his previous conclusion that "marriage and the family are not universal."[33]

⟪⟪⟪ Given the Supreme Court's holding in *Bowers v. Hardwick,* it is unlikely that the Court will recognize family groups consisting of homosexual partners any time soon. Hardwick challenged the constitutionality of a Georgia sodomy statute which he had been charged with violating for engaging in oral sex with another consenting adult in the privacy of his home. The Court framed the issue as

a colleague's kitchen at a party, I broke the cardinal rule of academic socializing—Thou Shalt Not Discuss Ideas—and vented my frustration. Someone casually suggested that I look into "network theory" in sociology. Maybe the members of the deathwatch did not belong to a nuclear family but instead belonged to a network. Maybe that was a way to figure out who deserved to be the paintiffs in my lawsuit and who did not, by throwing a net into the sea.

So I read up on networks. Conceptually, the network seemed to fit in somewhere between the family and the total social environment.

"whether the Federal Constitution confers a fundamental right upon homosexuals to engage in sodomy."[34] Laurence H. Tribe writes: "Six decades of privacy precedents from *Meyer v. Nebraska* and *Skinner v. Oklahoma* to *Griswold v. Connecticut* and *Roe v. Wade* were dismissed in two brisk paragraphs as having no relevance to this issue, since those cases involved rights related to 'family, marriage or procreation.'"[35]

Sometimes when things are darkest in federal constitutional jurisprudence, hope flickers in the state courts. *Braschi v. Stahl Assocs.*[36] examined a New York City rent and eviction regulation providing "that upon the death of a rent-control tenant, the landlord may not dispossess 'either the surviving spouse of the deceased tenant or some other member of the deceased tenant's family who has been living with the tenant.'"[37] The appellant had lived with a rent-controlled tenant for over ten years as a "permanent life partner."[38] They regarded one another, and were regarded by friends and family, as spouses. The two men regularly visited each other's families and attended family functions together. Furthermore, they shared finances, and the appellant was the beneficiary under the statutory tenant's life insurance policy and will. On the tenant's death, the landlord served the appellant with a notice to terminate since he was not a family member of the decedent. The Court of Appeals concluded that the term family

> should not be rigidly restricted to those people who have formalized their relationship by obtaining ... a marriage certificate or an adoption order. The intended protection against sudden eviction should not rest on fictitious legal distinctions or genetic history, but instead should find its foundation in the reality of family life.[39]

With a network, "some, but not all, of the component individuals have social relationships with one another. . . . They do not form an organized group, but there will be varying degrees of connectedness between them."[20] In a dispersed network, there are not many relationships among the component parts, whereas in a highly connected network, there are many such relationships.[21] While the concepts were not difficult to grasp, I wasn't certain how to apply them and, overall, my research was not very productive.

Perhaps the dead end was due to my lack of expertise and a visceral reaction to the ugliness of sociological prose. But it did lead me to some literature about the characteristics of the interactional process.[22] This literature suggested a different kind of organizational principle, based not on status, but on the content, directness, durability, intensity, and frequency of the interaction between the dying person and the member of the deathwatch.[23] It was a functional test, similar to the inquiry that some courts engage in when determining who should be allowed to have custody of a child—who should be granted the rights attendant to parenthood—who should be considered part of the family. ❮

Maybe I could convince judges to sit down and look not at the formal relationship the two parties bore to one another, but at their be-

---

❮ Natalia Ginzburg came up with one of the most beautiful ways to define a family that I have ever encountered:

There are five of us children. We live in different cities now, some of us abroad, and we do not write to one another much. When we meet we can be indifferent and aloof. But one word, one phrase is enough, one of those ancient phrases, heard and repeated an infinite number of times in our childhood. We have only to say, "We did not come to Bergamo for a picnic," or "What does sulfuric acid pong of?" for us to pick up in a moment our old intimacy and our childhood and youth, linked indissolubly with these words and phrases. One of them would make us recognize each other, in the darkness of a cave or among a million people. These phrases are our Latin, the vocabulary of our days gone by, our Egyptian hieroglyphics or Babylonian symbols. They are the evidence of a vital nucleus which has ceased to exist, but which survives in its texts salvaged

havior towards one another. Thus siblinghood, for example, would not qualify a potential paintiff, but a history of mutual regard and affection over a long period of time, the number and regularity of contacts between them, a record of honoring reciprocal obligations, evidence of freedom to exercise the rights and privileges of friendship, the right to confide and to be confided in, the right to hurt, and to be hurt, the right to forgive and to be forgiven.《 It would be like one of those tests that one finds in women's magazines: *Is Your Relationship an Intimate One? Do You Deserve Standing In Your Loved One's Deathwatch?*

from the fury of the waters and the corrosion of time. These phrases are the foundation of our family unity which will persist as long as we are in this world.[40]

It is difficult to imagine a court employing such a criterion as shared "texts salvaged from the fury of the waters and the corrosion of time" to define a family, but for me Ginzburg's test bears more truth than anything contained in official reporters.

《 A functional test for family status is not unheard of in the law. For example, the Oregon legislature allows someone who "has established emotional ties creating a child-parent relationship with a child" to petition the court for custody of the child or visitation rights. The child-parent relationship is defined in the statute as

a relationship that exists or did exist, in whole or in part, within the six months preceding the filing of an action under this section, and in which relationship a person having physical custody of a child or residing in the same household as the child supplied, or otherwise made available to the child, food, clothing, shelter and incidental necessaries and provided the child with necessary care, education and discipline, and which relationship continued on a day-to-day basis, through interaction, companionship, interplay and mutuality, that fulfilled the child's psychological needs for a parent as well as the child's physical needs.[41]

It all sounded like a lot of work,«« and I could see that opposition to an organizing principle would soak up so much judicial time and energy. The nuclear family was a much easier rule to apply, and judges might not have the skill, resources, or inclination to discover whether what looks like a single strand of thread is really a tangled knot. That is so often the way it is with good ideas: No one really likes them because they sound like a lot of work.

I was beginning to feel desperate about my lawsuit. Who were my paintiffs going to be?

«« Deeper values than just the ease of administration are undoubtedly at stake. The family traditionally has been the subject of constitutional protection. In *Moore*, the Court held that a local zoning ordinance which defined single-family dwellings to exclude a woman living with two grandchildren violated the due process clause of the Fourteenth Amendment: "Our decisions establish that the Constitution protects the sanctity of the family precisely because the institution of the family is deeply rooted in this Nation's history and tradition. It is through the family that we inculcate and pass down many of our most cherished values, moral and cultural."[42] While *Moore* declared the virtues of the family tradition and expanded them beyond the nuclear family, the Court in dictum spoke only of blood relatives ("uncles, aunts, cousins, and especially grandparents") when defining the constitutional "family." The Court has specifically refused to extend the concept of family privacy to groups of unrelated individuals living together in a single household.[43]

I hate making an argument based on familial privacy when the cases force me to accept such a narrow definition of family. I suppose I could take solace in Justice Brennan's decision in *Smith v. Organization of Foster Families for Equality and Reform (OFFER)*.[44] That case addressed whether a foster family deserved the same constitutional protection as a "natural" nuclear family. Justice Brennan discusses three elements that define a "family" and "contribute to its place in our society": biological relationships, emotional attachments, and origins entirely independent of the power of the State. Still, Justice Brennan's clear preference for a biological relationship in his discussion of these factors does not give me much heart or inspiration to make the argument.

"Do you know what really worries me about your paintiffs?"

It was several weeks later, and my friend and I were sitting alone quietly in the faculty library, grading papers, or so I thought. It was raining, a good day for a meaningless task. It had been weeks since we had discussed the deathwatch and whether its members should be able to bring their pain to court. I felt smug. I had managed to bother my friend enough with my problem that she had initiated the conversation on her own.

"What paintiffs?" I pretended not to know what she was talking about. Like someone with a secret passion who wanted to hear her lover's name spoken, I wanted my problem to come back to me through the voice of another. Besides, she always lent grace to my ideas—grace and termination. She would capture the flailing legs of my newborn child and gently fold them into the soft white fleece of a question mark.

"You know perfectly well what paintiffs. The Quinlans and the Cruzans, the members of the deathwatch." I had not fooled her. "Their pain is purely emotional, and the source of that emotional pain is the physical pain of another."

"I'm not so sure that I am willing to admit their pain is purely emotional," I responded. "For one thing, that pain could manifest itself in physical symptoms, and for another, those long, drawn-out 'medicalized' deathwatches can be a tremendous drain on family resources. Besides, there is the spiritual pain, the pain of watching someone you love in limbo, not being able to return to whatever version of God you believe in." I took a deep breath in recognition that I was about to tread on some of the more tender grass of our friendship. "I probably shouldn't say 'you,' since you may not recognize that spiritual pain because of your profound skepticism about its premises."

"Well, it just doesn't sit right with me," she said, ignoring my last comment, "letting people come into court and seek a remedy for watching the pain of another. Don't you have to be careful about granting them the status of substantive plaintiffs, when the defendants aren't really doing anything to them? I mean, what rights of theirs are being infringed upon? That's one of the things standing is for, you know." Today she was not sputtering, but was proceeding, civilly. "To be sure that the pain, as you put it, belongs to the plaintiff and not to somebody else. You've got to put limits on who can sue." "Is it time to yell Yazoo?" ❪

Several years earlier when a colleague had taken unexpectedly ill in the middle of a semester, I had fallen heir to the remainder of his Civil Procedure course. What a cruel twist of fate for those poor, unsuspecting first-year students who still harbored the illusion that their teachers knew something that they did not. If it had not been for that colleague's vulnerable constitution, I would never have known when to yell Yazoo, or even that one could yell Yazoo, in any meaningful fashion.

I sometimes wonder what others outside the law world would think about a constitutional theory known as the Yazoo doctrine. A "Yazoo" should be a soft drink, a plastic party favor to blow on, or a sneeze—but not a legal doctrine.

Despite the aggressive silliness of its name, the Yazoo doctrine once stood for something. It held that a litigant may only invoke his

---

❪ As with the development of substantive constitutional standards, courts have had to determine the nature and procedure of judicial review through a slow evolutionary process of interpretation. Part of the problem derives from the paucity of words to interpret. The text of the Constitution itself is characteristically terse about the conditions under which constitutional determinations may be made and who may obtain those determinations. It provides only that "the judicial power of the United States" shall extend to certain enumerated "cases and controversies," including those "arising under the Constitution."[45]

The Constitution also created the Supreme Court and limited its original jurisdiction, leaving Congress to authorize such inferior courts as it saw fit and to regulate the Supreme Court's appellate jurisdiction. Congress immediately enacted the Judiciary Act of 1789, authorizing Supreme Court review of certain state court constitutional determinations and establishing lower federal courts.[46] While the Act established the federal courts, it said little about the conditions appropriate to constitutional determinations, or who might obtain them.

own constitutional rights and immunities; he may challenge a law only if it applies to him.[24] The Yazoo doctrine rested on a view of constitutional adjudication that prohibited courts from declaring the meaning of the Constitution or from enforcing public norms. As Marshall insisted in *Marbury v. Madison*, the "province of the court is, solely, to decide on the rights of individuals."[25] Under this view, the judicial role in constitutional litigation was analogous to the judicial role in common law litigation.[26] Judicial concern was thus limited to the rights of litigants who had suffered an infringement of their individual rights. A plaintiff could only bring his own pain to court, not the pain of another, or the pain of a class of persons. ❪

❪ One way to view the deathwatch is to consider a lawsuit by its members as a class action. The class action, a nontraditional procedural device, challenges the individual autonomy of litigants in a typical lawsuit by providing a representative to litigate for or defend a class of persons who share a common interest in a lawsuit.

The class action arose to promote judicial efficiency, to provide access to the courts for small claimants, and to prevent inconsistent outcomes. The binding effect of a class action on all members of the class and the due process requirements that limit the use of this joinder device accomplish these policies.[47] Rule 23 of the Federal Rules of Civil Procedure provides authority and guidelines for bringing a class action in federal court.[48] Most state courts have adopted an identical or similar rule.[49]

Deathwatches occur in isolated, unpredictable circumstances and form small, ephemeral, and informal groups. They do not therefore lend themselves to the class action as a way of dealing with a multiplicity of law suits. Rule 23(a) sets out four requirements for a class seeking certification, which are augmented by two additional requirements imposed by the federal judiciary.

First, each class must be so numerous that joinder is impracticable. All the members of all the deathwatches at any given time would arguably satisfy this requirement. Obviously, the members of a single deathwatch are too few to invoke a class action.

Second, the class must have a common question of law or fact. Assuming that the issue for members of a deathwatch would invariably be the termination

Of course, it is no longer in vogue to view constitutional litigation as coextensive with private rights adjudication. No one would be deemed radical for asserting that federal courts do declare the meaning of the Constitution and enforce public norms.«« This change in view has resulted in the erosion of such doctrines as the Yazoo. Courts increasingly permit litigants who fall under a statute's valid application to assert its invalid application with respect to persons not before the court. The rules of third party standing have thus been reduced to rules of judicial discretion. Once the private-rights model

of life-sustaining medical treatment for an irreversibly comatose patient, the class might indeed have common questions of both law and fact.

Third, the class must state claims derived from the same events or resting on the same legal theory. The events of each deathwatch would be different, although the legal theory, if I could figure out what it was, would arguably be the same.

Fourth, the class must have representation that fairly and adequately protects the interests of the members. Presumably representation in the case of a deathwatch could meet this requirement.

Fifth, the class must be sufficiently identifiable. This is where I think the class action analysis for the deathwatch really falls flat on its face. The problems are already difficult if we look at a single deathwatch, as discussed above. If we address all of the deathwatches taking place in a given jurisdiction over a certain period of time, however, identifying members of the class would be impossible.

Sixth, the class must be represented by someone who is a member of the class to assure that the rights of the entire class are being adequately litigated. This does not pose problems for the deathwatch. In fact, in the termination of life-support cases, the petitioner tends to be a single member of the deathwatch, representing the interests of others who also gather around the bed.[50]

«« Owen Fiss writes: "[A]s pervasive a role as disputation may play in litigation, it is equally important to recognize that the *function* of the judge—a statement of social purpose and a definition of role—is not to resolve disputes, but to give the proper meaning to our public values."[51]

was rejected, more plaintiffs had access to the courts. Standing became reduced to a requirement that the plaintiff be injured in fact, and the courts interpreted injury expansively, to include economic and even aesthetic injury. A colleague's old class notes, etched in my brain.

If the standing requirement becomes more relaxed, does it become a kneeling requirement? Or if doctrines like the Yazoo disappear altogether, will litigants be able to lie down and roll into court, the way children propel themselves down a hill? And if we let everyone in pain sue from a horizontal position, won't there be a terrible pileup at the bottom of that hill?«

Is my friend right? Do we have to put limits on who can sue? Should derivative pain be something that the law recognizes—the pain of watching someone else's pain? Would that result in a house of mirrors?«« Next year would we have to recognize the pain of watching someone else's pain caused by watching someone else's pain?««« The law always seems to be shutting doors to avoid the risk of infinity.

« Large piles of people at the bottom of a hill are only a problem if each person litigates individually. If people organized into groups—indeed if collective litigation, rather than suits by individual plaintiffs, formed the basis of our legal system—we could potentially handle the large numbers. As is often the case, examination of another time and place can give us some insight into how different our own world might be if we operated from different premises.

Stephen C. Yeazell has explored the evolution of the class action and argues that its history should begin during the medieval period. More traditional histories of the modern class action usually begin with the procedure of the late seventeenth-century English Chancery and focus on corporation theory and the growth of the doctrine of individualism. Yeazell characterizes the seventeenth century as the transitional period of group litigation theory. The medieval period, Yeazell claims, contains the remote origins of the class action. Social organization in the Middle Ages centered on the group rather than the individual. Groups

FOR about a year of my life, I had to read to my daughter, over and over again, with the maniacal love for repetition that only a two-year-old has, a book called, *What's The Difference?*, by Bill Gilham. On one side of the page there is a photograph, and on the other the same picture appears, with one notable exception. One side has the child laughing; on the other, he is crying. One side has the child with long,

---

such as guilds, parishes, and village communities lent support and much-needed assistance in a harsh world.[52]

❝ This is just a variant of the "floodgates" argument, or the "there is no point at which such actions would stop" argument that was articulated in the famous California case of *Dillon v. Legg*.[53] California jurisprudence provides another formulation of the "floodgates" argument, one of my favorites. In a case decided before *Dillon*, which considered the same issue of tort liability based upon the "plaintiff's apprehension of negligently caused danger or injury to a third person," the California Supreme Court rejected liability, characterizing such an expansion of the duty of care to be an excursion into the "fantastic realm of infinite liability."[54] The "fantastic realm of infinite liability" properly belongs in the prologue of a *Star Trek: The Next Generation* episode.

❝❝ Permitting a bystander to recover for the negligent infliction of mental or emotional distress is a relatively new development in tort law. Traditionally courts would not compensate a plaintiff alleging mental distress unless the plaintiff could also prove accompanying physical injury.[55] Eventually courts allowed compensation for mental distress if the plaintiff suffered *any* physical impact, even without demonstrable physical injury. Most jurisdictions now permit compensation for the negligent infliction of mental distress to plaintiffs within the "zone of physical danger," even in the absence of physical impact. Recovery, however, requires some physical manifestation of the alleged mental distress.[56]

In *Dillon v. Legg*, the California Supreme Court extended the scope of the doctrine of negligent infliction of emotional distress and compensated a bystander outside the zone of danger. The court refused to engage in the "hopeless

flowing hair; on the other, her hair is braided. One side has the child standing in the sun; on the other, he is in the rain. "What's the difference?"

For months and months, my daughter dutifully played the game: Here he is laughing, and there he is crying; here her hair is long, and there her hair is in braids; here he is dry, and there he is wet. Then one day she asked, "Why is the boy crying?" She had made a subtle shift in intellectual stance that only a parent sitting on the bed reading the book for the thousandth time would notice. It was the shift from asking what the difference was to wondering what made the difference.

Perhaps it was the repetition, the saying over and over again, "What's the difference?," but somehow the structure of that inquiry has become imbedded in my own intellectual stance. I find that no

---

artificiality" of denying recovery to the mother "merely because of a happenstance" that placed her a few yards outside the zone of danger.[57] The case embraced foreseeability of risk as the primary consideration in determining whether the defendant owes a duty of care to the plaintiff and enumerated three factors for courts to take into account:

1. Whether plaintiff was located near the scene of the accident as contrasted with one who was away from it.
2. Whether the shock resulted from a direct emotional impact upon plaintiff from the sensory and contemporaneous observance of the accident, as contrasted with learning of the accident from others after its occurrence.
3. Whether plaintiff and the victim were closely related, as contrasted with an absence of any relationship or the presence of only a distant relationship.

The *Dillon* court applied an objective standard of foreseeability, inquiring "what the ordinary man under such circumstances should reasonably have foreseen." The *Dillon* court, like jurisdictions following the majority rule, confined its holding to cases in which the plaintiff's mental distress resulted in physical manifestations. In 1989, the California Supreme Court in *Thing v. Chusa* clarified *Dillon v. Legg*, holding that foreseeability alone was not sufficient to support a claim for negligent infliction of emotional distress.[58]

matter what I am looking at or thinking about, the thing or problem separates itself like a delicate piece of cloisonné into two pools of enamel, on either side of a smooth band of metal, sometimes silver and sometimes gold. Two identical pools of enamel, with one notable exception. "What's the difference?"

The factual answer is: On one side, the accident victim was the plaintiff's child. On the other, the accident victim was a stranger. From those facts, we could look up the rules in a number of jurisdictions and come up with the legal answer: One harm is compensable. One is not.

But with respect to that legal answer, once we make the shift from asking what the difference is to wondering what made the difference, the task becomes more difficult. It is not hard to see why witnessing the maiming of one's child should be compensable. After all, parental love is primitive and deep, and witnessing harm to one's child is worse than being harmed oneself. What is not so easy to understand is why witnessing harm to a stranger is not compensable. Although there is no emotional attachment to the victim, it is still disturbing to see the human body lose its integrity.

I once saw a man killed in southern France. I was on a camping trip with friends, and we were driving behind a car that was going too fast. The driver must not have seen the man up ahead on his bicycle. He was thrown off his seat and sailed high into the air, landing on his head in the road. His neck snapped like a stalk of broccoli, and his skull cracked open. As soon as the gendarmerie arrived, they covered his body with a blanket, but until they came, we stood around and stared helplessly at the lifeless form on the road. I had never seen the human brain before, but will never forget what memories look like: bloody cauliflower. I guess I got over it, but I suffered a loss from witnessing the breaking of another human being. It made me experience my own bodily fragility in a way that I had never felt before, and, in some ways, I have never again felt as solid or as whole or as certain of my own boundaries. I felt the loss of him too, deeply saddened, even though I had never known the face that once graced the front of his shattered head.

The legal rules about compensability for witnessing harm to others say something about the value that our culture places on love for family and love for strangers. We are expected to love our spouses and children very much, and strangers not at all. It is just a variant of the drowning baby rule. Most of the first year of law school, I wondered if I wanted any part of a legal system that imposed no duty on me to save a stranger's drowning baby.꜀ I was given leave to watch that baby slide under the surface of the water just because I did not know his name. This seemed wrong to me then, and seems wrong to me now.

But the underlying cultural value that divides family from stranger as appropriate objects of love, and therefore as sources of derivative pain, does not even seem to be invoked when it comes to the deathwatch. After all, most cases involving termination of life-support systems are brought by family members or close friends.[27] We are not talking about the pain of watching strangers die prolonged and

---

꜀ Prosser blames the law's refusal to impose on a stranger the duty to aid another human being in danger on the reluctance of courts to recognize "nonfeasance" as a basis for liability.[59] The examples discussed in Prosser's treatise are, at least to me, morally repugnant.

> The expert swimmer, with a boat and a rope at hand, who sees another drowning before his eyes, is not required to do anything at all about it, but may sit on the dock, smoke his cigarette, and watch the man drown. A physician is under no duty to answer the call of one who is dying and might be saved, nor is anyone required to play the part of Florence Nightingale and bind up the wounds of a stranger who is bleeding to death, or to prevent a neighbor's child from hammering on a dangerous explosive, or to remove a stone from the highway where it is a menace to traffic, or a train from a place where it blocks a fire engine on its way to save a house, or even to cry a warning to one who is walking into the jaws of a dangerous machine.[60]

> Correspondingly, there is no criminal liability for failure to render aid to another person who is in danger.[61] The Anglo-American position on criminal omissions is not necessarily shared by certain European codes. Many of those codes impose a duty to rescue someone in danger on anyone who could do so without endangering himself.[62]

difficult deaths. We are talking about the pain of watching our daughters and sons, our mothers and fathers, our sisters and brothers, and our loved ones and close friends die prolonged and difficult deaths.

On one side, the plaintiff witnesses a bloody accident in which his child is badly injured. On the other, the plaintiff witnesses his comatose child, curled-up in a fetal position, maintained on a respirator or nasogastric feeding tube, suffering interminably. "What's the difference?"

Even at the level of a two-year-old, I am hard pressed to come up with an answer. Maybe there is no satisfactory answer, no intelligent way to talk about the difference between one nightmare and another. Maybe we just need there to be a difference in order to draw a line; a line beyond which the law will not go. A way for us to say with certainty, some wishes cannot be granted. Some wishes must be made upon a star.

THERE is a large bulletin board outside my daughter's kindergarten classroom. It usually serves as a surface upon which to staple recent student artwork. The pictures tend to have a seasonal theme: *Sights of Summer, Winter Wonderland.* Or they might reflect a class project or field trip: *Our Visit to the Seashore; Why We Wash Our Hands; Growing Beans for Fun and Profit.* This spring, one of the teachers turned the bulletin board into a Wishing Wall. Each child was to make a wish, and then draw a picture of the wish as it came true. The wishes were sometimes funny, sometimes sad, and always revealing. Lots of the children wished for Porsches or other sleek machines. There were several wishes for cats and dogs. A few properly indoctrinated children wished for peace or an end to world hunger. I was somewhat abashed to find that my own daughter had wished for golden hair that touched the ground. My favorite wish was Matthew's. He wished for a magic pebble that would grant all of his future wishes.

The Wishing Wall drove me to the dictionary. A wish turns out to be a "feeling in the mind directed towards something which one believes would give satisfaction if attained, possessed, or realized." It commonly denotes a "desire for something not attainable by one's own effort" and is characterized as a "passive or inactive desire." A wish, according to the O.E.D., is "less emphatic than craving, longing, or yearning, but include(s) these as particular cases."

I began to wonder about my worry for the members of the deathwatch, and to worry about my wonder. I had been entertaining the notion of giving them some sort of legal recourse, of letting them sue the physicians and hospitals on their own behalf, of seeking to terminate life-support systems because of their own pain, and not because of the fictional pain of another. Maybe that notion was nothing more than wishful thinking.

Of course, in a sense, all lawsuits are a form of wishful thinking. The plaintiff may seek some reparation, some restoration of the status quo. Or he might ask the court to stop others from doing something, or for permission to do something to or for others in the future.〔 A plaintiff might express many desires: many cravings, longings, yearnings could make their way into a petition.

So characterizing lawsuits as a form of wishful thinking does not really advance the discussion. But assuming the role of the grantor of wishes does, and that is what judges do: They grant wishes. Lawsuits are expressions of a very particular kind of desire. They express desires attainable by evoking the power of the state. If a plaintiff is successful, there is an official mechanism for enforcing the judgment. It becomes a wish come true.

What must it be like standing at the Wishing Wall in the role of fairy godmother?〔〔 Looking at those expressions of childhood crav-

---

〔 Restitution means the "restoration of property or money taken from the plaintiff."[63] Punitive damages, as the name denotes, are punishment for particularly egregious conduct to discourage such behavior in the future. Punitive damages typically supplement other damage awards.[64] In seeking specific performance, the plaintiff requests the court to make the defendant actually perform according to the terms of the contract.[65] The injunction provides relief by compelling a defendant to act or refrain from acting in a given manner. Failure to comply with an injunction constitutes contempt of court and may result in fines or imprisonment.[66]

ings, longings, and yearnings, the discerning fairy godmother would begin to ask: Which wishes can be granted? Not all of them can be. She might be able to bestow a Porsche, or a pet, or the means to acquire them. But unless she is a deity, her powers are probably limited. She cannot, for example, grant my daughter a head of golden hair. Neither does she have the power to stop world hunger or the ravages of war. For some wishes, we would do better not to call on her but to use Matthew's magic pebble instead.

Besides, there may be other restraints upon a fairy godmother. Not all wishes should be granted. Assuming she has a conscience, granting some wishes may violate her sense of morality. And if she had tenure in her role of grantor of wishes, she may have to look to the future and consider the ramifications of granting a new kind of wish. If similar wishes start appearing on the wishing wall, there may be a drain on scarce resources: not enough Porsches or pets to go around. Or maybe she wants to protect her aesthetic sensibilities so as not to live in a world glutted with too many dogs and too many cars. A fairy godmother must think about many things if she intends to stay in her profession.

Courts, too, are grantors of wishes. Similarly, they must confront

----

◄◄ One interpretation of the Cinderella story, in which a fairy godmother plays a pivotal role, suggests it was a pagan anti-ecclesiastical allegory. Barbara Walker writes that "Ella was Hel, or Helle, daughter of Mother Earth, the Goddess with her regenerative fires reduced to cinders. Her ugly stepmother was the new church, [and her] ugly stepsisters were the church's darlings, the military aristocracy and clergy."

Walker also relates an early German version of the story in which Cinderella's real mother was the Earth. From beyond the grave, Earth, now dead, heard her daughter's prayers and sent her a "fairy tree" that produced golden apples and other beautiful things. This "'fairy godmother'... seems to have been a ghost of the mother, the dispossessed Great Goddess in retirement underground."[67]

(I do not mean to suggest that the fairy godmother in my text is a thinly disguised pagan goddess, although on some unconscious level she might be.)

the limitations of their powers and the restraints placed upon them by, among other things, morality, and the pressures brought to bear by consistency. A court must think about many things when confronted with a new kind of wish. Such things may exceed the boundaries of the petition, like ripples have significance to the pond way beyond that small displacement of water where the pebble dropped in.

But it is not always so easy to tell what kind of wish we have on our hands. What about my wishes on behalf of the members of the deathwatch? Are they the kind that cannot or should not be granted?

In order to answer those questions, I would have to answer my friend's questions from that windy March day. I would have to articulate the wishes, pour them into a word mold, give them shape and definition, and give them numbers for those who need enumeration.

CONSIDER the following hypothetical: The patient is a silent, curled-up daughter, the petitioners are members of her deathwatch, suing on their own behalf. The request for a judicial order might be made in one of two ways:

> Please order the doctors to terminate our daughter's life-support systems because we cannot bear the pain of watching her interminable dying.

Or, the alternative:

> Please order the doctors to release our daughter to us so that we can remove her from the health care facility and terminate her life-support systems because we cannot bear the pain of watching her interminable dying.

These hypothetical requests are not so different from requests that are typically made when members of the deathwatch sue on behalf of an incompetent patient. After all, no matter whose name is on the petition, the desired result is the same: the termination of the life-support systems. But when the members of the deathwatch sue as nominal, procedural plaintiffs, the courts employ a legal fiction: a pretense that the silent, curled-up daughter is doing the asking, and not the people who file the petition.

What would we gain by dispensing with the pretense? Judicial honesty. Recognition by the courts that the members of the death-watch are people in pain. Release from the awkwardness of fabricating intent for someone who no longer has any intent. Respect for a judicial system that confronts openly the reality of a situation, a judicial system that does not need the smoke screen of a legal fiction.⟨

But there is something more to gain from letting the members of the deathwatch sue on their own behalf: a higher likelihood that the petition to terminate the life-support systems will be granted. Increasingly high evidentiary standards must be met in order to justify the creation of fictional intent. *Cruzan* is a perfect example. The state of Missouri required "clear and convincing" evidence that Nancy Cruzan, before losing cognitive function, would have wanted to terminate the life-support systems had she known of her future situa-

---

⟨ No one in the history of jurisprudence hated the dishonesty of the legal fiction more than Jeremy Bentham. Bentham was no fan of the common law, which he thought was plagued with "tautology, technicality, circuity, irregularity, inconsistency.... But above all, the pestilential breath of Fiction poisons the sense of every instrument it comes near."[68] In another work, Bentham writes, "in English law, fiction is a syphilis, which runs in every vein, and carries into every part of the system the principle of rottenness."[69] Bentham particularly loathed the legal fiction because of its ability to make hidden changes in the law without legislation. It gave judges too much power to determine "what shall be morality as well as what shall be law."[70]

Jurisprudes of the early twentieth century took up Bentham's scathing attack on the legal fiction, although no one approached his level of rage or high concentrations of bile. Roscoe Pound classified the use of legal fiction as "spurious interpretation" which was to "make, unmake, or remake, and not merely to discover.... It is essentially a legislative, not a judicial process, made necessary in formative periods by the paucity of principles, feebleness of legislation, and rigidity of rules characteristic of archaic law."[71]

tion.⟨ Until new evidence was unearthed after the litigation, the petitioners on Nancy Cruzan's behalf could not meet that burden. They could not find a residue of the right words and, as a result, Nancy Cruzan was forced to stay alive. If there had been no legal fiction, the judge who heard the Cruzans' petition might have been free to let her quietly go. As it was, the highest court in Missouri, later affirmed by the United States Supreme Court, would not, perhaps could not, let her deathwatch come to an end.[28]

INHERITED from the utilitarian tradition, the cost-benefit analysis bids us to focus on our plans and to assess their costs and benefits

⟨ To effectuate the state's interest in the preservation of human life, the Supreme Court of Missouri in the *Cruzan* case adopted a strict standard of clear and convincing evidence for assessing the patient's former intent.[72] Under this standard, no one could make the choice to terminate life-sustaining treatment for an incompetent patient absent a living will or clear and convincing evidence of her former intent. In Nancy Cruzan's case, her statements to her housemate in a "somewhat serious conversation that if sick or injured she would not wish to continue her life unless she could live at least halfway normally,"[73] were deemed "unreliable for the purpose of determining her intent … and thus insufficient to support the co-guardians' claim to exercise substituted judgment on Nancy's behalf."[74] In a five-to-four decision, the United States Supreme Court upheld the Supreme Court of Missouri, holding that a state may apply a clear and convincing evidence standard in proceedings where a guardian seeks to discontinue nutrition and hydration of a person in a persistent vegetative state.[75]

Once the *Cruzan* case became a cause célèbre, three of her co-workers came forward and presented sufficient evidence of her former intent. At a hearing in November of 1990, the co-workers testified that they recalled Cruzan saying she would never want to live "like a vegetable."[76] This new evidence, plus new testimony from her doctor that her existence was "living hell," prompted

should we bring them to fruition.⟪ As lawyers, we do it every day. We look at a course of action, or at a rule, and ask, "If we decide to act one way instead of another, or if we decide to impose this limitation on our future actions, what will the upshot be?" ⟪⟪ There is the exhilarating side of the calculation: Who will be made happier,

---

Judge Teel of the Jasper County Probate Court to give permission for her feeding tube to be removed. Nancy Cruzan died twelve days later, at the age of thirty-three, with her family at her bedside.

⟪ The cost-benefit analysis focuses on the probable results of our action or the enforcement of our rules. Hence, it is a form of consequentialism, a doctrine holding that an action's value is always determined by its consequences; that is, only by referring to an action's result can it be justified.[77]

A "quality-adjusted life year (QALY)" is essentially a cost-benefit analysis, "a numerical description of the value that a medical procedure or service can provide to groups of patients with similar medical conditions." According to medical scholars,

> The concept of "cost per quality-adjusted life-year," as a guideline for resource allocation is based on six ethical assumptions: (1) quality of life can be accurately measured and used; (2) utilitarianism is acceptable; (3) equity and efficiency are compatible; (4) projections of community preferences can substitute for individual preferences; (5) the old have less "capacity to benefit" than the young; and (6) physicians will not use quality-adjusted life years as clinical maxims.[78]

A QALY "attempts to combine expected survival with expected quality of life in a single metric." Thus, "if an additional year of healthy life is worth a value of 1 (year) then a year of less healthy life is worth less than 1 (year)."[79]

⟪⟪ There are different kinds of utilitarianism. "Act" utilitarianism deals with particular actions, or situations when "an agent has a choice between courses of action (or inaction)."[80] Under an act utilitarian theory, we assess the "rightness or wrongness" of each individual action directly by its consequences.[81] "Rule" utilitarianism "does not consider the consequences of each particular action but con-

healthier, and wealthier from our decision and in what way?" Then there is the cold, dark, November side of the calculation: Who will be made sadder, sicker, or poorer from our decision and in what way? Presumably, if we remain true to the tradition, we will choose the course of action or the rule that will generate the greatest number of benefits for the largest number of people, that will maximize utility, as some are wont to say. ""

---

siders the consequences of adopting some general rule" and urges its adoption if the consequences of adopting it are better than those of adopting an alternative rule.[82]

" Sen and Williams characterize utilitarianism as an intersection between two different theories: consequentialism and welfarism. Under welfarism, the correct way to assess a state of affairs is to measure the aggregate welfare or satisfaction that all the individuals included in the calculation experience. Thus, utilitarianism as a moral theory recommends that we choose actions on the basis of consequences and that we assess the consequences in terms of welfare.[83]

"" Although utilitarianism has many precursors, most histories of utilitarianism begin with Jeremy Bentham. By "utility," Bentham meant
> that property in any object, whereby it tends to produce benefit, advantage, pleasure, good, or happiness (all this in the present case comes to the same thing) or (what comes again to the same thing) to prevent the happening of mischief, pain, evil, or unhappiness to the party whose interest is considered: if that party be the community in general, then the happiness of the community: if a particular individual, then the happiness of the individual.[84]

Mary Warnock, in an essay on John Stuart Mill, writes that "the word 'Utilitarian' appears to have been coined by Bentham":
> He used it first in a letter dated 1781, and again in a letter, dated 1801, in which he said, "A new religion would be an odd sort of thing without a name," and proposed "Utilitarianism." Mill, however, seems to have been unaware that Bentham used the word, for he claims to have taken it over from John Galt's novel "Annals of the Parish" (1821) where a character applies it to Benthamite views; and in the essay on Sedgwick's discourse to the University of Cambridge

As an intellectual endeavor, the cost-benefit analysis has always made me both profoundly tired and depressed. Even though my legal education was over many years ago, I still harbor resentment about having had the cost-benefit analysis imposed on my thinking process. It undercuts enthusiasm for new ideas. It fosters conservatism. It neutralizes the passions. It sucks the juice out of one's sense of injustice, leaving the pulp and rind of a well-reasoned decision—a well-reasoned decision that may not be the right thing to do.

Even though it makes me sad and weary, however, the cost-benefit analysis is still a part of the way I look at the world. So I am forced to look at the downside of my proposal: What would we have to lose by granting the members of a deathwatch the right to terminate their daughter's life-support systems? What are the costs of dispensing with the legal fiction that the request is being made by the silent curled-up daughter and not by her parents who are filing the petition?

The costs are high. Probably too high.

The most obvious cost would be the burden of judicial administration. I ran into that problem when I started to draw a circle of yellow chalk around the members of the deathwatch. Without a neat and tidy organizing principle like the nuclear family, the courts could spend all their time just trying to identify who the plaintiffs should be. There is the problem of how to deal with potential conflicts among the members of the deathwatch. What would a court do if half of the members wanted to terminate life-support systems and half did not? Would hours of judicial attention be spent just trying to compare relative degrees of intimacy? Because the group is informal, and the deathwatch ephemeral, there would be no internal structure

---

(1835) he feels it necessary to explain it in terms of adherence to the principle of Utility. The word "Utility" was in fairly common use as a technical term considerably earlier, and is to be found in the writings of Hume.[85]

Sen has a much more accessible definition, taking "utility ... to stand for a person's conception of his own well being."[86]

to deal with such disputes, just as there would be no institutional criteria to determine who qualifies to be a member and who does not.

Another cost of dispensing with the legal fiction is more difficult to put a price tag on. It is the problem that my friend alluded to when she said, "You've got to put limits on who can sue." This cost is generated by the tendency of ideas to migrate and by the unpleasant reality of human greed. If we expressly allow plaintiffs the right to assert a claim based on witnessing the pain of another, how can we prevent that idea from moving into new territory?

This might not pose a problem if courts limited the remedy to issuing orders to terminate life-support systems in carefully circumscribed situations. However, in recognizing new forms of harm, the legal mind likes selectively to pilfer bits and pieces of existing law to construct a new cause of action. In searching for analogous situations, courts would inevitably gravitate towards that area of tort law in which plaintiffs have sought, and been awarded, damages for the negligent infliction of mental distress caused by the plaintiff's witnessing harm to another. And damages mean money, both for the plaintiff and for the plaintiff's lawyer. If courts were cavalier about making doctors and hospitals pay damages for the harm caused by witnessing the pain of another, there would be an incentive for cre-

---

In a Louisiana Supreme Court case, *Lejeune v. Rayne Branch Hospital,* a member of a deathwatch sued a hospital for mental pain and anguish. *Lejeune* was not about the termination of life-support systems, however, it was about another kind of nightmare. Mr. Lejeune lay in a coma in the hospital. Shortly before his wife came into his room for her daily visit, rats had gnawed at his face. A student nurse tried to clean some of the blood away from the wounds, but the bites were still evident. In Mrs. Lejeune's deposition she stated: "They weren't cuts; you could tell it was eaten—eaten by little rounds, and there was blood, and it was all … he had some on his head, his face, his neck, and his nose. Now, you know that rodent went into his mouth because they would feed him through the mouth, and he had to breathe with his mouth open." The Supreme Court of Louisiana held that she had "sufficiently stated a cause of action" for mental pain and anguish against the defendant hospital.[87]

ative plaintiffs' lawyers to look for similar situations in which to sue. The contingency fee can be a catalyst to the imagination,⁣⁣ and an idea like compensation for derivative pain might indeed have a tendency to wander.

Although the cost of a nomadic idea might be difficult to assess, I am confident that the speculators of doom and gloom in the insurance industry could put some sort of dollar figure on a new kind of derivative pain. Similarly, someone could probably predict the administrative costs of courts having to identify plaintiffs or deal with intraparty disputes among the members of the deathwatch. Some costs, however, do not lend themselves to quantification. They take their toll on the human body and on the human heart.

Such could be the most serious cost of dispensing with the legal fiction: the risk of potential abuse. If we take our eyes off the patient and direct our gaze towards the members of the deathwatch, we might forget to ask whether that patient still had something to say. The scenario that I have just sketched of the late-twentieth-century deathwatch assumes a patient who has substantially lost cognitive function, a Karen Quinlan or a Nancy Cruzan. The medical determination of brain function and the legal determination of incompetency, however, are both capable of being manipulated.⁣⁣⁣ The pa-

---

⁣⁣ This insight I must attribute to my friend and colleague, Nicola Lee, Barrister at Law. One evening she was trying to explain to me how the practice of law in England differed from the practice of law in this country, and we lit upon the subject of the contingency fee. She contended that the institution of the contingency fee had an impact on the development of American law, providing an incentive for plaintiffs' lawyers to be creative in formulating new causes of action or in finding novel applications of the old ones. In England, where there are no contingency fees, barristers tend to be more conservative when initiating litigation. Actually, according to Nicola Lee, barristers tend to be more conservative about everything.

⁣⁣⁣ *In re Spring* is enough to make anyone nervous about the reliability of incompetency proceedings. The Massachusetts Supreme Court approved a lower

tient might be quite alive, both mentally and physically, but be too old or too annoying or too inconvenient or too expensive or too aesthetically unappealing or in some other way too much of a burden to have around. ⟨ Through the use of cooperative expert witnesses, such a patient could find that her medical care has turned into her deathwatch. ⟨⟨

---

court order permitting the petitioner, the ward's temporary guardian, to stop dialysis on a seventy-nine-year-old man thought to be incompetent due to "chronic organic brain syndrome." Two authors later pointed out:

> No psychiatric testimony was heard. Two written affidavits from physicians were presented which described Mr. Spring as suffering from chronic organic brain syndrome or senility. The signature on one affidavit was completely illegible; the other affidavit was based upon an examination of Mr. Spring conducted nearly 15 months prior to the appointment of Mr. Spring's wife and son as temporary guardians and their filing of the petition to terminate his hemodialysis treatments.... The only medical testimony concerning Mr. Spring's competency, or lack thereof, came from a kidney specialist at the institution where Mr. Spring received his hemodialysis treatment.... Based on this evidence, Mr. Spring was found incompetent and his family was authorized to order that his dialysis treatments be withdrawn.[88]

⟨ The same concerns about the risk of abuse were expressed by the Supreme Court in its rejection of due process and equal protection challenges to assisted suicide prohibitions. In *Washington v. Glucksberg,* Justice Rehnquist articulated the state's interest in protecting vulnerable groups, "including the poor, the elderly, and disabled persons," and quoted the warning of the New York Task Force on Life and the Law that "legalizing physician-assisted suicide would pose profound risks to many individuals who are ill and vulnerable.... The risk of harm is greatest for the many individuals in our society whose autonomy and well-being are already compromised by poverty, lack of access to good medical care, advanced age, or membership in a stigmatized social group."[89]

⟨⟨ With the high cost of medical care in this country, one of the greatest risks of abuse is the sacrifice of patients because their continued treatment drains re-

Even a judicial proceeding would not save her life. By the time the case reached the court's attention, the labels assessing the degree of mental capacity would already have been attached. Rarely, if ever, does a judge leave the sanctuary of the courtroom to see whether the curled-up daughter in that bed is truly silent.<<< Instead the judge

---

sources.[90] Soaring medical costs have been advanced in some instances as a "valid reason for putting someone to death by the proponents of rational and assisted suicides."[91]

Another factor is the "aging of the aged." As Schneider and Guralnick point out, "An unprecedented number of individuals are entering the ninth and tenth decades of life." This group of the "oldest old" is the fastest-growing in the United States. Things will really get tough when the "baby boomers" hit their eighties. In 2040, the average age of a baby boomer will be eighty-five years, and the level of Medicare spending for the population age sixty-five years and above could range from $147 billion to $212 billion, in 1987 dollars.[92]

Other risks of abuse derive from prejudicial attitudes toward the elderly, the diseased, and the disabled. No one can ignore the atrocities of recent history. During the autumn of 1939, Hitler instituted his "Euthanasia Program" in which over 275,000 people were gassed in killing centers. Most who were killed were deemed incompetent: the mentally retarded, the mentally ill, epileptics, the senile elderly, sufferers of neurological disorders such as Parkinsonism or multiple sclerosis, and other sick and handicapped people. Dubbed "useless eaters," their sacrifice was justified by a perverse form of welfare utilitarianism that sanctioned the killing of the weak so that others could flourish.[93]

By focusing on the rights of members of the deathwatch, our analysis shifts from the individual to the group. Any time this shift takes place, the risk of harm to the defenseless and vulnerable members of society arises. The risk is real; hidden biases against certain forms of illness, disability, indigency, unattractiveness, or any other difference may be tacitly plugged into a utilitarian calculation that results in discrimination, or worse yet, extermination.

<<< One notable exception was *In re President & Directors of Georgetown College*.[94] The U.S. District Court for the District of Columbia denied Georgetown Hospital's application for permission to administer blood transfusions to a

must rely on the professional training and credibility of the experts who have made the assessment. Sometimes a deposition of a doctor is a fait accompli.

By granting the members of the deathwatch standing to terminate life-support systems, we turn their silence into expression. My fear is that their voices would drown out whatever the patient might have left to say. After all, there is no guarantee that the members of the deathwatch will be good and true; they may have their own selfish reasons for wanting the deathwatch to come to an end. The incompetent person might be killed as a consequence of some unarticulated utilitarian calculation. The court might end up sacrificing her in the name of someone else's pain.

That would diminish us all. The loss of life and dignity is not only felt by the lamb, but also by those who lead the lamb to the slaughter. It is true that the use of the legal fiction may engender disrespect for a judicial system that cannot openly confront the reality of the situation. The members of the deathwatch are the paintiffs, and not the silent curled-up daughter. Furthermore, the use of the legal fiction may keep some deathwatches going interminably. But that may be

---

twenty-five-year-old woman who had lost two-thirds of her blood supply due to a ruptured ulcer. She and her husband refused to consent to the transfusions on religious grounds; they were Jehovah's Witnesses. The attorneys for the hospital applied for an emergency writ at 4:00 p.m. Judge Skelly Wright called the hospital to verify the attorney's representations, and "thereupon proceeded with counsel to the hospital," where he spoke to the patient's husband, Mr. Jones:

> He advised me that, on religious grounds, he would not approve a blood transfusion for his wife. I asked permission of Mr. Jones to see his wife. This he readily granted.... I then went inside the patient's room. Her appearance confirmed the urgency which had been represented to me. I tried to communicate with her, advising her as to what the doctors had said. The only audible reply I could hear was, "Against my will." It was obvious that the woman was not in a mental condition to make a decision.[95]

Judge Wright signed an order to administer the blood transfusions.

the way it has to be.℄ Although the members of the deathwatch may end up paying for use of that legal fiction, and that is a tragedy, the risk of abuse is a cost that I do not think we can bear.

So, once again, the cost-benefit analysis had silenced me, and I began a deathwatch on my own idea.

"*So* have you given up on them altogether?" She said one day at the pool while we were doing desultory laps. "Your paintiffs, the members of the deathwatch?"

"I guess so," I admitted reluctantly. "At least when I think of them legally."

It was several months later. I had become so disheartened by my own conclusions about granting the members of the deathwatch some form of legal recourse that I had lost faith in my original insights about their pain.

This happens to me a lot. It reminds me of picking chicory. You see something beautiful by the side of the road, a spray of periwinkle blue in the grass, and you want to pick it, to take it home. The wildflower book has warned you not to, that chicory does not take kindly

---

℄ Guido Calabresi come to a similar conclusion:

At the same time we make the decision of whom to burden, we are also are deciding whether we want to get accustomed, whether we wish to become callous, or whether, instead, if we think that as a society we would be better off if we continued to view some things as shocking, offensive, and even abominable.[96]

In this instance, by clinging to the legal fiction, we have decided to burden the members of the deathwatch, and, at the same time, we have decided to get accustomed to their pain. We do this because we are sufficiently worried that granting the members of the deathwatch their own cause of action might result in sacrificing innocent victims and that, as a society, we would be better off to remain deeply offended by the risks of abuse that I have described. Hence, we are willing to be callous about the pain felt by the families of Karen Quinlan and Nancy Cruzan.

to picking, but you do it anyhow. A few hours later, the chicory has collapsed. The crisp, jagged edges are limp, and the brilliant blue has turned to a sullen gray. My ideas, too, tend to faint against their glass prison when I pick them and try to arrange them in a vase; they wither and die. In fact, I had given up on trying to squeeze the members of the deathwatch into any kind of lawsuit. They had been relegated to that class of four-in-the-morning things, things out of my control.

"Well, that's too bad." She hugged the kickboard and pushed off from the edge of the pool, her legs flailing in a blur of water and air.

"What do you mean that's too bad?" I grabbed a kickboard and followed her in the water. I was annoyed. This was not the only time that she had done this to me. I would have an idea that could not withstand her scrutiny, and then she would not let it die a dignified death. She would not let it quietly slide down into the ravine of unworthy ideas, washed away by the gentle rain of indifference and neglect. Oh no, she had to torture it to death, submit it to a public execution.

"I just think it's too bad, that's all."

"But you were the first one to say that the members of the deathwatch shouldn't have any substantive rights of their own." I was kicking furiously to keep up with her, grasping tightly on to my kickboard.

"That's right, I did." We had reached the other side of the pool, and had stopped swimming. "Look, I can disdain the solution, but still admire the problem."

"The problem being?" At that moment, in that chlorinated sea, I could not remember what there was about the members of the deathwatch that had captured my imagination. The season had changed, and the chicory now lay under the ground. I could not remember its blue beauty in the light, or its splendid verticality.

"The problem being the law's failure to include the members of the deathwatch in the frame." My friend had just taken an introductory course in photography, and it seemed to radically alter the way that she looked at the world. Not only did she now see everything through a lens of a camera, but she was leaving words behind, consumed by an unexpected passion for the visual. "Those termination of life-support cases all focus on the face of someone who no longer cries, on the face of the incompetent dying person. The lens is telephoto, and the field of vision is so microscopic that the members of the deathwatch aren't included. The ones who are really crying aren't even in the picture."

"And what do you propose as an optic solution?" It was a good thing that I had an earlier lifetime as a photographer and could hold my own in technical banter.

"Maybe a twenty-eight millimeter lens. Something that still focuses on the face of the dying person but captures everything else around him. It's the lens of social context."

I wondered if that expression had been her own but did not want to offend her. "How sharply in focus would you have the members of the deathwatch be?"

"Not sharp at all. I'd want them in the picture, but as soft presences. An aura of human warmth and concern around the dying person, but without any formal recognition. You know," she grabbed her kickboard in preparation for departure, "if you insist that the law face this problem head on, in the middle of the frame, then you're stuck with the old picture. But if you let the law do its work like an artist, in the shadows and on the edges of things, you might still be able to do something about their pain. Don't desert your paintiffs yet, your members of the deathwatch." And she pushed off from the edge of the pool and disappeared down the lane.

Suddenly I loved my friend, old and new. The aqua-green water that enveloped her grew still, and I floated on my kickboard without moving, finding solace in her wake. I tentatively picked up another lens, the fifty-millimeter lens of our reality, and dared to look at my problem again, through the clear glass of her metaphor.

There they were, that splash of blue. I love the way the wildflowers come back in spring.

Left Hemisphere

Interlude

Over and over, I resisted the urge to ask the question. Over and over, I resisted the urge to outline an answer to it. I was not going to do it. I was not going to order my thoughts in a logical sequence. I was not going to make arguments, one, two, three. I was going to be a poet, not a lawyer.^c

And over and over, the argument kept appearing on legal pads and the backs of envelopes, written in a scrawl with a pencil, as if the illegibility and erasability of the words made them somehow less there. Worse yet, the argument kept falling into place behind those ominous numbers, one, two, three. Before I knew it, I was outlining an answer to a question, and could not stop myself from asking it.

QUESTION: What can the law do to alleviate indirectly the pain of the members of the deathwatch?

ᶜ In most animals, the two halves of the brain, or left and right cerebral hemispheres, are symmetrical in function; the human brain, however, is asymmetrical. In the 1960s, researchers at the California Institute of Technology, in particular a psychobiology professor, Dr. Roger Sperry, discovered that each hemisphere perceives reality in its own way. The function of language and language-related capabilities is located mainly in the left hemisphere. (This is true in approximately 98 percent of right-handers and about two-thirds of left-handers.) The left hemisphere operates "in a more logical, analytic, computer-like fashion," planning step-by-step procedures and processing information in a sequential, symbolic, and linear manner.[1] The right nonverbal hemisphere is intuitive; it apprehends forms and images and is not good at categorizing, naming, or placing things in sequential order. We use the right brain to imagine how things exist in space, to understand metaphors, to make art, to dream, and to create new combinations

ANSWER: Three things (of course, three things):

1. The law can redefine death.

2. The law can lower evidentiary standards regarding conversations about the circumstances of one's own death in recognition that the subject is a taboo in our culture.

3. The law can help create an environment in which a meaningful deathwatch can take place.

It is a hard fact to face: I am a lawyer, not a poet.

---

of ideas. Dr. Sperry argues that, "[O]ur educational system, as well as science in general, tends to neglect the nonverbal form of intellect. What it comes down to is that modern society discriminates against the right hemisphere."[2]

Even if the specialization of function in the cerebral hemispheres may not be so cut and dry, it is still useful to keep in mind that we have various ways of processing information and apprehending reality, and that how one approaches a problem will depend to a large part upon how one perceives it. Though our appreciation of the complexity of the neurophysiology of cognition and perception has deepened since the sixties, the metaphor of left-brain and right-brain thinking still makes sense to me. A lawyer will typically approach life from a left-hemispheric vantage point. A poet will not.

3

Moving Up the Brainstem

What can the law do to alleviate indirectly the pain of the members of the deathwatch?

THIS first suggestion is the most obvious and has been made by many others who have looked at the horrors of the late-twentieth-century deathwatch: The law can redefine death.

In the law, as in medicine, it has always been biological death that has commanded our attention. The cessation of the lungs and heart used to be what mattered. *Black's Law Dictionary* defined death as, "The cessation of life; the ceasing to exist; defined by physicians as a total stoppage of the circulation of the blood, and a cessation of the animal and vital functions consequent thereupon, such as respiration, pulsation, etc."[1] Once artificial ventilation became possible, however, the medical profession had to reconsider the definition of human death. The focus shifted from heart and lung activity to activity of the brain.

In a 1968 report, the Ad Hoc Committee of the Harvard Medical School to Examine the Definition of Brain Death specified a set of clinical tests which it maintained were sufficient for determining whether the entire brain was dead or the patient was in an irreversible coma.[2] It recommended that, excluding cases of hypothermia and the presence of central nervous system depressants, death should be declared when a patient exhibited three traits: unreceptivity and unresponsivity to external stimuli and inner need; no movements or

breathing; and no elicitable reflexes. A fourth condition, a flat elec-
troencephalogram (EEG) reading, should be used for its confirmatory value only. Once a patient met all three tests, the results of
which must be consistent over a twenty-four-hour period, the Committee recommended that death be declared and the respirator
turned off. The application of the report was carefully circumscribed
to be concerned "only with those comatose individuals who have no
discernable central nervous system activity."[3]

When Dorothy's house landed on the Wicked Witch of the East in
The Wizard of Oz, the Mayor of Munchkin City called the Munchkin
coroner to ensure that the witch is "morally, ethically, spiritually,
physically, positively, absolutely, undeniably, and reliably dead."[4] The
Harvard criteria, when applied, can do the same thing: they specify
a set of clinical tests that determines whether the entire brain of a comatose person is dead—or, in the words of the Munchkin coroner,
they tell us when someone is "not merely dead," but "really, most
sincerely dead." But the Harvard Criteria of whole brain death do not
apply to those patients who still have some residual nervous system
function. Those patients, like Karen Quinlan and Nancy Cruzan, are
not "dead" because they cannot meet the current definition. Their
cerebral function may be gone, but the lower brainstem function is
still hanging on.[c]

Other competing medical models provide definitions of human
death. Some prefer a definition that focuses on the loss of organic
function: "[A] human organism is dead when, for whatever reason,
the system of those reciprocally dependent processes which assimi-
late oxygen, metabolize food, eliminate wastes, and keep the organ-

Moving Up the Brainstem

---

[c] In a lovely footnote that in my mind belonged in the first paragraph of his article, Raymond J. Deverette pointed out that the word "brainstem" is a metaphor
borrowed from botany. Exploring the metaphor, Deverette points out the odd-
ness of saying that because the stem has survived, the brain is therefore alive:
"Now we do not say that we have a living rose when the stem is alive but the
blossom is dead, nor do we say we have a living or edible apple or grape when
the stem lives but the fruit is dead."[3]

ism in relative homeostasis are arrested in a way which the organism itself cannot reverse."[5] Others focus on whether the patient has regained consciousness.

All the medical models require doctors to prick limbs with needles, yell into deaf ears, shine lights into eyes that do not see. All entail a medical judgment based on an assessment of physical capacity, and, by and large, the conclusion can be justified by pointing to a chart. The incredible comfort of numbers tells us that we have done the right thing, the only thing, in considering this person a dead one.

In contrast to the premise of the medical models, some have argued that the task of defining death requires a moral, not a medical, judgment. Often the problem of defining death has been approached by examining the underlying notion of personhood. H. Tristram Engelhardt, for example, has argued that there are at least two notions of person. The first is that of the moral agent, the rational individual who bears rights and duties. The second is the social concept of person, an individual who, though perhaps incapable of rational or moral decision-making, can still engage in "at least a minimum of social interaction."[6] Children, the senile, the mentally retarded and mentally ill would all fall into this second category and are therefore bearers of rights, who must be treated with respect. One's life as a person and one's biological life can be distinguished, so that those whose brain function is deficient could be considered dead.[7]

The central question of these moral judgments is not so much, "How do we define death?" but, "When is it morally justifiable to treat a person as dead?" This question implies a deathwatch. Someone must ask that question: someone who is treating the dying person; someone who loves the dying person; someone who is responsible for the dying person; someone who must justify his decision to himself and to others. Unlike the medical models that have objective criteria, here we have value judgments to which we own up. It is impossible to justify the conclusion by pointing to a chart. There are no numbers in which to take comfort. Instead, this question must be answered by an essay—an essay that recognizes dying as a two-part relation, occurring within the context of a moral community. Such an essay would defend the behavior of one human being toward another.

Those who believe that the determination of death is a moral question often reject the medical definition of whole brain death. Robert Veatch, for example, has been a leading proponent of a "higher brain death" definition. He relies upon the Judeo-Christian notion of what it means to be a whole person, affirming that a human is of necessity an integrated unit of body and mind. According to Veatch, we should not be interested in "the death of particular cells, organs, or organ systems, but in the death of the person as a whole." "For purposes of simplicity," he explains,

> I shall use the phrase the capacity for bodily integration to refer to the total use of integrating mechanisms possessed by the body. A case for these mechanisms being the ones that are essential to humanness can indeed be made. Humans are more than the flowing of fluids. They are complex, integrated organisms with capacities for internal regulation. With and only with these integrating mechanisms is homo sapiens really human.[8]

The other higher functions of the brain, however, such as "consciousness [and] the ability to think and feel and relate to others," are so essential that "their loss ought to be taken as the death of the individual." Thus Veatch argues that death should be defined as the "irreversible loss of the embodied capacity for social interaction."[9]

Even though Veatch focuses on the human body's capacity, he is still squarely aligned with those who believe that the definition of death is a moral decision, not a medical one: "All that is at stake in the public policy debate over the definition of death is determining when death behaviors are appropriate."[10] Traditional death behaviors are those that society initiates upon the death of one of its members, such as preparing funerals, writing obituaries, and eventually burying and mourning the person. In a sense, the deathwatch is just an overture to these death behaviors—and possibly a form of dress rehearsal.

When faced with the patchwork of criteria for a medical and legal definition of death[11]—those currently in place and those proposed in legal, medical, and philosophical journals[12]—I am at loss to make an intelligent proposal for a new definition of death. It is work better left to those more qualified, and there are plenty of talented people to thrash out a new definition of death that we can all live with, or die with.[13] Chances are that technological advances will make whatever definition we settle on only a temporary solution.[14]

What I do hope will happen is this: that the Harvard Ad Hoc Committee's criteria from the late 1960s requiring whole brain death will be discarded for a definition that requires cessation of higher brain function only. Just when this will happen, I do not know—but the process may be slow.[15] Years ago, Robert Morison wrote about the desirability of moving slowly in this area: "It is not only probable, but highly desirable that society should proceed with the greatest caution and deliberation in proposing procedures that in any serious way threaten the traditional sanctity of the individual life. As a consequence, society will certainly move very slowly in developing formal arrangements for taking into account the interests of others in life-and-death decisions."[16]

Morison was right: we should move slowly in redefining death. Although I feel anguish for the members of the deathwatch, redefining death is something that should be done only after deep reflection. After all, we are searching for the right words to say: *This person is alive. That one is not.* The consequences that flow from such a definition are profound: it tells us what it means to be a human being—to be a person. We need to be very wary of those words; they must say exactly what we mean them to say.

4

Death Thought, Death Talk, and the Evidentiary Implications of Taboo

What else can the law do to alleviate indirectly the pain of the members of the deathwatch?

J U S T as members of the deathwatch hover over a dying person, so I hover over the subject of death. Death is not a subject that we meet face to face. We may talk and write around the subject of death, but we do not gather death into our arms. We do not feel its weight against our bodies; we do not look it in the eye. Instead, like strangers moving in and out of buildings, we brush up against death as we go about our business. Casual, unintentional encounters that do not implicate gravity. Oblique, fleeting encounters on other thresholds; silent nods in death's direction without the risk of intimacy.

W E had the conversation many years before his death. It was one of those close nights in August when the house was too small to hold us. My father and I had escaped together to the backyard. We were sitting on deck chairs in the dark, listening to the melancholy *chchchchchch* of the locust. Our gray cat had appeared from nowhere to join us, sitting silently on the edge of the ravine, his eyes flashing green and golden from some unknown source of nocturnal light. There was no breeze, but the evening air had an edge of coolness to it, a hint on the back of the arms that summer was coming to an end. The planet had started to tip backwards, away from the sun, and we were together on that journey, my father and I, those rasping locusts, and our cat. My mother was out singing somewhere.

I do not remember what book I was lost in that summer, but it was probably Jung. It does not really matter. I think everyone has an August night in his life where some book generates questions about the soul.

I asked my father if he believed in the human soul. His response was, as usual, Aristotelian.

"Yes," he said. "I believe in some spirit that lives and animates my body."

"And what will happen to that spirit when you die?" I pursued the subject, curious to hear his answer.

"What do you mean, 'What will happen'?" My father leaned over and picked up his beer that was nestled in the grass by his chair. "I don't think anything will happen. It will die when my body dies."

"That's it? You go and it goes?" I was disappointed, since I had recently come to a different conclusion and was seeking ratification.

"Yes, that's it. I am just a biological creature who lives in a body with a finite life span, and when it is over, I'll close my eyes and die. Then, I suppose, my body will be cremated, and you can sprinkle me in the ravine. It'll be good for the trillium." He laughed softly and took a swig of beer. "I'll finally be useful."

"I think there's more to it." I was shy to reveal my new beliefs, even to my father, particularly to my father.

"I expect you do, sweetie girl. That's because I am an Aristotelian, and you are not."

I was annoyed. My father had picked up several theories from his undergraduate education, and one of them was that there were two kinds of people in the world: those who belonged to the Aristotelian tradition and those who belonged to the Platonic tradition. It may well have been a useful tool with which to analyze his fellow man, but my father's theory had worn thin on his family. He brought it out all the time, and, much to our annoyance, it seemed universally applicable.

My brother rebelled against the theory with a countertheory designed to drive my father to distraction. There are two kinds of people in the world, my brother would say: those who believe there are two kinds of people in the world, and those who do not.

I⊤ has been a rough century to talk about the human soul.⟨ In the early part of this century, the positivists carved metaphysics out of philosophic discourse and devoted themselves to that which is knowable by our senses, one through five.⟨⟨ Nor does the law talk much

---

⟨ Alfred J. Ayer's *Language, Truth and Logic*, is the most famous articulation of philosophy's rejection of such metaphysical subjects as the future and past of the human soul. He begins by criticizing the "metaphysical thesis that philosophy affords us knowledge of a reality transcending the world of science and common sense."[1]

Metaphysicians produce sentences which are not verifiable by empirical evidence. While many metaphysical passages may have aesthetic or moral value, "[W]hat is important to us is to realize that even the utterances of the metaphysician who is attempting to expound a vision are literally senseless; so that henceforth we may pursue our philosophical research with as little regard for them as for the more inglorious kind of metaphysics which comes from a failure to understand the working of our language."[2]

⟨⟨ Thomas Nagel discusses the observation of Lucretius that it is irrational to fear death, since death is just the mirror image of our prenatal experience, and "no one finds it disturbing to contemplate the eternity preceding his own birth." Nagel argues that "if death is an evil, it is the loss of life, rather than the state of being dead, or nonexistent, or unconscious, that is objectionable. This asymmetry is important." I am not as certain as Nagel that prenatal and posthumous nonexistence are not analogous. But then, Nagel expressly wants to "leave aside the question whether we are, or might be, immortal in some form," and assumes,

about the human soul, except in the context of one's constitutional freedom to maintain beliefs about religion.⟨ And the medical profession is renowned for its reticence on spiritual matters, for keeping its gaze focused on the human body and not on what animates it.⟨⟨

Our collective reticence, however, does not mean that the subject is a dead one, not of vital importance to understanding the various attitudes towards the late-twentieth-century deathwatch. The pressures of intellectual fashion may push our thoughts about the human soul below the water's surface, but submersion does not necessarily

---

for example, that "none of us existed before we were born (or conceived), but few regard that as a misfortune." He also rather cavalierly states that "almost everyone would be indifferent (other things being equal) between immediate death and immediate coma followed by death twenty years later without re-awakening."[3]

⟨ The Court first articulated the "action-belief" doctrine in *Reynolds v. United States*. In that case, George Reynolds, private secretary to Brigham Young, appealed his conviction under the Morrill Act for practicing polygamy in the Territories. Reynolds argued that it was his religious duty to practice polygamy, and "that the failing or refusing to practice polygamy by such male members of said church, when circumstances would admit, would be punished, and that the penalty for such failure and refusal would be damnation in the life to come." The Court upheld the Morrill Act, announcing that the First Amendment makes freedom of *belief* absolute, but not freedom to act based on that belief. Although laws may not directly "interfere with mere religious belief and opinions, they may with practices." Thus, the law purposefully does not discuss the substance of an individual's beliefs about such things as the immortality of the soul, except perhaps to allude to them in the presentation of the facts.[4]

⟨⟨ Medicine in this century is viewed as a branch of science. Thus, like the positivists, the medical profession is only interested in phenomena which are empirically verifiable.

Physicians-as-scientists view their functions (observation, identification, description, investigation, and explanation of natural phenomena) within the the-

mean drowning. Our theory of ensoulment may still have enormous influence on our moral, legal, and medical behavior, even if those thoughts do not breathe the air.

Most of us believe in some theory of ensoulment, however inchoate, and, with apologies to my brother, my father was probably right: We do each belong to either the Aristotelian or Platonic tradition. I first read *The Phaedo* when I was seventeen. It was my season for leaving home, for shedding old beliefs and acquiring new ones, for pulling up the window shades to let the light flood in. In such a period of intellectual growth I first met Plato's theory of ensoulment. It had a great impact on me then, and, although I do not embrace all of it now, his theory still represents a rough version of spiritual truth for me.

Plato viewed man as having a dual nature; he is a composite being, consisting of a corporeal element, the body, and an incorporeal element, the soul. During our temporal existence, the soul is seen as attached to or incorporated in the physical matter of the human body. ⟪⟪ Plato always emphasized the element of control of the soul over

oretical confines of their discipline. They usually accept the notion of scientific law as a formulation of observed recurrences, order, relationships, or interactions of natural phenomena. Even theories to which they turn, while not, by definition, based directly on observable phenomena, must ultimately be validated by reference to confirmed experimental law—to observably simple and definitely true statements about the nature or behavior of natural phenomena.[5]

⟪⟪ In the *Phaedo,* Socrates characterizes the body as an "endless trouble to us." Our souls are infected with the evils of the body, with its lusts, appetites for foods and "fancies of all kinds," and susceptibility to disease. Worse yet, the body is "always breaking in upon us," causing turmoil and confusion in our inquiries, so that we are prevented from knowing the truth.[6]

One can only achieve knowledge of Plato's essential forms through a separation of the soul from the foolishness of the body.

It has been proved to us by experience that if we would have pure knowledge of anything we must be quit of the body—the soul in herself must behold

Death Thought, Death Talk, and the Evidentiary Implications of Taboo

the body.⁣ The soul is viewed as a navigator of a seagoing vessel. Upon death, the true essential person survives because of his identification with the immortal substance of the soul. Death is seen as a liberation. Once freed from the prison of its physical form, the incorporeal soul is capable of existing on its own, in one form of immortal life or another.⁣⁣ For this reason, Socrates can show indifference at the end of *The Phaedo* when Crito asks him how to bury his body: "In any way you like; but you must get hold of me, and take care that I do not run away from you."¹ Crito is not to be sorrowful as he buries the body of Socrates, because the soul of Socrates shall not remain, but go away and depart. Here is where Plato and I part company. He had an elaborate theory of the transmigration of souls in which I have never been able to believe.⁣⁣⁣ But it really does not matter what either Plato

---

things in themselves: and then we shall attain the wisdom which we desire, and of which we say that we are lovers; not while we live, but after death.⁷

⁣ In the *Alcibiades*, Socrates distinguishes between the user and the thing used. Analogizing to a shoemaker or a harpist, he notes the difference between the artisan or artist and the tools or instruments that he uses. Similarly, the true essence of the artisan or artist differs from the hands and eyes he uses to carry out his work. Because a man uses his body, he must therefore be something different from his body. The user of the body, Socrates concluded, must be the soul.⁸

⁣⁣ Socrates distinguishes the philosophic soul:
That soul, I say, herself invisible, departs to the invisible world—to the divine and immortal and rational: thither arriving, she is secure of bliss and is released from the error and folly of men, their fears and wild passions and all other human ills, and forever dwells, as they say of the initiated, in company with the gods.⁹

⁣⁣⁣ According to Socrates, what happens to the soul after death depends upon the degree of its purity at the time of departure. The philosophical soul who has striven during life to overcome the body in its quest for knowledge of the forms will be delivered to a divine, rational, and immortal world. The impure, polluted

or I believe about the afterlife. «««« What will happen upon our deaths will happen. We will just have to wait and see. What does matter, at least with respect to how we perceive our own deaths, is that we believe something will happen when we take our last breath. We can

---

soul who remained in love with the body has another fate, however. After death, such a depressed soul may be dragged down to the visible world and left to wander among the graves and sepulchers, still longing for the corporeal world. Eventually these doomed souls will be imprisoned in another body. Their physical form, Socrates warned, will be of the same nature they exhibited in their former lives. Thus, men who were gluttonous drunkards would pass into the bodies of asses and other lowly animals. The unjust, tyrannical, and violent would pass into the bodies of wolves, hawks, or kites. Temperate and just souls would pass into the bodies of social creatures such as wasps or ants or into the physical form of man again. From these happier souls would spring the just and moderate men of the future.[10]

Plato also describes the procedure for transmigration. After death, the soul of each person would be led to a gathering place for the dead to be judged on its former life. After judgment, the souls would be guided into the world below to "receive their due and remain their time." Eventually, another guide would bring the soul back to the visible world "after many revolutions of ages." Each soul would then be assigned to another physical form, a fitting habitation according to its degree of purity.[11]

If I turn out not to have a philosophical soul, and Plato's theory of the transmigration of souls turns out to be right, I can only hope to return to this earth as a cat in my own home. They really have it good.

«««« Milton describes the fate of the depressed souls of impure, lustful men:

[ß]ut when lust,
ßy unchaste looks, loose gestures, and foul talk,
ßut most by lewd and lavish act of sin,
Lets in defilement to the inward parts,
The soul grows clotted by contagion,
Embodies, and imbrutes, till she quite lose,
The divine property of her first being,

face our deaths with some degree of equanimity and curiosity because of our belief in the soul's immortality.

But for many people who live in the late twentieth century, this is not the case.« Like my father, they are Aristotelians. Aristotle was a biologist. He did not consider the soul to be in any sense a separate substance or entity, but rather the form of a particular living body.«« The soul-as-form stands in the same relationship to the physical body that the configuration of a statue stands to the materials from which

---

Such are those thick and gloomy shadows damp
Oft seen in charnel, vaults, and sepulchers
Lingering, and sitting by new-made grave,
As loath to leave the body that it loved,
And linked itself by carnal sensuality
To a degenerate and degraded state.[12]

« It is difficult to say if the decline in formal religious practice in many industrialized Western nations in the twentieth century represents a decline in religious beliefs as well. Writing about the Christian tradition in England, Ninian Smart suggests that the crisis in religious belief belongs more to "religious intellectuals," while "[s]omething like half of British people appear to believe in an afterlife."[13]

Smart attributes the intellectual crisis to three main roots, the second being "the effect of certain aspects of scientific thinking upon traditional ways of formulating Christian belief."[14] Scientific thinking had shaped my father's views on immortality and I suspect has also shaped the views of most members of the medical profession.

«« Aristotle started from the following principle, which ran through most early Greek philosophy: the soul makes living things alive. He was concerned, as a "student of nature," with all forms of life, not just with the human soul. According to Aristotle, the soul is the form of a living body, or "the first actuality of a natural body which has organs."[15]

The first actuality seems to be some sort of potentiality. Thus to speak of the soul is to speak of "the potentialities which a living thing has for different forms

it is made.⟨⟨⟨ As such, the soul is inseparable from the body.⟨⟨⟨⟨ Aristotle left no room in his theory for the immortality of the soul. Once the body has lost its vitality, it has also lost its soul. Body and soul are so intimately entwined that they live and die together.[2]

What I have presented is a rather crude dichotomy. I have only touched upon two traditions, and in a cursory fashion, at that.⟨⟨⟨⟨⟨

---

of life." These potentialities include the various faculties of living things: nutrition, reproduction, awareness, and rational thought. Aristotle believed they formed a hierarchy, with the higher functions being dependent upon those below.[16]

⟨⟨⟨ "Hence too we should not ask whether the soul and body are one, any more than whether the wax and the impression are one, or in general whether the matter of each thing and that of which it is the matter are one."[17]

⟨⟨⟨⟨ "That, therefore, the soul or certain parts of it, if it is divisible, cannot be separated from the body is quite clear; for in some cases the actuality is of the parts themselves."[18]

⟨⟨⟨⟨⟨ Descartes, a more modern philosopher, fits squarely within the Platonic tradition. Like Plato, Descartes believes that "our soul is in its nature entirely independent of the body, and in consequence it is not liable to die with it." As a student of physiology, Descartes departs from the Platonic tradition with his interest in science and mechanical principles. He equates living bodies with machines. Man-made automatons and brutes are considered pure machines, while man is seen as a machine with a mind. What distinguishes human beings from automatons and animals is the faculty of reason. Brute animals react only from the "disposition of their organs," not from reason.[19]

Furthermore, brute animals and automatons differ from man in their inability to arrange words and form statements by which they can make known their thoughts. Anthony Flew observes that this emphasis on consciousness and on the ability to use language as the criterion of thought is distinctly Cartesian. "It is to Descartes and not to Plato that we owe the typically modern view ... of the problem of body and mind as the problem of the relations between consciousness and the brain."[20]

Furthermore, I have confined myself to Western culture, not even nodding at the competing belief systems that exist in large parts of the world. ❨

But the deficiencies in my discussion go even deeper than that, and they are beyond my control. I have only dealt with the matter of the soul on the level of abstraction, and there is much more to it than that. It is one thing to subscribe to metaphysics intellectually, and another to believe in it consistently. It is possible to subscribe to Plato's views about the immortality of the soul in the daylight and break out in an Aristotelian sweat in the middle of the night.

In this century, traditional Cartesian dualism, or what Gilbert Ryle calls the dogma of the "ghost in the machine," has been challenged. With the scientific and philosophical recognition that mental and physical activities are not independent of each other, it no longer seems plausible to infer that there is some separate, invisible ghost inside who is running the machine.[21] At least with respect to my thoughts about death, my interest in Plato's theory of ensoulment, as well as in Descartes' theory, has more to do with theology than with the philosophy of mind.

❨ The Buddhist doctrine of rebirth differs dramatically from traditional Western concepts of the afterlife. Ninian Smart explains that

the individual is regarded as virtually everlasting, unless and until he attains liberation (nirvana), when there will be no more rebirth. The individual comes through a vast succession of previous existences. And will continue thus so long as he remains in the grip of craving and spiritual ignorance.... [T]he Buddhist doctrine of rebirth ... does not involve belief in a soul. There is no permanent self underlying physical and mental states.[22]

To attain Nirvana is to replace the imperfect states which make up the individual by a permanent state in which there is no person. The death of the individual is "the most fearsome sign of the impermanence" of the world, and the prospect facing the individual is seen "negatively as a succession of deaths." Thus one should not hope to attain individual immortality, but to transcend it. Nirvana is sometimes described as the "deathless place," since it is "beyond the realm of change and therefore of individual existence."[23]

In fact, most of us do all right when the death talk is abstract. We all know that death is part of the human condition, and this fact does sometimes enter into our conversations (although it is not a frequent intruder). No one invites the subject to come in, but no one denies it admission when it shows up at the back door, either.

But talk about a real death is another matter. That kind of talk is different. «And most of us never talk about our own deaths at all, except to ourselves, in the dark, in the dampness of Aristotelian sweat. Even then, the subject of our own death seldom makes a formal appearance. It does not become incorporated in our nocturnal dialogue about undone tasks, unpaid bills, the randomness of tornadoes coming our way. Rather, the subject of our own death waits outside, and looks longingly in through the window. It casts a shadow on all our other talk, and the darkness it sheds magnifies our little worries into grave concerns. It is not really talk about our own death, but non-talk. By not letting it into our sentences, even those muttered to the self at night, we try to deny that it is there. We cannot find the words to say that we might die today. «««

«« Ghassan Kanafani, a modern Arabic writer, notes the difference between talking about death in the abstract and talking about an actual death:
> What I want to talk to you about is death. Death that takes place in front of you, not about that death of which one merely hears. The difference between the two types of death is immeasurable and cannot be appreciated by someone who has not been a witness to a human being clutching at the coverlet of his bed with all the strength of his trembling fingers in order to resist that terrible slipping into extinction, as though the coverlet can pull him back from that colossus who, little by little, wrests from his eyes this life about which we know scarcely anything.

««« Freud believed that, due to our narcissism, "in the unconscious every one of us is convinced of his own immortality." Whenever we attempt to conceive of ourselves not existing, "we can perceive that we are, in fact, still present as spectators."[25]

THIS denial of our own death, and the resulting silence that surrounds the subject, came to be of more than academic interest to me.

Richard worked in the law library at school and, while at first I did not know him very well, he had helped me on several research projects. He was a gifted reference librarian, curious and intuitive. He was also very sick. He had started out with the flu one winter and his fever would not go away. It hung around for weeks and weeks, and when the doctor finally ran some blood tests, it turned out that Richard had lymphoma. He was thirty-one years old.

For months, Richard was in and out of the hospital for chemotherapy. During one dark period, his left lung suddenly collapsed and he ended up on a respirator in the ICU. He recovered, however, or so it seemed, and eventually came back to work. One sticky afternoon in July, I was invited back to technical services to celebrate a staff member's birthday. It was the usual fare: Carmella's cupcakes, Hawaiian punch, matching cups and napkins from Woolworth's, and a funny card signed by everyone. Richard and I sat together, perched on a cool radiator. I asked him how he was feeling.

"Fine, I guess. Tired. Okay, but really tired."

Then we talked about a movie I had just seen and something else that I don't remember. It was crowded in the room, and festive. People were milling around, laughing, talking, juggling cupcakes on their knees. I was about to get off the radiator and get some more Hawaiian punch when I heard Richard say, "I'd like to get one of those documents you were doing research on last year. You know, one of those living wills." ❴

"Oh, sure." I tried to sound casual.

"You know, just in case. I don't know if you knew it or not, but last spring my lung collapsed and they put me on a respirator. I don't ever want to be on one of those things again. Ever. I would rather just

---

❴ The living will is a written directive, executed while the patient is competent, stating preferences about such things as termination of life-support systems and withdrawal of food in the event the patient later becomes incompetent.[26]

die."[3] He said all of this rather matter of factly but did not look at me. I did not know what to say, so I just rattled the ice cubes in my paper cup. "So anyhow," he said after an awkward silence, "I'd like to get one of those."

"I'm sure we can find a living will form somewhere in the collection. I don't have one, Richard, but they aren't hard to find."

"Okay, I'll look." And that was all he said.

Richard and I had many subsequent conversations during that summer, but he never again mentioned the living will. He continued to work in the law library until the middle of August, when his fever came back to haunt him. His recovery had been an illusion. He went into the hospital for more tests and stayed for some experimental chemotherapy. One Monday morning I came to the library to learn that Richard was again in the ICU. On a respirator.

I called his mother to see how he was, and she said that when Richard's lungs had failed him, the doctors had put him back on the respirator. He was acutely agitated, and seemed to want to tell her something. Richard had written my name on the chalkboard that the nurses had given him to communicate. She wondered if I knew why, and I told her of our conversation of several months back, sitting on the radiator in technical services at a staff member's birthday party. She was frantic. There was nothing she could do for her son, and she wanted to do something. Anything.

Could I bring one of those living wills to the hospital?

I went to the card catalog, and within a few minutes I found a book with the living will form. I photocopied it and brought the form to the hospital, and his mother led me into the ICU. Richard was lying all alone in a dark cubicle. From the eyes down, the respirator had taken over his face, making him look like some kind of exotic, elephantine creature.⁴⁴ With each pseudobreath, it inflated him, over and over again, jerking him across the bed as if he were the mario-

---

⁴⁴ Paul Schilder writes: "The transformation of one thing into another is the specialty of the so-called demons."[27] The fact that a respirator is attached to the human face through a green plastic mask from which protrudes a long green ele-

nette of some mad puppeteer. What I saw was violence, and a total, complete absence of control.

As far as I could tell, when I engaged his eyes, Richard seemed happy to see me, and nodded when I showed him the living will. I could get no one to witness its execution. The nurses had been instructed not to participate in the signing of any documents, and I was referred to the hospital's legal department. It all seemed so pointless there in the corridor of the ICU, staring at an empty form whose legal effect was dubious to begin with,[4] its purpose already defeated, and my friend Richard exactly where he did not want to be. But his mother was looking at me with such expectation, as if by witnessing the signing of the living will, we could somehow make Richard live. And Richard had nodded.

So I got a pen, and we smoothed the document over the chalkboard, and Richard signed the damned thing. He slipped into a coma that afternoon and was dead before the sun went down. He never got off the respirator.

With the fierce egocentricity of a survivor, I felt responsible. I should have pursued that conversation and have often asked myself why I did not. It would have taken just a few minutes to go to the card catalog on that sticky day in July and find Richard a living-will form, the same few minutes it had taken on the day that he died.

Perhaps it was the informality of the occasion: Carmella's cupcakes and the Hawaiian Punch. Perhaps it was the tenuousness of our relationship: a friend I knew from work. Perhaps it was my own inability to deal with the request: denial of Richard's death and of my own. Perhaps I just did the wrong thing.

I have had to live with that failure for a long time. Richard died over ten years ago. Eventually I gave up blaming myself for those last few days he spent on a respirator in the ICU. If he really had felt that

---

phantine tube is difficult to ignore. Masks transform the human body into something else. These transformations often occur in fairy tales, where animals can change into human beings, or human beings into animals. Watching such a transformation of a familiar face can be a disturbing experience.

strongly about life-support systems, I told myself, he would have gotten the living-will form himself. After all, he certainly had the research skills. Besides, there were many times after that conversation on the radiator at which Richard could have broached the subject, and did not. It was up to him to instigate the conversation, not me. I was just a co-worker, not his lawyer or best friend. Such were my rationalizations.

I have often wondered why Richard chose me to reveal his thoughts to about the respirator. Perhaps he knew the nature of my research and assumed that I would be able to find a living will. That seemed like a logical explanation, but just beneath the layer of words that sought to make sense of things, it made no sense at all. I might be able to follow a map in the law library, but Richard was a cartographer. Perhaps he chose me because there was no risk in his revelation. It was an opportunity to speak the truth, without suffering the consequences. Speaking the truth is never cheap. It always costs somebody something.∁

Why had he not told his mother how he felt about the respirator? Under almost any scenario, his mother was the one who would be there at the moment of decision; she was certain to be a member of his deathwatch. She would have been in the best position to carry out his intent.

But would she? I did not know Richard's mother well, though well enough to know something of her despair. Richard may well have calculated the cost of telling the truth to his mother and decided that it was too high. Not only would the conversation itself have been incredibly painful, with its implicit acceptance of failure, but carrying out its intent might also have been too much for her to bear. It was a heavy burden to place on a mother, instructing her not to put her son on a life-support system when she was clinging to his life. Also Rich-

---

∁ I have always been leery of our enshrinement of the truth as the ultimate ideal. One of my favorite quotes comes from Otto Rank: "[F]or the time being I gave up writing—there is already too much truth in the world—an overproduction which apparently cannot be consumed!"[28]

ard's request might have interrupted the flow of her prayers, and he might not have wanted to do that.

The fact was that Richard did not want to die. He found the contemplation of his own death a terrifying thing.⟨ He called me once, late at night, before his last hospitalization, and wanted to know whether I believed in God. I think he was under the misapprehension that I was a rational person, and that if a rational person could believe in God, then maybe he could too. I was not up to the task. My own beliefs were so idiosyncratic that I could not give Richard what he needed, a transfusion of faith. During the course of that conversation, however, I discovered how truly frightened he was. Here was someone who had not come to terms with his own mortality. That was probably not unusual for a man age thirty-one, but his illness had taken Richard's rather commonplace fears and elevated them into a spiritual crisis. He needed to talk to someone.

In our culture, the subject of death—in particular, one's own death—is taboo.⟨⟨ Richard was in a panic, but customary patterns of

---

⟨ In *The Denial of Death*, Ernest Becker writes: "[T]he idea of death, the fear of it, haunts the human animal like nothing else: it is a mainspring of human activity—activity designed largely to avoid the fatality of death, to overcome it by denying in some way that it is the final destiny for man."[29] Becker devotes much of his book to showing that the fear of death is universal.

> The fear of our own death is so great that we actually repress the idea: Therefore in normal times we move about actually without ever believing in our own death, as if we fully believed in our own corporeal immortality. We are intent on mastering death.... A man will say, of course, that he knows he will die someday, but he does not really care. He is having a good time with living, and he does not think about death and does not care to bother about it—but this is a purely intellectual, verbal admission. The affect of fear is repressed.[30]

⟨⟨ The *American Heritage Dictionary* defines taboo as (1) a prohibition excluding something from use, approach, or mention because of its sacred and violable nature; (2) an object, word, or act protected by such prohibition; (3) a ban or inhibition attached to something by social custom or emotional aversion; (4) belief

conversation did not provide him with a graceful way to initiate talk about that panic. He once made an appointment with a priest in the hospital, but it was a man he did not know, the priest was in a hurry, and Richard was very shy.

Besides, talk about our own death rarely takes place in a formal setting. It does not wear a tuxedo, the way we dress up our words in drafting a will, when we commit to writing what we want done with our property. Talk about what we want done with our bodies in the event of terminal illness almost always wears blue jeans and a T-shirt, and is spoken softly, in casual, even haphazard, circumstances. Too much fear and superstition surround those words, and they cannot bear much scrutiny. After all, to the speaker of those words, there is a risk in saying them. For Richard, to articulate his intent about life-support systems was to ensure the inevitability of their use. To say those words was to make them come true.

Is it any wonder, given the climatic conditions, that there was no rain, that no words of intent showered down upon his mother, his doctor, or his lawyer in written form, or public, oral declarations? Is it any wonder that Richard chose to reveal himself to someone he did not know very well, at a birthday party at work, while sitting on a radiator?

Now here is the wonder: that Richard managed to crack the hard, dry surface of his silence at all.

THERE is a direct relationship between our theory of ensoulment and our attitude toward death. If we subscribe to some version of the

---

in or conformity to religious or social prohibitions; (5) a proscription devised and observed by any group for its own protection—*adj.,* excluded or forbidden by use, approach, or mention.

Radcliffe-Brown explains that the English word taboo derives from the Polynesian word, *tabu,* which means simply "to forbid" or "forbidden" and can apply to any sort of prohibition. Thus, the word may express a rule of etiquette, a chief's order, or an injunction to children not to touch something.[31]

Platonic tradition, and truly believe in spiritual immortality, then we might welcome death, or at least face it with stoic resignation. But if we believe in the Aristotelian notion that our soul will be buried with the body, that could indeed create a dark, moist environment in which the wild orchids of desperation might grow.

These are generalizations, of course, but I make them just the same.ᶜ I am aware there are exceptions. For example, one could believe in an afterlife and also in eternal damnation. Then, depending upon one's propensity to sin, the contemplation of death could inspire holy terror. Similarly, I have known some peaceful and content Aristotelians. My father was an example. It really did not seem to bother him that someday he might end up fertilizing the trillium. Still, I think the generalizations are more true than not. Beliefs about the soul's continuation, or lack thereof, affect our attitude towards death. This is not a very ambitious claim.

There is also a direct relationship between our attitude toward death and its status as a taboo subject. A taboo is something forbidden, and taboos come in many different forms. They may be proscriptions against certain behaviors,ᶜᶜ or against eating certain

---

ᶜ In one of my favorite essays, "But I Generalize," Joseph Epstein extolls the virtues of generalizations and their importance to "civilized discourse." Perhaps I am so fond of the essay because he used as an example a variant of my father's generalization about people falling into two categories. "[T]here is something appealing in the finitude of them. If there are only two types or categories or kinds—or even if there are four or five—then the world suddenly seems so much more intellectually manageable."[32]

ᶜᶜ Some of our behavior, thought to be motivated by superstition, is in fact motivated by taboo. Radcliffe-Brown gives the example, in contemporary England, of someone accidentally spilling salt. Though it is considered unlucky, he can avoid misfortune by throwing salt over his shoulder. "[H]e ... takes precautions and goes through a ritual in order that he may escape the danger and be restored to his former ritual status."[33]

foods,⟪⟪ or touching certain sacred or profane objects or persons.⟪⟪⟪ But taboos can also be what Levi-Strauss called "linguistic prohibitions."[5] ⟪⟪⟪⟪ In a given culture, certain words or subjects may be forbidden in public discourse. Someone with Victorian sensibili-

---

⟪⟪ The biblical rules found in Leviticus and Deuteronomy are perfect examples of dietary proscriptions:

> Every animal that parts the hoof and has the hoof cloven in two, and chews the cud, among the animals you may eat. Yet of those that chew the cud or have the hoof cloven you shall not eat these: the camel, the hare, and the rock badger, because they chew the cud but do not part the hoof, are unclean for you. And the swine, because it parts the hoof but does not chew the cud, is unclean for you. Their flesh you shall not eat, and their carcasses you shall not touch. Deut. 14:6–8

⟪⟪⟪ Some cultures proscribe touching a corpse. Radcliffe-Brown cites the Polynesian belief that a person who touches or carries a corpse is in danger of "the misfortune … of illness" and discusses other cultures' similar proscriptions against touching a newborn baby.[34]

⟪⟪⟪⟪ Radcliffe-Brown discusses linguistic prohibitions, found in Australia as well as in America, involving speaking the names of the dead. For example, "the Wik Munkan forbid any mention of a name or names for three years after the death of their bearer, that is, until his mummified body has been burnt." Similarly, some names, such as those of a man's dead sister or his wife's dead brother, may never be mentioned. "An inquirer committing the blunder of asking them is supplied with a substitute name which means literally 'no name', 'without name' or 'the second born.'" In some cultures the dead are given a new proper name, known as a "necronym," to avoid breaking the taboo. Necronyms sound to me a great deal like the euphemisms we use, such as "passed on" or "passed away," to say that someone died, presumably to avoid a linguistic prohibition.[35]

Freud has a lot to say in *Totem and Taboo* about the prohibition against uttering the name of a dead person and about the "taboo upon the dead." One explanation for the taboo is a fear "of the presence of or of the return of the dead person's ghost…. [T]o utter his name is equivalent to invoking him and will

ties, for example, may consider the mention of sexual activity or birth to violate a taboo.⁴ Geoffrey Gorer has theorized that there has been a shift in prudery during the last century, with death replacing sex as the forbidden subject.⁶ ⁴⁴ His explanation of the linguistic prohibition on the subject of death is the same as mine: People no longer have a system of belief that includes spiritual immortality.

The reasoning goes something like this: If the predominant attitude toward death in a culture is one of fear, then death becomes the subject of a linguistic prohibition—a taboo.⁴⁴⁴ There are risks in violating a taboo. Much like a formal legal system, our informal, traditional codes of conduct often carry sanctions for the breaking of unwritten rules.⁴⁴⁴⁴ By referring to death, and in particular to one's

---

quickly be followed by his presence." Freud believed that the taboo had developed from our ambivalent feelings toward the dead person. We may indeed feel an unconscious satisfaction from the death of a loved one, and this "can explain the idea that the souls of those who have just died are transformed into demons and the necessity felt by survivors to protect themselves by taboos against their hostility." Eventually the ambivalence becomes apparent when, as time goes by, the demons of the recently dead disappear and are replaced by ancestors who are to be venerated. Mourning performs a "psychical task.... [I]ts function is to transform those demons into friendlier spirits who can be revered and appealed to for assistance."³⁶

⁴ I have often noted that in social situations pregnancy and birth are considered inappropriate topics of conversation in "mixed company." It is deemed "girl talk," something that the women may discuss freely among themselves in the kitchen but not out in the living room where the men most often reside. This has always struck me as odd, since for me, the bringing into the world of a new human being has infinite fascination.

Mary O'Brien has pointed out that the subject of birth has seldom been held to be as profound as the subject of death. Death appears on the male agenda, but "birth [is] not and will not become, a worthy subject of male philosophy."³⁷ Virginia Held writes that symbolic representations of giving birth are rare: "Imaginative representations of birth from the point of view of a woman contemplating it, or of a woman experiencing a pregnancy … or of a woman giving birth, are unfamiliar cultural constructions."[38]

((Geoffrey Gorer, in his essay "The Pornography of Death," points out that in the mid-Victorian era it was birth and intercourse that were the "unmentionables," whereas death was "no mystery." Children were not only encouraged to think and talk about death, but to attend the deaths of others; it was a "rare individual who, in the 19th century with its high mortality, had not witnessed at least one actual dying."[39]

In the twentieth century, Gorer argues, prudery has shifted. Sexual intercourse has become more mentionable, and "death has become more and more 'unmentionable' as a natural process." Gorer sees a connection between the shift of taboos and the shift in English religious beliefs, since "belief in the future life as taught in Christian doctrine is very uncommon today." He recommends that we "give back to death—natural death—its parade and publicity, readmit grief and mourning" in order to do away with this "modern pornography of death."[40]

(((In *The Magic Mountain*, Thomas Mann alludes to the taboo nature of death. A popular old man in the sanitorium, known as the "gentleman rider," died after weeks of critical illness. When a nurse "discreetly communicated the sad event" to Hans Castorp, the protagonist, he rebelled against the "prevailing system of secrecy" by insisting on viewing the gentleman rider's mortal remains. At the dining hall, Castorp

> tried to introduce the subject of death at table, but was met with such a flat and callous rebuff on all sides as both to anger and embarrass him. Frau Stroer had been downright gruff. What did he mean by introducing such a subject—what kind of upbringing had he had? The house regulations protected the patients from having such things come to their knowledge; and now here was a young whippersnapper bringing it up at table.[41]

((((Ironically, given his role in forming the tenets of liberal thought, emphasizing individual freedom to pursue one's interests without interference from the state as long as no harm is caused to others, John Stuart Mill also reminds us of the sanctions that society may impose on an individual who strays too far from

own death, one runs the risk of conjuring it up, or invoking it.« In breaking the taboo, the speaker endangers himself by making himself vulnerable to the evil that prompted the taboo. If that risk is of no threat to the speaker, then the subject can be openly spoken of. In this instance, if the appearance of death does not rattle our bones, then there is no reason for silence on the subject. Simply put, the less fear we have about something, the more likely we are to talk about it. The converse is true as well: the more fear we have about something, the less likely we are to talk about it. Once again, this is not a very ambitious claim.

Anyone who does not believe me should spend some time in Ireland.

---

the accepted path. In "On Liberty," he argues that, while the state may not have the authority to intervene and stop certain socially unacceptable behavior, the citizens do have the power to punish the offender; society can ostracize a violator of social norms.[42]

« Radcliffe-Brown defines "ritual avoidance" or "ritual prohibitions" as rules of behavior "associated with a belief that an infraction will result in an undesirable change in the ritual status" of the offender. Rules of avoidance almost always accompany cultural rites associated with birth and death. A baby or corpse, the object of ritual avoidance, has "ritual value," and there may be a taboo against touching it. Many things can have ritual value, including "a person, a material thing, a place, a word or name, an occasion or event," or even a period of time. The members of a given culture generally agree as to the ritual value of certain things. If a taboo is broken, the person who broke it must restrict his behavior. He "may not use his hands to feed himself," for he is "in a state of danger." Nor may others touch him, because he can be dangerous to others. He himself becomes taboo by having broken the taboo.[43]

I am arguing here that the very subject of death, especially one's own death, has ritual value; it is the object of ritual avoidance, in that speaking of it puts the speaker in danger. The danger is that the offender may now suffer an undesirable change in her ritual status. That is to say, she may become vulnerable to death and put others in danger of death by having become taboo herself.

My husband's family lives in county Wexford, and every summer we take the children and rent a house for an extended visit to the Irish grandparents, aunts, uncles, and cousins. The first time I went to Ireland I was struck by the frequency with which death, and the dead, were mentioned unflinchingly in casual conversation.

On my first visit, I tried very hard to learn all the branches of the family. It was not an easy task. My mother-in-law came from a family of nine. I found that I could keep the relationships straight if I thoroughly understood the preceding generation, so I started by learning the children's names and the birth orders of both sets of my husband's grandparents. As I met each aunt and uncle, and began to have a face to attach to the name, I moved on to their spouses and children. To tell the truth, after almost twelve years, I am still working on the children of their children. With over seventy first cousins to master, and many repetitions of the same name, it is a miracle that I have remained sane. A few rules have saved me. For example, when in doubt, his name is Andrew.*

The real problem for me at first was to determine which of the aunts and uncles were dead. My confusion sprang from the freedom with which death, and the dead, were talked about around the kitchen table. On the first visit, I was having trouble identifying Father Ger. Father Ger was an older brother of my mother-in-law, a Sinnott. He was obviously much loved, a practical joker and a confidant to many. The one photograph I had seen of him showed a handsome young man in a priest's collar, hands thrust rakishly into his pockets, legs crossed, a greyhound at his feet, and an engaging smile that demanded one in return. I had heard many Father Ger stories and was looking forward to meeting him. About two weeks into the visit, I heard my mother-in-law refer to her brother Ger and then say

---

* There is a time-honored Irish custom of naming the eldest son after his paternal grandfather and the second son after his maternal grandfather. The eldest and second daughters are similarly named after their paternal and maternal grandmothers.[44] Thus, on my husband's father's side all the eldest boys are named Andrew, after their paternal grandfather.

quietly, "God have mercy on his soul." For the first time, it dawned on me that I was not going to meet Father Ger, on this trip or any other. He had died in 1957.

In my defense, I had not been tipped off about Father Ger's death by any visits to his grave.⁣⟨ Many of the other deceased members of the family, including the grandparents, were buried in the village churchyard. They were visited at least once a week, on the way to or from Mass. It was as if the dead were still a part of the community. Dying marked a sort of transition, but not the kind that I had been accustomed to in my own culture. Where I come from, once a person dies, he more or less ceases to be the subject of conversation. Even in intimate family settings, where a dead person might be talked about openly, he has been relegated to the status of memory, a static position. In Ireland, however, the dead do not disappear or become frozen in the same way. Somehow they are still with us as active, silent participants, and no one seems to find anything disturbing about their presence. On the contrary, having them around is rather comforting.⟨⟨

The same thing is true about the subject of death in Ireland. While it is not dwelled upon, when it does come up in conversation, the

---

⟨ Father Ger was buried in the parish in which he served rather than in his family's parish. This is not an uncommon practice in Ireland. Similarly, nuns are usually buried with other members of their religious order.

⟨⟨ The following passage from the work of Henry Scott Holland was recently read at the funeral of one of our most beloved Irish aunts:

Death is nothing at all. It does not count. I have only slipped away into the next room. Nothing has happened. Everything remains exactly as it was. I am I, and you are you, and the old life that we lived so fondly together is untouched, unchanged. Whatever we were to each other, that we are still. Call me by the old familiar name. Speak of me in the easy way which you always used. Put no difference into your tone. Wear no forced air of solemnity or sorrow. Laugh as we

speaker's tone of voice does not change. He maintains eye contact, and there are no awkward silences or clumsy efforts to move away from a subject that should never have been mentioned. You can talk about death over a cup of tea if you have to, need to, or want to. Although I have often heard sadness expressed in the mention of someone dying, I have never heard an echo of fear or desperation.

The closest thing to trepidation that I ever heard about dying was from my mother-in-law. At a family gathering, we were talking about irrational worries, and my mother-in-law confessed that she was pathologically afraid of being buried alive. As a child, she had once read about a man who had been in a coma and appeared to be dead, but in fact was not. He had been waked and buried, and later was discovered to have regained consciousness while in a coffin, under six feet of dirt. To this confession, her nephew, Father John, quipped, "Don't worry, Aunt Nan. We'll know if you've stopped talking for more than five minutes, you've got to be dead."

The anecdote has become a bit of family folklore; my daughters will hear the story over and over again, long after their grandmother is gone.

What accounts for this attitude toward death in the corner of Ireland that I have come to know? My intuition is that it comes from a strong religious faith and a firm belief in the immortality of the soul. The Catholic theory of ensoulment, when embraced wholeheartedly, makes death a mundane topic, even one that can generate a joke at a family gathering. Because death has spiritual meaning and is

---

always laughed at the little jokes that we enjoyed together. Play, smile, think of me, pray for me. Let my name be ever the household word that it always was. Let it be spoken without an effort, without the ghost of shadow upon it. Life means all that it ever meant. It is the same as it ever was. There is absolute and unbroken continuity. What is this death but a negligible accident? Why should I be out of mind because I am out of sight? I am but waiting for you, for an interval, somewhere very near, just round the corner. All is well.[45]

theologically a joyous occasion, there is no reason to avoid mentioning it in conversation.ᶜ The subject is not taboo.

It is no quirk of fate that the Catholic religion has been at the forefront of articulating when it should be permissible to withhold extraordinary care from terminally ill patients.ᶜᶜ Nor is it surprising that the Catholic tradition allows the burden on the family to be taken into account when determining whether a particular treatment is ordinary or extraordinary. Where the belief system exists that takes away the fear of death, it is possible to shift the focus from the dying person to the members of the deathwatch.ᶜᶜᶜ For the dying person, the journey is almost over. Those who are left behind must be ministered to. They are the ones who must contend with sorrow and pain, not the soul who is about to take flight. Ireland could teach us something about how to face our going out. If we could shatter the silence that surrounds the subject of death, we might be able to confront the taboo. Confronting the taboo would make for better deaths, and making for better deaths would help alleviate the horrors

---

ᶜ Catholics find their beliefs about the immortality of the soul in the New Testament. "The principle of life is the spirit, the soul," and "death is the giving up of the spirit." Catholics are "consoled by the many biblical assurances that we will rise with Christ to a new life in God the Father who prepared our reward from all ages."[46]

ᶜᶜ Catholicism makes a distinction between "extraordinary" and "ordinary" care when determining what care can be withheld from terminally ill patients. This distinction has a long history in Catholicism, where it was used prior to the discovery of antisepsis and anesthesia to decide whether a patient's refusal of treatment should be classified as suicide.[47]

> Ordinary means of preserving life are all medicines, treatments, and operations, which offer a reasonable hope of benefit for the patient and which can be obtained and used without excessive expense, pain or other inconvenience.... Extraordinary means of preserving life ... mean all medicines, treatments, and operations, which cannot be obtained without excessive expense, pain, or other inconvenience, or which, if used, would not offer a reasonable hope of benefit.[48]

of the late-twentieth-century-deathwatch. It would be an improvement in the human condition; a benefit for us all, and something to aspire to.

But for the people in power, confronting the taboo must be more than just an aspiration. Those people who orchestrate the death of others—who have jurisdiction over the human body, who judge death talk, who design death spaces—have a duty to confront the taboo. This duty runs not only to the dying person, but also to those who gather around him.

DOCTORS more or less run the dying show. Because of their medical monopoly on what takes place in hospitals and other health-care facilities, their attitudes toward death shape the contours of the late-twentieth-century deathwatch. Like other kinds of death talk, their attitudes will rarely be spoken of or written down, but they do not need to be. Like DNA, they encode the dying experience without

---

<<< Pope Pius XII has spoken about the family's responsibility to the patient:
The rights and duties of the family depend in general upon the presumed will of the unconscious patient if he is of age and *sui juris*. Where the proper and independent duty of the family is concerned, they are usually bound only to the use of ordinary means.

Consequently, if it appears that the attempt at resuscitation constitutes in reality such a burden for the family that one cannot in all conscience impose it upon them, they can lawfully insist that the doctor should discontinue these attempts, and the doctor can lawfully comply.[49]

The Sacred Congregation for the Doctrine of the Faith endorsed this stance with its May 5, 1980, "Declaration on Euthanasia," approved by Pope John Paul II. It asserts:

It is also permitted, with the patient's consent, to interrupt these means (provided by the most advanced medical techniques), where the results fall short of expectations. But for such a decision to be made, account will have to be taken of the reasonable wishes of the patient and the patient's family, and also of the doctors who are specially competent in the matter.[50]

expression, and, obedient to the genetic command, the medicalized deathwatch unravels itself in a designated way.

The taboo on the subject of death is even more pronounced in the medical profession. There is often a conspiracy of silence about death in a hospital, a reluctance to express in words the fact that a patient is dying. In the early 1980s, there were some chilling cases in which "Do Not Resuscitate" orders ("DNRs") were conveyed by attaching purple adhesive dots to the patient's nursing records, or by circling the patient's name in red on the chart. Mistakes in applying dots and circles to the wrong person's name, and disputes over who should have the power to add color to those charts, resulted in much more stringent requirements for the ordering of DNRs.[7] ⟨ It was as if the doctors and nurses needed another form of symbolic representation, something besides words, to communicate their orders about an impending death. I was reminded of those dots and circles when reading about a practice in a large, urban hospital. There was often a time-lag at this hospital between the death of an indigent patient and the transportation of the body to the morgue. To alert other hospital workers that there was a corpse inside a room, the door would be

---

⟨ A grand jury, investigating cases in which resuscitation was ordered withheld from two patients, criticized La Guardia Hospital in Queens. The hospital staff there conveyed "Do Not Resuscitate" orders by attaching a purple decal to the patient's nursing record. In an attempt to escape the legal risks of withholding CPR from dying patients, they would then discard the purple decal along with the record when the patient died.

New York Hospital identified patients whom it did not intend to resuscitate by circling their names in red on the chart. The hospital was charged in a civil suit when an intern refused, against the protests of a family member, also a physician, to resuscitate an eighty-seven-year-old patient for whom the family had not authorized DNR orders. It must have been quite a horrible scene: a family member and physician ordered a "crash cart" but was restrained by a hospital intern who refused to resuscitate the woman, pointing "to her chart, which had a red circle drawn around her name, signifying that she should not be saved."[51]

closed, and often a slip of white paper would be taped to the door, a silent, wordless announcement that a death had just occurred.[8]

Another sign of the taboo nature of death, even in the medical profession, is avoidance of the dying person. Not only do health care workers not want to talk about a patient who is dying, but often they do not want to talk to a patient who is dying. Of course, this kind of avoidance behavior is not confined to health care workers; it is just a manifestation of what has come to be called "death anxiety." « An early study of avoidance behavior attempted to identify the relative degree to which college students would distance themselves socially from a dying person. The researcher found that white subjects would avoid dying persons to the same extent that they would avoid "blacks or gamblers."[9] Most would not want to have a dying person as a friend. Similar studies in health care settings show that doctors and nurses are also guilty of fleeing from a dying patient, perhaps due to

---

« Psychological literature defines, in various ways, an empirically measurable theoretical construct known as "death anxiety." Kastenbaum and Aisenberg, for example, define the fear of death as the "fear of extinction, annihilation, obliteration, or 'ceasing to be.'"[52] Choron isolated three different types of death fears: fear of the event or process; fear of what comes after death; and fear of ceasing to be.[53]

Various measurement techniques seek to quantify the amount of death anxiety an individual has. The two most commonly employed direct measures are the Templer Death Anxiety Scale and the Collett-Lester Fear of Death and Dying Scales. The Templer Scale is a unidimensional measure which more often correlates with fears of one's own death and dying than with fears of the death and dying of others. The Collett-Lester Scales attempt to assess four distinct fears: fear of death of self; fear of death of others; fear of self dying; and fear of others dying. Both scales require subjects to rate statements about death and dying. For example, the Collett-Lester Scales ask subjects to rate their degree of agreement or disagreement with a statement like, "I would not mind dying young." The Templer Scale asks subjects to respond True or False to similar statements.[54] One of the major problems with these empirical techniques is their inability to measure the largely unconscious quality of death anxiety.

their own anxieties about death.⟨ They distance themselves; they express anger at the patient; they limit conversations; they avoid contact altogether, intellectualizing the patient's condition so they no longer have to deal with him as a person.⟨⟨ The effect on the dying person can be devastating. The abject loneliness of the situation,⟨⟨⟨ the depersonalization,⟨⟨⟨⟨ and the denial of any kind of significant social role⟨⟨⟨⟨⟨ are forms of social death which seem far more abhorrent than the biological death which the health care workers are avoiding. There are reasons, obvious ones I suppose, why medical profes-

---

⟨ Commentators have suggested that practicing medicine itself generates a higher degree of death anxiety than the general population experiences. One study reports that a group of eighty-one physicians was more fearful of death than groups of medical students, healthy persons, and terminally and seriously ill patients. The medical student group was less fearful of death than the physician group, but more fearful than the other groups studied.[55] Data suggests that "continued experience in the medical profession did not facilitate the mastery of one's fear of death, but rather appeared to enhance it."[56]

⟨⟨ David Sudnow has written about the treatment of patients in hospitals. A patient may be treated as "socially dead" though they are not yet biologically dead. Social death he defines as "that point at which socially relevant attributes of the patient begin permanently to cease to be operative as conditions for treating him, and when he is, essentially, regarded as already dead." He gives the example of a nurse closing the eyelids of a dying woman in preparation for her status as corpse, it being apparently more difficult to close the lids after rigor mortis sets in. This practice allowed the nurse to wrap the body more efficiently when the woman actually did die.[57]

⟨⟨⟨ In an article about group therapy with the terminally ill, the authors reported that "the most basic anxiety of many group members was not so much a fear of dying, of finiteness and nonbeing, but of the absolute utter loneliness that accompanies death." While existential loneliness could not be allayed by therapy,the psychiatrists felt that "secondary interpersonal loneliness that is a function both of the shunning of the dying person and his/her self-imposed isolation" could be handled capably in the group. Nurses, doctors and other medical personnel would often subtly "cue the patient" that her illness was terminal. Dying patients experienced a "hushed shrinking away, a tendency to be less intimate, a slightly greater distance." One patient initially realized the gravity of her illness when her doctor began ending his meetings with her by solemnly shaking her hand instead of "giving her a gentle pat on the fanny" (a remarkable observation on several different levels).[58]

《《《《 Just becoming a patient in a hospital, regardless of one's terminal status, can lead to the psychological phenomenon known as "depersonalization." This phenomenon, a feeling of loss of ego, has more specifically come to mean "a state in which the individual regards himself, and particularly his body, as a foreign object. He is estranged from his own body and does not experience it as belonging to himself. There are associated feelings of being without will and being like a machine."[59]

Depersonalization can occur chronically in severely disturbed people, but also occasionally in normal people, often as a response to stressful or degrading situations. One psychologist researched political prisoners in Nazi Germany who had once been substantial citizens but were being treated as criminals. They frequently reacted with depersonalization symptoms, such as feeling that their face or limbs did not belong to them. The denial of part or all of the body was a symbolic denial of the criminal role assigned to them. The same psychological phenomenon can happen to anyone who leaves his social role behind him to become a patient in a hospital. This is particularly true if one is dying and the hospital workers exhibit avoidance behavior.[60]

《《《《《 The denial of a social role for the dying person cannot be discussed in an historical vacuum. Erik H. Erikson argues that it is all too easy to discuss intellectual history as if it has no influence on the development of our psychological profiles, and urges us to analyze the "individual's ego identity in relation to the historical changes which dominated his childhood milieu." While a child has a number of "opportunities to identify himself, with real or fictitious people of either sex, with habits, traits, occupations, and ideas … the historical era in which he lives offers only a limited number of socially meaningful models for workable combinations of identification fragments."[61]

sionals might not deal well with death and dying. After all, most of them consider themselves to be in the business of saving lives,❝ and it is easy to see how they might perceive the death of a patient to be a failure—a public, professional failure.❝❝ An article about heart surgeons in New York State published mortality rates as evidence of a doctor's skill.[10] It was a telling comment on our culture that survival rates would stand out as the sole criterion by which we would judge a doctor. There was no corresponding chart of sensitivity, tact, or a willingness to respond to not only the medical needs of the patient, but to his emotional, spiritual, and social needs as well.❝❝❝

The increased medicalization of death and the shunning of the dying person by both medical professionals and laymen have provided no socially meaningful role for the dying person. This has caused a psychological crisis for the dying person which must be understood in its historical context.

❝ In Brian Clark's play, *Whose Life Is It Anyway?*, Dr. Emerson treats a young sculptor who was paralyzed from the neck down in an accident and has chosen not to continue his life. When another doctor suggests that someone in his patient's situation might wish to die, Dr. Emerson categorically states, "No, Clare, a doctor cannot accept the choice for death; he's committed to life. When a patient is brought into my unit, he's in a bad way. I don't stand about thinking whether or not it's worth saving his life, I haven't time for doubts. I get in there, do whatever I can to save life. I'm a doctor, not a judge."[62]

❝❝ John Hinton writes about the issues of self-esteem that confront a doctor who has a terminally ill patient:
Being human, the doctor can be hurt when forced to acknowledge that his patient is going to die. Perhaps as his medical experience lengthens he is less aware of the hurt he first felt earlier in his career when his patients died; but although the situation becomes bearable it can still perturb. He must admit to the person most concerned that he is now impotent to do what is desired so much, to save his patient's life. The doctor's ability to cure and bring relief usually sustain him in his work—and in his own self-esteem. He can feel very threatened at having to admit failure to a person who is depending on him.[63]

That should come as no surprise, however. We are all obsessed with beating death, and our own attitudes promote and perpetuate the attitudes of our healers. It is a symbiotic relationship, one in which miracles are demanded and often delivered.⟨⟨⟨⟨ When the miracle does not happen, the failure must be felt acutely by the miracle worker. There is a lot at stake in that failure, most of it having to do with the death of a patient and not the death of a human being. It is understandable, therefore, that medical professionals would be even more vulnerable to the taboo of death talk—understandable, but not forgivable. The facts are that people die, and they do so while being cared for by doctors and nurses. Because the power to determine the circumstances of death resides almost entirely with medical professionals, there is a duty to chart carefully the course for a patient riding through those narrow straits, a duty not to let the patient crash into sheer cliffs, hurdle over wild waters alone, or languish in

⟨⟨⟨ My indictment against the medical profession is, of course, general. Many nurses, doctors, and other health care professionals have spoken and written about the importance of attending to the members of the deathwatch as well as to the patient. For example, some hospitals and hospices offer what is sometimes referred to as "Bereavement Service," which includes counseling for family members both before and after the death. At St. Christopher's Hospice in London, the Bereavement Service maintains contact with the family for an average of eighteen months after the death. Families and close friends are "assisted in working out their bereavement through reality assistance, emotional support, and simple talking-out."[64]

⟨⟨⟨⟨ Symptomatic of a "demanding" era, groups have even formed that are devoted to the goal of beating death altogether. For example, a publication originated in California (where else?) called *The Immortality Newsletter*, whose motto was "Death is an imposition on the human race and no longer acceptable." This denial of death generated the cryonics movement of the 1970s, in which people chose to have their bodies frozen in liquid nitrogen when they died, with the hope of being revived in the future, when medicine would presumably have found a cure for their fatal illnesses.[65]

the doldrums of artificial life-support. That duty runs to the family and friends of the dying person, to the members of the deathwatch. The death belongs to them as well.

Ultimately, the medical profession must confront the taboo. Words must be found to communicate the fact of the death so that a proper deathwatch can take place. Words of disclosure to the patient and his family.« Words about life-support systems that allow the patient to manifest his intent before losing competency.«« Words that help to turn the fear inside out, just by virtue of their having been spoken. Words of consultation««« and of sympathy.««««

Lawyers too must confront the taboo, but in a different way.

« A trend has developed toward more open disclosure to patients, including disclosure of a bad prognosis. A 1961 study found that almost 90 percent of doctors had a "strong and general tendency" not to tell their patients of a cancer diagnosis.[66] Sixteen years later, more than 97 percent of doctors said they routinely disclosed a cancer diagnosis to patients.[67]

A one-sided disclosure from doctor to patient may not actually do much to confront the taboo on the subject of death. In *The Silent World of Doctor and Patient*, Jay Katz argues eloquently for doctors and patients to move beyond the narrow confines of the doctrine of informed consent, which only requires the doctor to recite a litany of medical risks to the patient. Instead, the doctor and patient must have a dialogue in order to arrive at appropriate medical decisions, a dialogue which admits the inequalities of the parties. The doctor knows more about the disease, and the patient knows more about his needs. The conversation must be built on trust. "This trust cannot be earned through deeds alone. It requires words as well. It relies not only on physicians' *technical* competence but also on their willingness to share the burden of decisionmaking with patients and on their *verbal* competence to do so."[68]

«« It always made me angry that my friend Richard's doctor did not initiate any conversations with him about any sort of living will or other advance directive regarding life-support systems, considering his gloomy prognosis. Apparently, it is not uncommon for doctors to fail to take the initiative in this way.[69]

Doctors have also complained, probably justifiably, that the legal profession

IT seems as if we are going to have to live with the pretense that the decision to terminate life-support systems belongs to Karen Quinlan or Nancy Cruzan. Dispensing with that pretense appears to be too costly; too much is at stake. To make the pretense palatable, however, courts have imposed certain standards of proof on the manifestations

has not done a very good job of communicating the law to the medical profession. Michael Flick has commented that "[b]oth what the law is and how it is applied are largely mysteries to doctors, who get their information about law from newspapers and medical journals. In the retelling of the law, commentators inevitably simplify and put a gloss on it."[70]

《《《 Words of consultation are particularly critical to family members who may be bearing a large part of the burden of caring for the dying patient. Dr. Wallace I. Sampson has some excellent medical advice for families who have decided to bring a patient home to die. Among the subjects he covers are pain control, ways to deal with bowel and bladder dysfunction, and the patient's need (or lack thereof) for food and water. Sampson also has some advice for doctors on how best to support and assist the patient and family: "People seem to want to regain control of their lives and of their deaths. Except in smaller towns, medicine has not been geared to home care, so we need to reorient ourselves to the desires of people who want to die at home." In a sense, Sampson's is a "how to" article on the logistics of bringing back the nineteenth-century deathwatch.[71]

《《《《 Occasionally a doctor will directly address the emotional needs of the members of the deathwatch. While Dr. G. E. Burch focuses on the welfare of the patient, he also writes about the fears and anxieties of family members and discusses the need for physicians to meet regularly with the family and to allow frequent and lengthy visits to the bedside of the dying person. He suggests that doctors often appear to family members as "primarily concerned with the use and operation of complex, frightening, awful apparatus with stern, serious, and grim automatons in attendance." Dr. Burch admits that the additional burden of responding to concerns of the family of the sick "can annoy the doctors at times, but this is part of caring for the sick, part of the practice of medicine."[72] Dr. Burch may attend my deathwatch anytime.

of the patient's former intent. In applying those standards, the taboo nature of death talk must be taken into account.

Consider the evidentiary standards New York and Missouri imposed on the members of the deathwatch. To prove that the patients, if competent, would have refused life-sustaining treatment, those states have adopted a "clear and convincing" standard of proof.[11]

Mary O'Connor was a seventy-seven-year-old woman who suffered from dementia as a result of several strokes. Although the condition "substantially impaired her cognitive ability," she was not in a coma or a persistent vegetative state: "she was conscious, and capable of responding to simple questions or requests sometimes by squeezing the questioner's hand and sometimes verbally."[12] She could not understand complex questions, however, such as those dealing with her medical treatment. Her doctor doubted that she would ever regain significant mental capacity because the brain damage was substantial and irreparable.[13] Mary O'Connor was a widow, with two adult daughters, Helen and Joan, both of whom were practical nurses. After her first stroke, she went to live with Helen, but, when she suffered a second stroke, she lost her gag reflex and had to be put into a nursing home. Because she could not eat, O'Connor became so ill that she had to be transferred to a hospital, where her doctors wanted to insert a nasogastric feeding tube to keep her from dying of thirst and starvation. Her daughters opposed the insertion of the tube, stating that this was against their mother's expressed wishes that "she did not want her life prolonged by artificial means if she was unable to care for herself."[14]

At trial, James Lampasso, a former co-worker and longtime friend of Mary O'Connor, testified that he first discussed artificial means of prolonging life with her in 1969. At that time, Lampasso's father was dying of cancer and had informed him that he would not want to continue life by any artificial means if he had lost his dignity and could no longer control his bodily functions. O'Connor had wholeheartedly agreed, saying, "'I would never want to be a burden on anyone, and I would never want to lose my dignity before I passed away.'" Lampasso also noted that O'Connor was a "'very religious woman' who 'felt that nature should take its course and not use further artificial means.'" During two or three subsequent conversations, O'Connor stated that it was "'monstrous' to keep someone alive by using 'machinery, things like that' when they are 'not going to get better'; that she would never want to be in the same situation as her husband and Lampasso's father, and that people who are 'suffering very badly' should be allowed to die."[15] Mary O'Connor had been a member of two deathwatches: her husband's and her step-mother's. One daughter, Helen, testified that after her father was hospitalized with cancer, her mother said that she never wanted to be in a similar situation; "she would not want to go on living if she could not 'take care of herself and make her own decisions.'"[16] Helen testified that later, after O'Connor had been hospitalized for a heart attack and had finally been discharged, her mother said "that she was very glad to be out of the hospital and hope[d] she would never have to be back in one again and would never want any sort of intervention, any sort of life-support systems to maintain or prolong her life."[17] Mary O'Connor's other daughter, Joan, gave similar testimony, describing her mother's statements on this subject as "less solemn pronouncements": "'It was brought up when we were together, at times when in conversations you start something, you know, maybe the news was on and maybe that was the topic that was brought up and that's how it came about.'"[18]

The New York Court of Appeals held the members of the death-watch, in this case the daughters, to the very high evidentiary standard of "clear and convincing" evidence with regard to their mother's intent.[19] The usual standard of proof in a civil case is a "preponderance of the evidence"; in a criminal case, the burden is "beyond a reasonable doubt." In the mist, between the two standards of proof, floats this standard called "clear and convincing" evidence. In this context, the New York Court of Appeals described it as "proof sufficient to persuade the trier of fact that the patient held a firm and settled commitment to the termination of life supports under the circumstances like those presented."[20]

When the New York Court of Appeals applied the evidentiary standard of "clear and convincing," the daughters' testimony in *O'Connor* could not meet the burden of proof. The court noted that

Mary O'Connor had never discussed the withholding of food and nutrition; nor had she indicated whether she would feel the same way if the refusal of medical treatment would have produced a painful death. Both daughters admitted that their mother had never discussed what she would have done under those precise circumstances.[21]

Nancy Cruzan's parents ran into the same high evidentiary hurdle in Missouri when they sought to withdraw her nasogastric feeding tube. Nancy's statements, made at age twenty-five in a "somewhat serious conversation with a housemate friend that if sick or injured she would not wish to continue her life unless she could live at least halfway normally," also did not meet Missouri's standard of "clear and convincing" evidence.[22] Like the daughters in *O'Connor*, the members of Nancy Cruzan's deathwatch faced a familiar problem, harking back to *Quinlan*. Her statements about life support were too general, too hypothetical, too lacking in specificity.

The writers of those state appellate opinions, however, treated the subject of death just like any other subject about which a court might have to infer intent. They did not indicate that what was being talked about was any different from what kind of chickens a restaurant might want to buy, or what kind of windows an owner might want to put in his house.[23] Chickens, windows, death—the subject matter is all the same, in texture, in color, in density.

To my mind, Mary O'Connor's statements did not seem to be too general, too hypothetical, or too lacking in specificity. Judge Simons, who wrote a dissent to *O'Connor*, agreed with me. While he was willing to adopt the standard of "clear and convincing," he was also willing to accept the trial court's finding that Mary O'Connor's family had met that burden of proof, that "Mrs. O'Connor did not wish any artificial means used to prolong her life under these circumstances."[24] He also noted that she had participated in several deathwatches of close family members, that she had consistently expressed the view that artificial means should not be used to sustain life, and that some of those statements had been made after a hospitalization for a serious illness.

Similarly, the conversations that Nancy Cruzan had with a roommate, and the conversations that Karen Quinlan had on several occasions with family members and friends, do not strike me as too general, too hypothetical, or too lacking in specificity. To its credit, the Supreme Court of New Jersey later stated that Karen Quinlan's statements were "certainly relevant to shed light on whether the patient would have consented to the treatment if competent to make the decision."[25] Some have suggested that there is a lot of hidden sexism in these appellate cases regarding the termination of life-support systems; that the moral agency of women, and thus their statements of intent, are taken less seriously than those of men.[26] That makes a lot of sense to me.

It is in Justice Brennan's dissent in *Cruzan* where the taboo nature of death is dealt with honestly. Justice Brennan's dissent is also where the members of the deathwatch are acknowledged, and their pain openly recognized. After describing the physical deformation and dependency of a patient in a persistent vegetative state, he wrote, "Such conditions are, for many, humiliating to contemplate, as is visiting a prolonged and anguished vigil on one's parents, spouse, and children. A long, drawn-out death can have a debilitating effect on family members."[27] He opposed the standard of "clear and convincing" evidence on several different grounds, one of those being the exclusion of any testimony from family members and close friends regarding what Nancy would have done.[28] In fact, Justice Brennan argued that intimate conversations with those family members and close friends may be "the best evidence available of what the patient's choice would be. It is they with whom the patient most likely will have discussed such questions and they who know the patient best."[29]

Finally, Justice Brennan urged us all to look at the nature of death talk. While the majority suggested that only living wills or equivalently formal directives could meet the high standard of proof, Justice Brennan pointed out that most people do not behave that way about their own deaths. Ignorance about the legal requirements, denial of the possibility that such a thing could happen, and denial of their own mortality all contribute to an absence of formality about their intent regarding life-support systems. No inference of lack of intent, Justice Brennan argued, should be drawn from the failure to write it down:

> Too few people execute living wills or equivalently formal directives for such an evidentiary rule to ensure adequately that the wishes of incompetent persons will be honored. While it might be a wise social policy to encourage people to furnish such instructions, no general conclusions about a patient's choice can be drawn from the absence of formalities. The probability of becoming irreversibly vegetative is so low that many people may not feel an urgency to marshal formal evidence of their preferences. Some may not wish to dwell on their own physical deterioration and mortality.[30]

Justice Brennan ended his dissent by disparaging the legal fiction that the Supreme Courts of Missouri and the United States were trying to effectuate Nancy Cruzan's intent. Instead, "[t]hey have discarded evidence of her will, ignored her values, and deprived her of the right to a decision as closely approximating her own choice as humanly possible. They have done so disingenously in her name, and openly in Missouri's own."[31]

Justice Brennan's remarkable dissent is followed by another, by Justice Stevens. Justice Stevens also brought the members of the deathwatch into the circle of constitutional consideration. His contribution, in my mind, is to tie their presence to the spiritual component of death. Borrowing an elegant turn of phrase from Justice Harlan, Justice Stevens made a beautiful analogy: "[J]ust as the constitutional protection for the 'physical curtilage of the home . . . is surely . . . a result of solicitude to protect the privacies of the life within,'" so too "the constitutional protection for the human body is surely inseparable from concern for the mind and spirit that dwell therein."[32] While admitting that the constitutional significance of death is difficult to describe, he explained that

> not much may be said with confidence about death unless it is said from faith, and that alone is reason enough to protect the freedom to conform choices about death to individual conscience. We may also, how-

ever, justly assume that death is not life's simple opposite, or its necessary terminus, but rather its completion. Our ethical tradition has long
regarded an appreciation of mortality as essential to understanding
life's significance.[33]

Justice Stevens then cast his eye on the members of the deathwatch.
Nancy Cruzan's interest in life included "an interest in how she will
be thought of after her death by those whose opinions mattered to
her. There can be no doubt that her life made her dear to her family,
and others. How she dies will affect how that life is remembered."[34]
He argued that the state of Missouri should have deferred to the
members of the deathwatch, not directly as I had originally planned,
but indirectly, working in the shadows and on the edges of things as
my friend had suggested.

The trial court's order authorizing Nancy's parents to cease their
daughter's treatment would have permitted the family that cares for
Nancy to bring to a close her tragedy and her death. Missouri's objec-
tion to that order subordinates Nancy's body, her family, and the lasting
significance of her life to the State's own interests. The decision we review thereby interferes with constitutional interests of the highest
order.[35]

As I said, those are remarkable dissents.
Do others sometimes feel, as I do, that they were born at the
wrong time? That their feelings and thoughts are so out of sync with
the majority opinion, whatever the issue may be, it is almost guaran-
teed to be alien to them? That they may as well skip the front part of
the decision and go directly to the dissent? That the dissent will be
the place where the truth will emerge, where wisdom will be found,
where there will be resonance with what is in their hearts?
I am grateful for those dissents. It is so important for me to see Supreme Court justices acknowledge the difficult and risky nature of
death talk; to address the members of the deathwatch and their pain;
to dare to put the spiritual meaning of death in the same sentence
with the Constitution. It is also important for me to hear the argu-

ment that the standard of "clear and convincing" evidence is too high, considering that talk about one's own death is taboo in our culture. It makes me feel a part of the human family, and not alone. It is like the wonder of literature, when a writer captures something that you have said to yourself in the dark silence of the night, certain that you alone felt and thought that way. A flood of relief comes from the revelation that you are not unique, that the same words have formed in other minds, that when you cannot sleep because of what happened to Karen Quinlan, Nancy Cruzan, Mary O'Connor, and their families, your insomnia is shared—and justified.

I am grateful to those dissents, and worried about my longevity. The women in my family live forever. Justice Brennan has died, and Justice Stevens is an old man. If I stay out of sync and live long enough, what will happen to those dissents? I can bear the alienation from the majority opinion, but I will not be able to bear a silence at the end.❨

❨ Perhaps I will even outlive this genre of constitutional decisionmaking, where opinions are structured in this fashion, with texts divided into "majority opinions" and "dissents." I may already have. Lately I find that I lose my bearings when reading Supreme Court cases—my briefing methods are out of date. I am looking for what "the Court held," and there no longer seems to be a "Court," but rather one short solo piece, a confident trumpet blast, which is then followed by a polyphony—and sometimes a cacophony—of concurring justices. The votes may be unanimous, as with the recent rejections of due process and equal protection challenges to assisted suicide bans in Washington and New York, but the opinions are fractured, splintered things.[73] Perhaps dissents like those in *Cruzan* are an endangered species, the classical dualism of the majority and dissenting opinions yielding to a postmodern jurisprudence with multiple explanations, interpretations, and justifications for almost everything. As a reader, I feel endangered as well. Invariably, I have brought the wrong tool to the analysis: a knife to chop the onion. What is now needed is some sort of peeler—an instrument designed not for the creation of bite-sized, crisp, sharp edges, but for the teary task of exfoliation.

And so, that is how lawyers should confront the taboo of death talk. We should implicitly recognize the taboo in our application of evidentiary standards to former conversations of incompetent patients. It is not the time for rigor and heightened scrutiny. It is a time to let Richard express his concerns about life-support systems to a co-worker, sitting on a radiator, drinking Hawaiian punch. It is a time to let Mary O'Connor tell her daughters and her friends about the horrors of the deathwatches she has seen. It is a time to let Karen Quinlan tell her sisters about the nightmare of watching family friends die terrible, lingering, painful deaths. It is a time to let Nancy Cruzan tell her roommate that she does not ever want to die that way. It is a time to defer to the members of the deathwatch and to give credence to their words about words whispered to them in the night.

5

Law and the Architecture
of Ritual Space

What else can the law do to alleviate indirectly the pain of the members of the deathwatch?

THE deathwatch serves a ritual function,« sending a member of the community on his way, and fortifying the survivors against the threat of change; it conquers the anarchy of death and restores order to the universe—and to the community.«« The deathwatches of the nineteenth century took place in the bedroom of the dying person, as portrayed in Munch's painting. What had once been the private domain of the individual was turned into a place for community ««« and consecration. The bed would be moved to a central location, and chairs would be placed around the bed to permit visitation. The cur-

---

« Lawyers deal with conceptual language, and the functions of language and ritual are often at odds. Roy Rappaport writes: "The distinctions of language cut the world into bits ... into categories, classes, oppositions, and contrasts. It is in the nature of language to search out all differences and to turn them into distinctions which then provide bases for boundaries and barriers." Rappaport contrasts conceptual language with the function of ritual "to unite, or reunite, the psychic, social, natural, and cosmic orders which language and the exigencies of life pull apart."[1]

« "Ritual" has been defined in a number of different ways. Sir Edmund R. Leach, a cultural anthropologist, suggests an expansive definition, applying it to all stereotypical, symbolic behavior that serves to communicate information about a culture's cherished values.[2] Another common definition of ritual, one favored by psychoanalytic theory, refers to all nonrational or formalized symbolic behavior as "ritual," as distinct from pragmatic behavior that is rationally related to the achievement of some end.[3]

Other anthropologists are interested in the religious meaning of ritual symbolism. Victor Turner defines ritual as "prescribed formal behavior for occasions not given over to technological routine, having reference to beliefs in invisible beings or powers regarded as the first and final causes of all effects."[4] Evan M. Zuesse defines ritual as "those conscious and voluntary, repetitive and stylized symbolic bodily actions that are centered on cosmic structures and/or sacred presences."[5] Does it matter which definition of "ritual" we adopt for purposes of the deathwatch? I do not think so. The behavior exhibited in a deathwatch qualifies for the more expansive definitions. It is formalized behavior that has social meaning, in that it transmits the culture's values and unifies individual participants into a genuine community. But the behavior exhibited in the deathwatch meets the narrower definitions as well. There is no getting around the fact that a member of the community is dying, that a life force is waning, or transmuting, or moving on. In recognition of that fact, certain rituals are performed during a deathwatch that refer to invisible beings, cosmic structures, or powers that are regarded as the first and final causes; someone or something in the transcendental realm is invoked or addressed.

««« Sally Falk Moore and Barbara G. Meyerhoff define the communities that engage in secular rituals rather loosely:

> Secular ceremony certainly often takes place outside of community in the sense of "corporate group" and outside of community in the sense of "common culture." There are secular ceremonies invented and produced for persons who have come together just for one particular occasion. The participants even may be of different cultures.[6]

The members of the deathwatch may in fact, and more than likely will, be part of a larger, more permanent community. They may also form one of the more ephemeral communities, however, that Falk Moore and Myerhoff refer to here.

tains would be closed,⟨ and candles would be lit. The sickroom was transformed.

Dying is a rite of passage. In his seminal work *The Rites of Passage,* Arnold van Gennep distinguished among three phases in a rite of passage.[1] The first phase, known as "separation," clearly demarcates sacred time and space from profane or secular time and space. With formal institutions, separation is accomplished by the construction of a special building, such as a church or a temple, and by the holding of religious services that are beyond or outside the time that measures our everyday lives. Since the timing of death in the nineteenth century could not be controlled, the decline of the human body dictated when the deathwatch began.⟨⟨ Similarly, since dying took place in informal settings, there were no special buildings devoted to the

---

⟨ Closing the curtains creates an enclosure, a demarcation between profane and sacred space. Mircea Eliade writes that all sacred spaces are enclosed, one reason being to preserve the "profane man from the danger to which he would expose himself by entering it without due care. The sacred is always dangerous to anyone who comes into contact with it unprepared, without having gone through the 'gestures of approach' that every religious act demands." The sacred enclosure is also analogous to city walls, originally used as a "magic defense, for they marked out from the midst of a 'chaotic' space, peopled with demons and phantoms … a place that was organized, made cosmic, in other words, provided with a 'centre.'"[7]

⟨⟨ Although the timing of death cannot be controlled in the way a periodic, religious occasion can be scheduled, Eliade would still argue that sacred time, as well as sacred space, is implicated in a deathwatch. Death is an event, and as such, "every event (every occurrence with any meaning), simply by being effected in time, represents a break in profane time and an irruption of the Great Time." Profane time is "the time in which meaningless actions come and go." Not all sacred, religious time is reproduced periodically, since "any time may become a sacred time." Just as any space can become sacred, "so too sacred time, generally established by communal feasts set by the calendar, may be attained at any time and by anyone, simply by repeating an archetypal, mythical gesture."[8]

deathwatch. However, the rituals of moving the bed chairs, closing the windows, and lighting the candles accomplished the same thing —the creation of sacred space.[3] «««

This sacred space was created in preparation for the next stage of a rite of passage, known as "transition."[4] During this intervening phase, which van Gennep referred to as a "margin," or "limen," meaning "threshold" in Latin, the ritual subject, the dying person, passes through a period of ambiguity in which normal social relations are discontinued, rights and obligations are suspended, and cosmological concerns become of central importance.«««« During this phase, in the nineteenth-century deathwatch, dying words would be

««« Eliade's sacred space can be described as "a defined place, a space distinguished from other spaces. The rituals that a people either practice at a place or direct toward it mark its sacredness and differentiate it from other defined spaces."[9] The functions of sacred space are dual: first, to provide places of communication with divinity, i.e., places where people can go to meet the gods; and second, to be a locus of divine power.[10]

«««« Victor Turner built upon van Gennep's theory of liminality, extending it far beyond its original sense of an intermediate stage in a rite of passage. For Turner, liminal personae could become an enduring category of people who inhabit the edges of social boundaries: poets, clowns, shamans, and monks. Turner writes:

> The attributes of liminality or of liminal personae ("threshold people") are necessarily ambiguous, since this condition and these persons elude or slip through the network of classifications that normally locate states and positions in cultural space. Liminal entities are neither here nor there; they are betwixt and between the positions assigned and arrayed by law, custom, convention, and ceremon[y] ... .Thus, liminality is frequently likened to death, to being in the womb, to invisibility, to darkness, to bisexuality, to the wilderness, and to an eclipse of the sun or moon.[11]

Some people live their lives in these liminal positions. (In the legal profession, the academic plays the court jester, "betwixt and between.") During a rite of passage, however, all participants are in a sense liminal; by engaging in ritual activity, they separate themselves from their everyday roles and statuses.

said, old grievances forgiven, property distributed, promises extracted, and confessions made. It was a time for extraordinary utterances, words said outside the normal boundaries of social intercourse, a time of change and of confusion. By its very nature, the liminal stage of a rite of passage is threatening to the community; certainly this was true for the members of the nineteenth-century deathwatch. The constituency of the group was about to change: A member was on the verge of departure, and in the vacuum he left behind, there was chaos, a lack of order and definition.《

The third and final phase of a rite of passage, "reaggregation" or "incorporation," is also accompanied by symbolic acts: closing the eyelids, covering the face, and reciting prayers to send the soul on its way.[5] This third phase places the ritual subject in a new, well-defined position in the society. In the nineteenth-century deathwatch, the new position was that of ancestor.《《 His body became a corpse and was subject to a new set of rules for its handling and final disposition.《《《

《 According to Walter O. Weyrauch, any change in membership in a small group, whether that change is the birth of a child, marriage, or the death of a member, strains its internal cohesion. A change such as a death "inevitably affects the group as a whole and the relationships among the participants. Every relationship within the group must be readjusted, and the newly formed group as a result is not identical to the original conjugal group."[12]

《《 When I refer to the dying person's new status as "ancestor," I have of course picked a term that has familial connotations. I do not mean to limit my remarks to familial deathwatches. The new status might just as easily be described as that of "deceased friend or loved one."

In many cultures, however, ancestor worship plays a significant role. Joachim Wach writes that death rituals "which revolve about the departed are designed to remove pollution and other evil consequences and to propitiate the deity and thus obtain the favor of the spirit of the deceased.... Either the departed is considered to have gone and is therefore prevented by a series of rites from returning and upsetting the newly achieved equilibrium of the surviving group, or he con-

The rituals of the nineteenth-century deathwatch, the prescribed symbolic acts performed by the entire community, represented some sort of constancy to a community that was threatened by change. «««« The deathwatch gave the members of the community an excuse to gather, and, once in each other's presence, it gave them something to say and do, a way to express grief and a way to deal with the burden

---

tinues even after death to be regarded as a highly revered, howbeit invisible, member of the group." It is possible that the high regard in which his family holds Father Ger is just another version of ancestor worship.

««« Under Jewish law, a person moving from life to death actually has an interim status. *Goses* is the name given to a dying person, and in the Talmud, different rules apply to a *goses* than to a living person. For example, the *goses* should not be touched for fear that his departure might be inadvertently hastened. Furthermore, a *goses* should not be left alone, and it is a great *mitzvah* to be present at the departure of the soul. Candles are usually lit in the presence of a *goses* to symbolize the flickering out of the human soul.[14]

Once the *goses* achieves the status of corpse, a different set of rules apply. For example, someone, preferably the firstborn son, should close the eyes of the dead.[15]

«««« Sally Falk Moore explains the function of ritual:

Rituals, rigid procedures, regular formalities, symbolic representations of all kinds, as well as explicit laws, principles, rules, symbols, and categories are cultural representations of fixed social reality, of continuity. They represent stability and continuity acted out and reenacted: visible continuity. By dint of repetition they deny the passage of time, the nature of change, and the implicit extent of potential indeterminacy in social relations. Whether rituals, laws, rules, customs, symbols, ideological models, and so on, are old and legitimated by tradition, or newly forged and legitimated by a revolutionary social source, they constitute the explicit cultural framework through which the attempt is made to fix social life, to keep it from slipping into the sea of indeterminacy.[16]

of one's own body at an awkward time.⟨ Each participant knew his role before entering the dark, candlelit room, and that certainty of script was more than just a consolation. The deathwatch represented to its members a promise of order and a restoration of normal social relations. It became a polar star to focus upon, a steady, unblinking point of light in the dark maelstrom of impending death.

Except for the rules about testamentary dispositions, the law did not have much to do with the substance of these rituals. As we have seen, however, the law does help define the temporal limits of the deathwatch. In this century, and in the past, we have tacitly agreed to gather together for this rite of passage, to stop looking at the clock. But no ritual can go on forever; we must eventually return to ordi-

---

⟨ One function of a deathwatch is to prepare the survivors psychologically for the death and attendant grief. One study investigated the relationship between families' anticipation of a member's death and their adaptive behavior after the death. Families who were psychologically prepared for the death of a member made earlier arrangements for the body to be removed, behaved less emotionally, and expressed fewer feelings of guilt. Those families who had not engaged in a deathwatch, or for whom the death was a surprise, displayed extreme emotional behavior, such as "vomiting, screaming and fainting," and often refused to accept the reality of the death pronouncement.[17]

The study also investigated the function of a hospital "quiet room," on the same ward but apart from the deceased patient's room, to which the family could go to be alone after the death. The room provided "an appropriate place and the needed time for personal reflection, reaction, further clarification, and emotional expression." Families who had engaged in a deathwatch and were expecting the death used the room less often than those who were psychologically unprepared for the death. In part, the study concluded that family visits should be encouraged since they build "expectancy via exposure to the situation and increased opportunity for acquisition of information." The author also recommended the hospital hire a "grief therapist," a nurse or family counselor who would help the "family to enter into or continue through the grief process." Such a "grief therapist" would arguably serve the same function as a spiritual leader in a nineteenth-century deathwatch.[18]

nary time. By redefining death and by recognizing that death talk is taboo, the law can help bring the attenuated deathwatch of the late twentieth century to an end.

The law can, however, do something more to alleviate the pain of the members of the deathwatch. It can help create an environment in which a meaningful deathwatch can take place. This the law cannot do alone. Lawyers have to talk to members of the medical profession and to the architects of ritual space. There is a logistical problem to such a conversation, however. It is difficult to talk to people who are not there.

EVERY semester, after several weeks have gone by and I have begun to recognize the faces that look out at me, I give a speech about the importance of coming to class. It is not a very inspired speech, but it is heartfelt. I always feel a bit silly at its end,⟪ since the speech was given for the benefit of those students who are not there. The students who share my views about the importance of coming to class are already sitting before me. I suppose an analogue is the spiritual leader who admonishes his flock about the wages of sin, knowing full well that the sheep inside the gate are already convinced. The real sinners are out of earshot, wandering the fields unattended, bleating their way straight to ovine hell.

It is all a problem of audience. How do you convince others to take a certain course of action if they are not there to hear your words? In this instance, their absence is not due to truancy or sin, but to intellectual isolation. I propose that lawyers and doctors and architects get together to help alleviate the pain of the members of the deathwatch, but we rarely talk to one another, or read each other's words. I know there are a few curious souls who cruise outside of their discipline. After all, I am one myself. But my participation is that of an

⟪ On days when I am feeling formidable, I admit to my students that I feel a bit silly, and on days when I am feeling fragile, I do not. Feeling fragile is a virus that attacks women law teachers in particular.[19]

eavesdropper. I like to perch on the edge of other professions because I am nosy and lonely. I like to know what they are thinking about, since so often when I stay at home I have to think alone.

But eavesdropping is solitary and passive and does nothing to bridge the gaps between the professions. Even with the occasional exchange of footnotes, the fact remains that doctors talk and listen to doctors; lawyers talk and listen to lawyers; architects talk and listen to architects. And no one talks or listens to poets. We are very insulated from one another. Indeed, one of the goals of professional education is to provide students with a vocabulary that ensures that what they have to say will be understood only by other members of their guild.

The problem goes deeper than that, however. We learn a way of looking at the world that makes it difficult to see things through any other prism. We also begin to believe that our profession has a monopoly on solutions. No matter what the problem is, most doctors believe that the solution lies hidden in the secrets of nature, in attaining a perfect understanding of the human body. Most lawyers believe that the solution lies hidden in the secrets of language, in finding the perfect words to address the situation. Most architects believe that the solution lies hidden in the secrets of design, in conceiving of the perfect space. All poets know that the solution, if there is one, lies hidden in the secrets of the human heart, where perfection is unheard of.

WE were expecting as visitors for the weekend an old friend from Columbus, Colin Fink, his wife Nancy, and their two children. Colin is an architect in upstate New York. Here was an opportunity to talk to someone who was not a lawyer, to someone who designs spaces for a living. Maybe we could discuss what our respective professions could do about the horrors of the late-twentieth-century deathwatch, what lawyers and architects might do together to alleviate the pain of its members.

With four small children under one roof, it was not easy to find an island of silence upon which to embark on an adult conversation.

When such an island finally appeared on the horizon, I found Colin sitting on a lawn chair in our living room, reading. He put his book down and asked me what I had been working on, and I tentatively started in on the deathwatch.

Colin was interested. The firm with which he had once been associated, the Research and Design Institute (REDE), had been hired in the late 1960s as a consultant for the design of a thirty-bed extended care unit to a county hospital.[6] The premise that bed rest is essential to post-operative care had been replaced by a theory advocating early ambulation and "self-therapy."[7] The hypothesis was that patients would heal better and faster if they were actively involved not only in their own recovery but also in the recovery of others.

This hypothesis proved to have a profound effect on the design of the Borda Wing, as it came to be called. The REDE team was concerned that conventional hospital corridors would discourage early ambulation because there just was not enough room in the narrow hallways for people to move around. The team recommended that the corridors be used not only for getting from one room to another, but also as communal areas, capacious enough to accommodate any combination of recuperating patients, some of them in wheelchairs or stainless steel exoskeletons. The architects went to work, and instead of designing the hallways for solitary nurses, they made them wide enough so that patients could congregate in groups, share experiences, and give support to one another while bodies were on the mend.

The corridors in the Borda Wing were eighteen feet wide, rather than the standard six to eight feet. The communal spaces included two nourishment centers available for staff and patients, and patients could eat whenever and with whomever they pleased. There were game tables, reading and writing stations, alcoves for private telephone conversations, and sunny dayrooms at either end of the corridors to provide a "destination point," otherwise known as someplace to go. Privacy was respected, but the therapeutic emphasis was on collaboration. Everyone was encouraged to live out in the open as active members of a healing community.

It was an interesting conversation, but too short. Colin's presence was required in the backyard, and I never really got to ask him how he would design for the deathwatch. It was too short, but long enough to give me a flash of insight: architects approach problems differently from doctors and lawyers.

First, architects are obsessed with function: what is it this building is supposed to do?« Usually the answers are quite simple. For example, this building is supposed to provide shelter for a family; or this building is supposed to provide a place to learn; or this building is supposed to provide a place to care for the sick and restore them to health.««

Armed with a concept of what the building is supposed to do, ar-

---

« Suzanne K. Langer argues that this obsession with function ("What is it this building is supposed to do?" "Provide shelter? comfort? safekeeping?") has confused architects about the status of architecture. "Some have regarded architecture as chiefly utilitarian; others have treated it as an 'applied art.'" Others, such as Louis H. Sullivan, Laszlo Moholy-Nagy, and Frank Lloyd Wright, have "tried to meet the prosaic demands of utility by making function paramount, believing that genuinely appropriate forms are always beautiful."[20]

Architecture does more than just provide shelter. According to Langer, it also creates an "ethnic domain," an image of a culture and a

physically present human environment that expresses the characteristic rhythmic functional patterns which constitute a culture. Such patterns are the alternations of sleep and waking, venture and safety, emotion and calm, austerity and abandon; the tempo, and the smoothness or abruptness of life; the simple forms of childhood and the complexities of full moral stature, the sacramental and the capricious moods that mark a social order, and that are repeated, though with characteristic selection, by every personal life springing from that order.[21]

«« Colin Fink quarrels with my statement that architects are obsessed with function. He writes, "In defense of architects, a good architect should not be obsessed with anything. The beauty of good architecture is the beauty of poetry—the ambiguity, multiplicity, and flexibility of a design."[22]

chitects start out with some expectations about how the human beings who will use the building are going to behave. This requires them to focus not so much on the behavior of any given individual, but on the behavior of a group of individuals. While it is true that the basic unit is still the human body, most buildings are designed with the idea that more than one human body will use the space, and that the patterns of use are predictable. In homes, for example, at least in our culture, people usually sleep in bedrooms that are located towards the back of the house, and gather together in large rooms towards the front. In schools, teachers usually stand up and talk in the front of the room, and pupils sit down and listen.«« In hospitals, sick people usually lie down in beds, more or less grouped together by disease, and their family and friends sit down to visit them. Most of these expectations are culturally determined.

At a deeper level, there are hypotheses about how best to achieve the maximum function of a building that embrace a certain view of human psychology. All of these hypotheses begin with the premise that people are affected by their environment; that the dimensions, floor plan, orientation, light, colors, and textures, all of the attri-

---

««« It has always bothered me that the architecture of law schools seems to demand that classrooms be designed like large, fixed-focus cameras, the teacher occupying the focal point at the bottom of the pit and the students placed on ascending tiers, with the seats invariably screwed to the floor to assure the maintenance of this unpleasant status quo. When I first started teaching at Touro, we had just moved into an old junior high school building, and my first classes were held in a large, level room which had been the cafeteria. The students sat in folding chairs, and we moved them around a lot. The balance of power was always changing, as was the way in which we saw the world and each other. As we remodeled the building and struggled toward accreditation and acceptance in the academy, the ABA required us to screw the chairs to the floor. Now we eat bad hot dogs in that room, and I find myself teaching at the bottom of a pit.

butes of any given building, will have an impact on how people think and feel and interact in that environment.⟨

How people think and feel and interact in a hospital or other health care facility became relevant when Norman Cousins, among others, convinced us that healing is dependent on the patient's state of mind.⟨⟨ Cousins further insisted that a patient's environment has a "large part to do with getting the best out of health care."[8] These ideas had an impact on hospital design.⟨⟨⟨ It became a shibboleth in

---

⟨ Consider the following statement regarding the design of environments for special groups of people such as the elderly, disabled children, or homeless people: "Architects of such facilities agree that the most important aspect in designing for any special population is the creation of an environment that is sensitive to the needs, feelings, and dignity of the people who will use the space."[23] While such a statement seems almost trite in an architectural journal, it is difficult to imagine a similar goal being articulated in either law or medicine.

⟨⟨ Interest in the relationship between a patient's mental state and the healing process, with its implications for the design of hospitals, hardly started with Norman Cousins. For example, the ideas and architectural principles of the Austrian visionary Rudolph Steiner, the founder of Anthroposophy, the "science of the spirit," have been influential among some architects and designers. Danish-born Eric Asmussen has concentrated on anthroposophical architecture in hospital design since 1960. Asmussen designed the hospital that is part of the Rudolf Steiner Seminary at Jarna, near Stockholm. He strove to create "a stimulating environment which inspires the healing activity for which the building was intended. Windows, for example, are shaped as keyholes suggesting connections with the 'spiritual in the universe.' The resulting harmony brings equilibrium to the patient, who by being sick, is out of balance." The architecture itself serves as therapy, on the theory that the environment can encourage healing.[24]

⟨⟨⟨ Cousins's book, Anatomy of an Illness, is one of the most well-known expressions of a holistic approach to incurable illness. After its publication, St. Joseph's Hospital in Houston was the first to develop special facilities based on his ideas. They created a living room for cancer patients, an "airy open space with comfort-

the architectural literature that the design had to promote the healing process, as the architect struggled to come to terms with his obsession: what is it this building is supposed to do?

Architects started asking questions like these: Does it matter how many doors a patient must open in order to be out in the world?((((Does it matter if a patient has another human being to make eye contact with when he enters a health care facility?(((((Does it matter if

able furniture, a television with video cassettes of old comedies ... a place to paint or play the piano." Cousins reported that at least "a dozen hospitals ... have taken similar steps to reduce the institutionality of a medical environment and make it more homelike for patients and families alike in recent years."[25]

((((A relationship exists between a patient's vulnerability to death and changes in physical environment. Studies of transfers of the frail elderly from one setting to another show that such moves may threaten their health:

One of the most reliable predictors of death among the elderly who have been transferred is the loss of desire to penetrate the social and physical environment. The number of times a person needs to go beyond his or her boundaries—or have someone penetrate theirs—in order to remain alive can be fixed. These numbers of penetrations become the most accurate predictor of death among the aging who have been transferred from one setting to another.[26]

(((((One problem with the architecture of spaces designed to house new medical machines is the tendency of architects to want to "celebrate the technology" by exposing the hardware. For example, the architects of the Center for Non-Invasive Diagnosis at the University of New Mexico in Albuquerque had to fight the urge to "express the building as a giant machine (which it actually is)." Instead, the Center is "quite domestic in scale," reflecting the architecture of the American Southwest. The architect, Glade Sperry, Jr., felt it was "important to have human contact on entering the center, and the receptionist's desk is positioned so that one immediately makes eye contact." While the exterior reflects "the palette of the desert, the interiors are cool and restful—rose, gray, mauve, and tan." The goal is to minimize the "frightening experience" of "being pushed through a magnet and emitting radio signals."[27]

there is room on the maternity ward for the father to sleep?« Does it matter whether the lighting is diffuse in the ICU? Does it matter whether the pulsating life-support systems hang naked from the walls?«« Does it matter if a bedbound patient can see a tree?«««

Even questions of power are raised in projects like the hospital wing that Colin's firm helped design. The hypothesis there shifted part of the responsibility for the healing process from the medical

---

« Until recently, maternity units in hospitals were judged on clinical efficiency. In Wythenshawe Hospital, an older hospital in Manchester, England, there was "no attempt to provide a domestic atmosphere or to make unobtrusive the clinical equipment such as gas outlets, cot, scrub-up trough." There was space for about five witnesses, such as pupil midwives, the husband, and later, medical students. While the husband could witness the birth, his extended stay was not anticipated.[28]

Compare this to a maternity unit in the Stirling Royal Infirmary, which seeks to provide "every amenity for the patient": the labor suite has a lounge, where the patient may remain during the early phases of labor, and later on, in the first-stage delivery rooms, the husband is not only welcome, but an overnight room is provided for him.[29]

In another new design for a birthing room, a Chicago-based architecture and interior design firm created suites at West Suburban Hospital in Oak Park that serve as labor/delivery and recovery/postpartum care rooms (LDRP) for normal and high risk births. The suite also serves as a "homey living/dining/bedroom for visiting, and even family sleep-overs in a reclining lounge chair." The medical equipment needed for the birth, such as oxygen, air, and suction vacuum, for use in case of emergency, and an examining light, all disappear after the baby is born. The bed converts into a labor table, then a delivery table, and then back to a bed. The family is invited to participate in the birthing event, and the room's design helps to "bridge the gap between pregnancy and parenthood."[30]

«« In designing an innovative intensive care unit, Orlando Diaz-Azcuy was aware that there were four essential elements to consider: "the medical staff; the patient; the family; and the technology." Diaz-Azcuy hid most of the ICU equipment in "office style cabinets" in the wall when it was not in use. He also pro-

professionals to the patients themselves. By shifting that responsibility, there was a corresponding shift in power; how the therapy and course of treatment were going to proceed became more a joint enterprise than a dictatorship. In the Planetree Model Hospital Project in San Francisco, to give another example, a designer challenged the traditional nursing station with its high counters and lack of accessibility, claiming that such bastions emphasize "territoriality and convey a strong 'us versus them' mentality." The nursing work areas were therefore located informally along the perimeter walls, and in the middle of this area tables were provided for patients to look over their charts and discuss them with nurses, doctors, or family members. A patient library in the twenty-five-bed unit "symbolically convey[ed] the importance of openly exchanging medical informa-

---

vided for a private toilet and sink that were hidden from sight, and he calculated where the window should begin so that the patient could see the outside world from his bed. He designed what was called the nurses' "Observation Wall," "built from Varilite panels that change from clear to water-white at the patient's discretion to ensure privacy." Instead of having lighting installed in the headwall, Diaz-Azcuy provided for soft, ambient lighting, with several additional lighting sources that could be operated by dimmer according to either the patient's or medical staff's needs. The curtains were a yellow stripe, and the wood paneling was made of white oak. His overall goal was to create "humanistic and sensitive designs."[31]

≪≪ Roger S. Ulrich, a geographer at the University of Delaware, has suggested that trees can actually reduce costs in hospital care. He examined the postoperative care records of two groups of patients who were virtually identical except that some had looked out onto a brown brick wall from their hospital beds, and some onto a small stand of deciduous trees. On average, patients who could see the trees spent nearly twenty-four fewer hours in the hospital, needed less attention from nurses, and took fewer doses of expensive drugs. Ulrich argues persuasively that hospital design should take into account the quality of the patients' views from the windows.[32]

tion." As the space was redesigned, the power relationships were re-defined.[9]❨

As I said before, architects approach things differently from doctors and lawyers.❨❨ Unlike architects, most doctors do not deal with patients as members of a community. There is one human being, and only one, at the end of the stethoscope. Even then, in light of the specialization within medicine, it is sometimes difficult to get a doctor to see that one human being instead of just the body part in which he is interested.❨❨❨ Lawyers deal with humanity in the same way; the tenets of liberalism have forced upon us the unit of the individual, and

---

❨ To me, the most radical innovation in the Planetree unit did not have to do with design, but with time. The power to set the schedule for waking and visiting was returned to the patient. Every evening the nursing staff asked the patient when he would like to be awakened, instead of rudely waking him at 6.00 a.m. to take his temperature. Similarly, the patient was the one to decide who would visit and when.[33] These seem like such little things, but anyone who has spent time in a hospital knows that these little things are what get you down. They are what diminish you as a human being.

❨❨ I realize that I may be speaking of only a handful of progressive architects. Probably just as many are designing hospitals in the more traditional style. Furthermore, some new movements in design strike me as a step backwards. I felt a chill run down my spine when I read about the new phenomenon of "medical malls." One such mall is in Tucker, Georgia, a suburb of Atlanta. The mall has 120 licensed beds, with "an inpatient care area connected to the administrative and business office by an open atrium." Since the offices did not have to meet the stringent hospital codes, the mall is very cost effective. Dr. Roger Panther, president of Quorum Health Resources, Inc.,describes the layout of several medical malls he has developed: "The core of the mall has an outpatient entrance leading to a central reception area.... More than simply an open area for traffic, the reception area doubles as functional space for waiting, reception, admitting, information, and dining. The multi-purpose atrium design stresses natural lighting and an airy atmosphere with interior landscaping, skylights, and on-the-mall eating areas for visitors and staff."[34]

our procedural apparatus has reinforced that limitation by making it difficult to listen to more than one voice at a time.

Because architects do not look at human beings in isolation, they have given a lot more thought to the deathwatch and to how to alleviate the pain of its members. We have a lot to learn from them.

WHAT does it mean to be at home? I looked up the word, and the first six definitions listed in the *American Heritage Dictionary* read like a piece of poetry:

Unfortunately, I have had a recurrent nuclear holocaust dream in which I always find myself living out the last few days of my life, with my small children, in the Walt Whitman Mall in Huntington, New York. I was not happy to see that medical malls are on the horizon. Maybe I *will* someday die in a room next to an escalator, with indoor trees, a phony roaring fountain, and the malevolent hum of muzak in my ears.

‹‹‹ A monologue in Wallace Shawn and Andre Gregory's movie, *My Dinner with Andre,* comments on the narrow focus that a medical specialist can have. Andre's mother had been dying in the hospital, and a specialist who had been consulted about a minor problem with her arm failed to see the rest of the patient:

You know, we had gone to the hospital to see my mother, and I'd been in to see her, and I saw this woman that looked as bad as any survivor in Auschwitz or Dachau, and I was out in the hall sort of comforting my father, and this doctor who was a specialist in a problem she had with her arm went into her room and came out just beaming and said to us, "Boy, don't we have a lot of reason to feel great? Isn't that wonderful how she's coming along?" Well, all he saw was her arm. That's all he saw. And I mean, here's another person who's existing in a dream. Who on top of that is a kind of butcher who's committing a kind of familial murder, because he comes out of that room, and he psychically kills us by taking us into a dream world, you see, where we become confused and frightened, because the moment before, we saw somebody who looked already dead, and now here comes the specialist who tells us that everything is great.[35]

home (hōm) *n* : (1) a place where one lives; residence; habitation (2) the physical structure or portion thereof within which one lives, as a house or apartment (3) one's close family and one's self; a person's most personal relationships and possessions: house and home (4) an environment or haven of shelter, of happiness and love (5) any valued place, original habitation, or emotional attachment regarded as a refuge or place of origin (6) the place where one was born or spent his early childhood, as a town, state, or country.

Such a lot of work for one small word, and each competing definition is beautiful in its own way. With so many meanings, it explains how I can feel at home in my little grey house, or at home with my family, or at home at work, or at home in Columbus, Ohio, or even at home in my own mind.

But, at the moment, I am thinking more about a home space, an actual place in which to live, and ultimately to die. A book by Gaston Bachelard got me thinking about home space; what it means to have one and what it means not to have one. In *The Poetics of Space*, Bachelard writes, "All really inhabited space bears the essence of the notion of home." The phenomenologist of the home has his task set out for him: He must "say how we inhabit our vital space, in accord with all the dialectics of life, how we take root, day after day, in a 'corner of the world.' For our house is our corner of the world. As has often been said, it is our first universe, a real cosmos in every sense of the word. If we look at it intimately, the humblest dwelling has beauty."[10]

What does it mean to take root, day after day, in a corner of the world? For me, it means waking up in my own bed by the dim light of the dawn, making the solitary journey to the kitchen to put the kettle on, the cats at my feet, music from the radio humming in the background, knowing that the people I love the most in the world will soon join me in the kitchen, with their clatter and clutter and morning demands. For a brief, precious moment of time, we will inhabit our home space together before we all go out the door.

That door. We all go out of it in the morning and come back through it at the end of the day. That door means everything to the definition of my home space. It creates a boundary between my family and the outside community. It keeps in our family secrets, our rituals, our words of love, and our words of frustration. It houses both our dreams, and sometimes our fears. That door defines the outer edges of our intimacy.❝

That door. We all go out of it in the morning and come back through it at the end of the day. Not only does it keep things in, it also keeps things out. Each of us who inhabits the home space within has control over the use of that door; it provides the power to exclude. Even though it is only a piece of wood, hanging tenuously at times from two hinges, it is a symbol to all who stand before it that permission must be granted before entering.❝ And when we open that door to a friend, we do so knowingly and willingly, because of our decision

❝ Examining the significance of the human body in architecture, Kent C. Bloomer and Charles W. Moore have discussed the symbolic meaning of "the house." At the "edges of the house," where the house dweller leaves and enters, a reorientation from a place of one or a few people to a place of many people is necessary:

> Even as the primary body boundary exists between the world of the individual and the community, the house boundary exists between the family and the community. The entryway, therefore, becomes an extraordinarily sensitive region of the house boundary, a landmark which must respect and reinforce the feelings and identity of both the inside and outside communities.... The architectural boundary exists to encourage and ritualize activities which are sacred to the family, and its destruction or exaggeration can sap the vitality of both the family and the public domain in which it resides.[36]

❝ About the "essence" of the house, Christian Norberg-Schultz has this to say:

> Let us only say a few words about the "essence" of the house. To find a common denominator for all houses (buildings) may seem futile. If it makes any sense to talk about the "level of houses," however, it ought to be possible. In fact, all treatises on architecture from Alberti to Venturi in some way or other have attempted to solve the problem. It was pointed out above that essentially the house brings us "inside." The essence of the house as architecture, therefore, is interior space. In the city we are still "outside," although we have left the open landscape. In the house we are alone with ourselves, we have withdrawn.

that, for a time, we do not mind redefining the boundary of our private domain.

Without that corner of the world, that vital space to take root in day after day, the world would be, and is for many, a cold and heartless place.

THE only good place to be sick is at home.

Once I was trapped on my back in a hospital for four months, and I can still remember my incessant yearning to return to my home space. Day after endless day, I would say to myself and to others, "All I want to do is go home." I wanted my own bed, my own window looking out on my own tree, my own sheets, my own cats, my own tea cup, my own bathroom, my own door. That door.

I hated having no door to close in the hospital, being subjected to the unannounced entrances and exits of strangers.⟨ I hated the nurses coming in and out, and those constant bodily invasions, perpetrated against me according to someone else's schedule. I hated visiting hours, when sometimes people I did not choose to see chose to come

When we open our doors to others, it is our free decision: we let the world come to us, rather than looking at it outside. "Domestic peace" has been a basic right since remote times.[37]

⟨ A room in an institutional setting like a hospital will always be subject to intrusions by others since it is one small unit in a much larger public space. Not only does the occupant of a hospital room lack the power to exclude others, but he also lacks the power to inhabit the public space beyond the few square feet allotted for his body. A hospital room therefore probably qualifies as a "cell." According to Βloomer and Moore, the distinction between a house and a cell is fundamental. Whereas in a house, a family expects to be able to occupy all its parts, a cell denies the occupant "access to the whole of the place which contains the cell. The front door of a prison, for example, is not accessible to the occupants of its cells, nor are the attics, cellars, and grand interior meeting places available to the tenants of most modern apartment 'complexes.'"[38]

see me. I hated having other very sick human beings in beds eight feet away, with their own parade of visitors, their own medical traffic, and their very different universe on the television. I hated having always to be pleasant, since I knew too well the price for petulance: a decline in the quality of nursing care. For anyone with a chronic illness, the mentality must be that of a survivor; in a conscious act of will, the prickly parts of one's personality must be wrapped in the velvet of submission. Day after day, night after night, all I wanted to do was to go home, and, unlike many times when wishes came true, when I finally did go home, there was no sense of disappointment. All I had yearned for were little things, and the little things were all still there, waiting patiently for me: my bed, my cats, my tea cup, my tree, now leafless from the winter winds.

Sickness brings with it a vulnerability of spirit, a fragility that makes us want to turn away from the world and crawl into our own beds. It is a great irony to me that our need to be at home is greatest when we are sickest, yet that is the time in our culture when we are bodily removed from our homes. Just consider what it means to crawl into your own bed.⟨⟨ My Irish mother-in-law, for example,

---

⟨⟨ The history of where we lay ourselves down to sleep, or to die, is interesting. In Europe, until the late Middle Ages, most people slept on loose bedding or on the ground. Beds were a luxury, a sign of wealth and rank. For example, the ranking individual in a household slept in a bed with elaborate accouterments, in particular a canopy. This "Bed of Estate," much like the Chair of Estate, would be used only when official visitors were received. A simpler bed would be used for less momentous sleeping.[39]

In the eighteenth century, beds became smaller, less elaborate, and more accessible to the average man. In England, the typical bed was a simple four-poster with draw curtains. A smaller canopy bed known as the "field bed" became more popular in America. Beds of the Empire periods tended to be low, chunky blocks, usually undraped. The "sleigh bed" was of this type. Modern springs and mattresses have replaced heavy wood framing; most contemporary bed designs use only enough framing to raise the bed from the floor. Canopies, if they are used at all, have become merely decorative.[40]

when she goes to bed at night, goes to the bed that she was born in, to the bed that her brothers and sisters were born in, to the bed that her mother died in, to the bed that her great-grandmother died in. My babies, her grandchildren, have many times crawled into that dark wooden bed to read books with her, to be near her soft, sweet skin that always smells of roses. Someday, she herself will die in that dark wooden bed.

Does it matter where we conceive our children? Where we give birth to our children? Where we lie down to sleep? Where we lie down to die?

Just consider what it means to crawl into a hospital bed. The mattress is enclosed in thick, brittle plastic that resists the weight of a human being.⟨ It is a hot, sweating thing, made bearable only by the intervention of rough, white cotton that only stays in place if the envelope is not opened. Its frame is metal, and it is not committed to any certain place, but migrates on wheels at the whim of some-

---

⟨ Those horrible mattresses are intended to serve laudable goals of sanitation and patient hygiene. Although one guidebook to the design of long-term care facilities states as its "main thrust" the "creation of an environment which promotes a feeling of well-being, of independence, of individual worth, and an atmosphere which engenders the continued growth of the resident," on a previous page under "Odor Control," the book states: "Proper selection of furnishings will also go a long way toward eliminating this disagreeable problem. Mattresses should always have waterproof ticking. Seating used by residents should also be covered in materials that shed or repel liquids." The authors even suggest, "Some mattresses are also available with a germicide impregnated in the ticking, the value of which may be subject to question."[41]

All this may be well and good for patients who are incontinent or highly contagious. However, for the dying patient who is neither, it seems a shame to force him to live out his last few days afloat a poisoned, rubber mattress. Are comfortable, disposable mattresses that more closely resemble a normal bed an impossibility? During my own lengthy hospital stays, I would gladly have paid for my own mattress, if the hospital would have permitted it. As it was, I had to fight for the privilege of keeping my own pillow. If the goal of

one other than its occupant. It has the terrible potential of becoming a prison, with shiny parallel bars that wait poised below the mattress line. They brush against your calves when you get up to roam around, a chilling reminder of their function, to capture and retain. The crime committed: illness. The theory of punishment: isolation. Although few of us crawl into the bed that bore us, those of us who are lucky enough to live in a home space have a place to lie down at night to call our own. I want to die in that place, if I can. But if I must die in a bed that belongs to another, I do not want it to be in one of those hospital beds. I do not want my body lifted from a plastic platform to a plastic bag. I do not want to be rendered untouchable by a barrier of chrome.

To me, the answer to those questions is obvious: It matters where we crawl into bed, whether we are sleeping, making new life, healing, giving birth, dying, or just having a nap. It matters a lot.❝❝

And the only good place to be sick is at home.

---

long-term care design is truly to promote the resident's feeling of well-being and individual worth, some attention ought to be paid to treating a reclining human body as something other than a generator of odor-causing fluids and germs.

❝❝ Christian Norberg-Schultz explores the "lowest level of existential space, that of furniture and objects-for-use."[42] The fireplace, which has since ancient times been the very center of the dwelling, and the table, the place "where the family joined to form a 'ring,'" are extremely important. However,

[T]he bed represents the centre even more convincingly, being the place from where man starts his day, and to which he returns in the evening. In bed, the circle of the day, and of life, is closed. The bed, therefore, par excellence, is the place where man "comes to rest," where his movements find their goal. Boll-now also points out that man's active relationship to the world is characterized by his vertical position; he takes a "stand." To sleep means to give up this position and return to the very "point of departure." When the Chateau de Versailles was centralized on the bed of Louis XIV, it symbolized more than a mere demonstration of power.[43]

WHAT is the relationship between a home space and the ritual space that is needed for a meaningful deathwatch?

We cannot create the ritual space needed for a meaningful deathwatch without a home space. Ritual requires the demarcation of ritual space from secular space, and there can be no demarcation without the power to transform. Ritual also requires a community, and there can be no community without the power to include and exclude. Those powers can only be exercised in a home space. If there is no home space, there can be no ritual space, and if there is no ritual space, then the deathwatch lacks meaning.

Having a home space means, among other things, that those who inhabit it have control over what transpires within. This includes the power to transform the environment. If for whatever reason the inhabitants of the home space wish to make a room which is normally light, dark, they can do so. If they wish to change the configuration of the furniture, they can do so. If they wish to unplug the telephone and turn off the television, they can do so. If they wish to fill the room with music or prayer, they can do so. In a home space, there are no institutional impediments to the creation of ritual space. There is a door, and behind that door the members of the deathwatch can gather. There is freedom behind that door.

That door. Having a home space also means that its inhabitants can shut that door, or they can choose to open that door selectively, to invite in friends and family. That door redefines the community; it draws the circle around the members of the deathwatch, not some arbitrary legal category. Control over that door, and who goes in and out, allows the inhabitants of the home space to create their own circle of intimacy, without which ritual cannot take place. There is a relationship between a home space and the ritual space needed for a meaningful deathwatch, all having to do with that door.

Recognizing that relationship is something that the law could do to alleviate indirectly the pain of the members of the deathwatch. There is this obvious suggestion: If possible, we should help those people who want to die at home, or who want to care for their dying family members or friends at home, to do so. The idea is not new; no wheels need be invented. There is already an institution in place to facilitate such a home death. It is known as a hospice. Although the words "hospice" and "hospital" share the same etymology,⟨ and the institutions share the same history, they have come to mean very different things. In the ancient civilizations of India and Egypt, as well as in early Greece and Rome, the public facilities for the care of the sick were located in temples.[11] Bodily and spiritual health were regarded as the same thing.⟨⟨

In Western Europe, during the medieval period, religion was again the dominant influence in the establishment of healing institutions. During the Crusades, "hospices" or "hospitals" sprang up all over Europe alongside monasteries to provide food, temporary shel-

---

⟨ The word *hospital* ultimately comes from the Latin *hospes,* meaning "a guest." The French hospice developed from the Latin *hospitium,* which meant the location where a guest was received, and the English words *hospital, hostel,* and *hotel* come from the old French *hospitale.* Thus, the words *hospital, hostel, hotel,* and *hospice* were all originally used in the same sense.[44]

⟨⟨ In a summary of the history of hospice care, Kenneth Cohen comments that both ancient India and Egypt had crude facilities that we might characterize as hospitals. Buddha is believed to have appointed a physician for every ten villages and built hospitals for the crippled and the poor as early as the sixth century B.C., according to Cohen. His son also built shelters for the pregnant and the ill. In early Egypt, medical treatment was usually dispensed in the home, but some therapy was also available in the temples. Egyptian doctors and priests were often the same, since little distinction was made between science and magic. In ancient Greece, sanctuaries for the sick, where they were ministered to for both their physical and spiritual woes, were dedicated to Aesculapius, the Greek god of medicine. These Aesculapia had large spas; gymnasia for "gymnasiotherapy"; amphitheaters for entertainment; libraries; and rooms for patients, visitors, attendants, priests, and doctors. Aesculapia spread throughout Greece and into the Roman empire.[45]

ter, and medical care for travelers and pilgrims.⁽ A number of military facilities provided for the care of sick and exhausted crusaders. In the early medieval period, monks and clerics performed the role of healers, because they were the only ones with a semblance of education and were bound by vows of charity. In 1163, a Church edict forbade clergy from performing any operation that necessitated the shedding of blood. The result was a sharp curtailment in the medical activities of religious leaders, and the barbers took over surgery. Centuries later, even though the hospitals are still dominated by the successors of the barbers, religious leaders have returned to the hospice, to treat the spiritual ills of the weary travelers within.[12]

The "modern concept of hospice care dates back to the late 19th century, when an associate of Florence Nightingale opened a home for the terminally ill in Dublin."[13] It is not easy to define a hospice, because it is often not a place, but an outpatient program for the terminally ill and their families. In 1978, the National Hospice Organization adopted the following definition of hospice, which is as good as any:

> Hospice is a medically directed, nurse coordinated program providing a continuum of home and inpatient care for the terminally ill patient and family. It employs an interdisciplinary team acting under the direction of an autonomous hospice administration. The program provides palliative and supportive care to meet the special needs arising out of the

---

⁽ Pestilence and disease were particular problems during the Crusades, and there were a number of monastic and military hospitals and hospices for the care of sick and exhausted pilgrims and crusaders. The first reference to beds being provided for patients was in the foundation charter of the Knights Hospitallers, dated 1113, which set up seven resthouses for sick or wounded pilgrims on their way to the Holy Land. Leprosy was another contributing factor in the establishment of hospitals in the twelfth and thirteenth centuries. "Lazar houses" were developed to segregate and treat those afflicted with leprosy. They were generally crude structures, isolated on the outskirts of town, which served to check the spread of the disease.[46]

physical, emotional, spiritual, social and economic stresses which are experienced during the final stages of illness and during dying and bereavement.[14]

One of the greatest virtues of hospice care is that it takes care of the terminally ill person in his home space. In fact, the hospice takes care of everyone who inhabits the home space.[15] This is one instance where the architect's approach of looking at human problems in a social context prevails. The patient is not seen as an isolated, autonomous individual, but as a member of a family and a community. The pain of the members of the deathwatch is not only expressly recognized, but addressed. Most hospices provide counseling for friends and family members before and after the death of the patient, sometimes for longer than a year, and there is evidence that bereaved survivors of hospice patients experience much less painful and protracted periods of mourning.«« The patient too does not suffer the isolation and loneliness that often come with a hospital death.««« He

«« In a recent study of bereaved survivors whose family members had received hospice care from a hospital-based hospice program, survivors reported that "routine, pre-death, work of the hospice team had a noticeable and positive impact on their subsequent well-being in bereavement." The study included a new clinical tool called the "10-Mile Mourning Bridge," which represents the grief process. Conceptually, bereaved individuals successfully cross the bridge when "they are able to reinvest their emotional energy into new interests and relationships."[47]

««« In their study of three extended care wards in a Veterans' Administration Hospital, Reynolds and Kalish found almost no social interaction among the patients: "Many patients lie mute in bed; others, sitting in wheelchairs by their beds all day, say little or nothing to their roommates." In the solarium, the researchers found "seven wheelchairs facing in seven directions, no one facing anyone else, no one talking or even watching the jumping unclear images on the TV screen." Many patients had no visitors, even at the time of their death, and many others had guardians or socially distant relatives who only showed up when they died.

is restored to the center of the circle, in his own home space, and his dying and his deathwatch once again have social meaning. He does not die alone.〉

Sometimes hospice care takes place outside the home,〉〉 for a variety of reasons,〉〉〉 and it is in the design of inpatient care hospices that architects have shown themselves to be light years ahead of doctors

---

There were no chairs at the patients' bedsides, and ambulatory patients sometimes used wheelchairs to assure themselves of a place to sit down. The staff controlled the temperature and lighting. Lights were turned on at 2:15 a.m. to change incontinent patients, and all patients were awakened at 4:00 a.m., even though breakfast did not arrive until 8:00 a.m. Reynolds and Kalish described the smell of the ward as "objectionable at first, although one becomes adjusted to it in a few minutes."[48]

〈 Dr. Timothy Quill recommends that the principles of hospice should guide the debate about physician-assisted suicide rather than the principles of acute medical care in which "we often ask people to endure considerable suffering in the interest of prolonging their lives."[49] Of particular value is the hospice principle of nonabandonment:

But the most profound value of hospice care is nonabandonment—the commitment to work with people no matter where their illnesses take them, through their deaths. It may take health care providers in a direction where hospice principles and the double effect clearly guide medical intervention, but it also may take them to a place where the decision is not clear. Our commitment as physicians caring for people who are dying is to continue to stay with them and to creatively problem solve, no matter what happens. Nonabandonment is a fundamental principle of hospice care.[50]

〈〈 While home care may be ideal, one doctor has noted that for many patients it is not possible. Many patients cannot afford home care; many patients do not have family; and, for those patients who do have a family, "work or other obligations may restrict the time a family can spend on the patient." Dr. Kerstein has urged that more hospice care be made available, recommending that hospices be affiliated with major universities so they could be used to teach and provide re-

and lawyers in their concern for members of the deathwatch. St. Christopher's Hospice in London was the model. Consider the following description of St. Christopher's:

> There are mainly wards, with few private rooms. Each bed has a colorful curtain around it, and there are some transparent partial panels. Personal touches, such as flowers, paintings, comfortable lounge chairs, and wood, give a feeling of warmth. In addition to the wards, there are family rooms for visits and a large room for group activities. . . . Each patient brings his own personal belongings. Hospital gowns are not used. Bedside cabinets are of wood. The beds are simple and low enough for easy egress and ingress. Five huge, down pillows are supplied each patient. . . . Children of all ages, including infants, are permitted to come and go freely in all wards, hallways, and dayrooms. . . . [T]he actual event of death is managed with dignity. The dying patient is not isolated behind curtains. All patients in the ward area are aware of what is transpiring. The lack of suffering, in fact the absolute absence of patient distress, is the unique factor permitting the staff and other patients to overcome their fear of death.[16]

search data in sociology, nursing, and theology, as well as undergraduate and graduate medicine. This "combination of disciplines would allow this supportive group to be more realistically aware of the patient and of his family life-style."[51]

❮❮❮ Despite the hospice movement, it is not clear that the medical profession has truly changed its attitudes and practices toward the dying patient. One study reviewed medical charts to study the terminal care practices at a hospital and two in-patient hospices. As might be expected, the hospital patients had more diagnostic tests and laboratory charges. In all three institutions, however, it was unusual to find physicians' notes about the patients' families or nonmedical aspects of the illness.[52]

The study distinguished between "curative" therapy and "palliative care."[53] "Palliative care" has become a euphemism for "hospice" in American hospitals. When my great-aunt was dying of cancer in St. Luke's Hospital in New York City, she told me that she had received a call from a nurse in the "palliative care" unit. She then asked me where in the body the "palliative" was located.

The first freestanding hospice in the United States was a project of Hospice, Inc., a New Haven, Connecticut, nonprofit group.[17] Lo-Yi Chan was the architect, and he was particularly challenged by the problem of achieving a proper balance between isolation and privacy.《 Experience in English hospices had shown that the dying patient actually needed company more than privacy, since privacy came to signify isolation and abandonment. Chan found that the space requirements for hospices differed from those of an acute care facility or a nursing home because of the importance of "interdisciplinary care and family participation."[18] Thus, Chan designed the rooms in the New Haven Hospice to have approximately twenty feet around each bed to accommodate visitors and family members. Here was an architect who recognized the importance of the deathwatch and offered its members a legitimate space to stand in.《《 Perhaps I make

《 Lo-Yi Chan is one of many architects who have turned to the problems of hospice design. William Breger, the architect of an addition to St. Mary's Hospital in Bayside, Queens, a palliative care unit or hospice for dying children, has also been sensitive to the needs of the members of the deathwatch. The unit accommodates ten terminally ill patients aged two to sixteen with life expectancies of up to one year. At a washer/dryer area, families could "meet and share their thoughts." There was ample space for visitation, and relatives could place convertible chairs next to the beds so they could "stay overnight and maintain hand-to-hand contact with the child." Grieving parents could retreat to a lounge on another floor so their behavior would not upset the patients. In hindsight, Breger would have expanded these facilities.[54]

《《 When the University of Michigan overhauled its health-care facilities in 1980, it studied the use of the hospital by the "forgotten users," the patients and their families. Not only did the researchers look into the nonmedical needs of the patients, but they were also concerned about visiting friends and family:

> While the inpatient is whisked from admitting to the cocoon of his room, his illness, and his treatment, it is his companions or visitors who brave the confusions and complexities of the establishment to find the patient's room, the nearest telephone, restroom, or cup of coffee, or a place to await medical verdicts.[55]

too much of twenty feet of floor space, but, on a symbolic level, those twenty feet represent for me a glimmer of hope that the horrors of dying alone in the late twentieth century might come to an end.

How could the legal profession help people who want to die at home, or who want to care for their dying family members or friends, to do so?««« First, they could get involved in projects that would create more hospices. Despite the desirability of hospice care, and even its cost effectiveness,«««« there simply are not enough hos-

---

Many in-patient hospices have open visiting hours and permit overnight guests. Space for extra beds in the patient's room is provided, and extra chairs can be brought in when the deathwatch finally takes place.[56]

««« Many consider hospice care to be, as Robert Miller writes, a "credible response to the assisted-suicide movement." A survey done in the early 1990s indicated that most hospice staff members would not participate in an assisted suicide. Miller exhorts us to remember that the hospice movement teaches us to "learn to accept the truth of our ultimate fate, that pain, loss and death are part of life." He continues,

> We cannot eliminate death. Euthanasia serves only to avoid dealing with death. The real goal is to eliminate the suffering of the dying. Hospice workers and palliative care experts are working to relieve this suffering. They are in need of better drugs, more research, and better access for all to good palliative care. They have not asked for permission to kill their patients. Killing people is not the mature way to deal with dying, and not the best way to relieve suffering.[57]

«««« Dying under hospice care is much cheaper than dying in a hospital. Medicare currently pays $400 to $500 a day for a bed in a hospital, compared with $93 for at-home hospice services, which account for 90 percent of the total, and $250 for care in a residential hospice. In addition, since the hospice philosophy is to let death occur naturally, Medicare hospice benefits cover only symptom management and pain control. Expensive life-sustaining treatments such as resuscitation and surgery are not allowed. Hospice care has grown by 17 percent a year over the past five years, and almost one in five non-sudden deaths are now taking place under hospice care.[58]

pices to go around. For many, if not most, terminally ill patients in this country, hospice care is not available; in particular, there is a scarcity of inpatient hospice beds. Lawyers are often involved in the development of health care facilities, and recognition by the legal profession that a hospice is an option for the care of the terminally ill could go far in promoting the hospice movement.⁣⟨

Second, the legal profession could be instrumental in developing a national system to make hospice care available to those who cannot afford to pay.⟨⟨ As it now stands, there are gaps in Medicare cover-

---

⟨ Lawyers could be more aggressive in recommending hospice care to clients for whom it would be appropriate. Close to three-fifths of the families interviewed in one study had received no information about hospice care after a diagnosis of terminal cancer. Data from physicians confirmed that they were not giving information about hospice care to terminally ill patients and their families. The study did not even mention lawyers, presumably because they were not identified by families as a source of information. As a group, "friends" most often communicated information about hospices.⁵⁹

⟨⟨ In the Health Care Financing Administration (HCFA), the bureaucracy that oversees Medicare and Medicaid and pays for the care involved in 65 percent of the deaths in the United States, there has traditionally been a dichotomy between curing and caring for a patient. Until recently, hospitals could only receive reimbursement for curative care; hospital codes were categorized only by disease. Under new guidelines, there is a new category, a palliative code which means care "designed only to keep a dying patient comfortable."⁶⁰ This new code will enable hospitals to provide government-paid comfort care for the dying. (Previously, Medicare benefits were limited to hospices in cases when the patient had less than six months to live and chose palliative over curative care.)

These new guidelines may ensure that dying and deathwatches will continue to take place in hospitals, instead of in hospices or at home. Bruce Vladeck, the administrative director of the HCFA, admits that "unnecessary suffering and emergency intervention still are imposed on terminal patients in hospitals," citing a recent study in the *Annals of Internal Medicine* which found that four in

age for hospice care; dying younger adults and children are not eligible.⁣⟪⟪⟪ Thus, even if there were a hospice, many of the patients who might benefit from its services are too poor to bear the cost alone.⟪⟪⟪⟪ Perhaps amending the existing federal scheme is not the answer. After all, the hospice movement was in many ways a reaction against the dehumanizing experience of a hospital death. The tradition in England was a freestanding hospice facility unaffiliated with a hospital. That tradition did not survive the journey across the Atlantic, however. Most hospice care in this country is affiliated with a hospi-

---

ten patients were in severe pain during the final three days of life, and that "measures to cure rather than to comfort were used despite preferences expressed by 10 percent of the dying."[61]

⟪⟪⟪ One gap in the insurance coverage for hospice care involves younger people who are dying and not eligible for Medicare. Although some private insurance companies provide hospice benefits, and hospice programs frequently try to provide services on a sliding fee scale, the expense can still be prohibitive.[62]

Until recently, children have had very little in the way of hospice care, despite the fact that approximately 100,000 children die annually in the United States. Most hospice programs in the early 1980s could not accept children as patients.[63] Children's Hospice International (CHI) was formed in 1983 to improve the availability and quality of hospice care for children. CHI serves as a training and conference center, publishes training manuals, and supports efforts to expand awareness of the benefits of children's hospice care. A children's hospice in Alexandria, Virginia was "designed to feel like home, complete with playrooms and toys ... 14 beds for children and space for visiting parents."[64]

⟪⟪⟪⟪ While nine out of ten healthy Americans want to die at home in their own beds, the chances of that happening are slim unless the government puts more resources into hospice care. Hospice care makes up only 1 percent of the Medicare budget. Under current policy, patients who are certified as terminally ill (having less than six months to live) qualify for four hospice benefit periods, and at the end of each one the patient must requalify. If hospice care is no longer considered appropriate at the end of the fourth period—if, for example, a cancer pa-

tal,[19] and there have been instances in which the existing funding system and criteria established by third-party payers have forced the hospice to fit the hospital mold.« Hospicizing the hospital may end up hospitalizing the hospice. Instead of building upon the structure that generated the problem in the first place, we may need to get out a shovel and break new ground.

Third, the legal profession could help develop licensing standards for the other professionals who work in hospices to ensure quality care and to avoid the risk of abuse by greedy and exploitative individuals who might want to get rich quick from the death racket.««

Fourth, lawyers could help fashion creative solutions that combine some form of hospice care with already existing health care faci-

---

tient goes into remission—the patient may never again qualify for hospice care benefits under Medicare.

This means that people want to be certain they are really going to die before signing up for hospice benefits. A deathwatch begun in a hospice, but thwarted by a revival, could ensure a hospital death later on down the road. Hospice administrators are very "wary of taking in patients who may not be dying fast enough."[65] Thankfully, this policy on hospice benefits is under reconsideration.[66]

« For example, St. Luke's Hospital Center, a teaching facility in New York City, was one of the first to establish a hospital-based team that provided a combination of home care and inpatient services. St. Luke's did not group the hospice inpatients together in a special unit. Instead, it assigned them to various floors in the hospital, fearing that the hospital might otherwise lose its standing with third-party payers as an acute-care facility.[67]

«« Most states have licensing requirements for hospices. However, there are not always licensing requirements for the professionals who work in hospices. Nurses are a perfect example. The nursing profession has seen proposals to educate and certify nurses in hospice care. These nurses would receive special training in such things as pain management, home pain management, instruction of family members in home care, crisis management, and bereavement counseling. One article proposed two levels of hospice education. The first level would cer-

lities.⟨⟨⟨ The Mayo Clinic, for example, has purchased a hotel across the street from its surgical facility and discharges patients to spend a few days there.[20] The family can then come and stay with the patient, administer medication, and care for him, but if complications arise, immediate medical attention is available across the street.⟨⟨⟨⟨ Such a move across the street to an environment that is more like a home space might be a possible solution for families who cannot care for

tify the nurse as a "hospice nurse certified" who would deliver patient/family hospice care; the second level would certify him as a "hospice nurse advanced" who would educate and administer hospice care programs.[68]

⟨⟨⟨ Michael Kearney, a physician from St. Christopher's Hospice in London, argues that hospice care should not be seen as an alternative or complementary movement in medical care, but as a concept that has broad implications within existing patterns of medical care:

Hospice does not mean "bricks and mortar" but a concept of care that can be applied in different ways in different settings. The aim of the hospice movement is not to monopolize care of the dying but to disseminate the concept of care back into the general medical services so effectively that it will eventually make itself redundant.... As a movement in health care in the United Kingdom perhaps its greatest significance lies in the fact that it is happening *within* the existing pattern of health care. The hospice movement is neither an alternative nor a complementary movement but an attempt to broaden the vision and scope of existing medical care from within.[69]

⟨⟨⟨⟨ The University of Texas M.D. Anderson Cancer Center in Houston, Texas, has built a new patient-family facility, the Jesse H. Jones Rotary House International. Unlike the Mayo Clinic arrangement, patients are not *discharged* to Rotary House; rather, it operates as a hotel. The facility has been designed to provide a comfortable, homelike atmosphere for patients and their families while also taking into account the patients' physical needs. Guest rooms are larger than industry standards to accommodate wheelchairs and medical appliances. A resource center offers education programs for patients and family members on how to care for themselves and cope with their disease.[70]

the dying person in the home. It would allow a meaningful death-watch to take place, yet the medical services of a hospital would be only a few steps away. In New York State, to cite another example,[21] there has been a move for hospices to enter into contracts with individual nursing homes to provide care for terminally ill nursing home residents.« These kinds of creative solutions require complicated negotiations, exchanges of promises and expectations; in short, they require the skill and imagination of legal minds.

So lawyers do have something to contribute: setting up the legal relations that create a space in which a meaningful deathwatch can take place. We are professional wordsmiths, and our words are instrumental. We can make things happen with our words: words of contract, words of legislation, words of persuasion and legitimization. Our law words can help carve out of the universe a warm space in which our fellow human beings can gather upon the death of one of their own.«« That warm space is called home.

« A 1989 federal law permitted Medicaid reimbursement for hospice patients living in nursing homes.[71] In May 1991, the New York Department of Social Services implemented an interim system whereby hospices could be reimbursed for care inside nursing homes in New York. Before this, nursing home residents in New York were not eligible for hospice care.[72]

One local health-care industry analyst estimated that the new law could more than double New York hospice business in the state's eighty hospices. The state would reimburse hospices with patients in nursing homes at 95 percent of the nursing home rate. At that point, the contract between the hospice and the nursing home would determine how the nursing home would be reimbursed for its care of the patient. If the patient were eligible for Medicare coverage, the federal government would pay the cost of hospice care in the nursing home. This would prevent the transfer of terminally-ill nursing home residents to hospitals where "they are likely to be subjected to aggressive and costly life-extending medical procedures."[73]

«« In a moving essay, Dr. William G. Bartholome, a terminally ill physician, writes about the "withdrawal rituals" that he has planned, including rereading sections

THERE was one other thing Colin said that keeps ringing in my ears. It is a high-pitched sound, and unpleasant, like tinnitus. He said this:

In a way, the inability to have a meaningful deathwatch in a hospital is your own fault. I don't mean you personally, but the fault of lawyers. Most doctors I know are panicked about being sued. If the doctor opens the door and lets a lot of people into the room to watch the patient die, somebody's cousin is going to be a lawyer, and before you know it, the doctor will end up in court. I wouldn't want to open that door either. It's like inviting an audience in to witness your failure, your inability to keep out the ultimate uninvited guest, the specter of human death.

Those words are still humming in my head, disturbing my equilibrium. There is some truth to them. Although I like to think the law could alleviate indirectly the pain of the members of the deathwatch, the lawyer might just bring the deathwatch to an end. After all, his relationship with human failure is parasitic; he needs someone to stumble in order to survive. And as long as the doctor per-

---

from the *Tibetan Book of the Dead*, meeting with family members, looking over photographs from a rich and satisfying life, listening to music, and sharing the experience with his wife and children. The knowledge that hospice care will be available to him is clearly a source of great comfort.

I will have made—for both myself and for my family—arrangements to be cared for during this process by a hospice. I have seen the kind of care they can provide to the dying and their families. I am a believer. I also know that these hospice professionals will recognize, respect, and actively support my withdrawal rituals.... I am fortunate to have a loving spouse, a supportive family, a home in which to die, and more. Given access to the level of sophisticated end-of-life care that is now available through hospice, and given the encouragement and support in creating and sustaining a wide range of rituals of withdrawal, Americans should also be the least likely people on the globe to see suicide or assisted suicide as the only ways to determine the nature and time of their deaths.[74]

ceives death to be such a failure, he is never going to let the lawyer into the room.

Perhaps as lawyers we could make a small gift to the members of the deathwatch—a small gift, but one from the heart. Just as judges should be generous to those who engage in death talk, so should we be generous to those who take care of them. When we ourselves become members of a deathwatch, when we enter the ritual space to attend, we should leave our law words behind.

There are times in life, and in death, when no one needs our dutiful prose. Only our prayers and our poetry.

Coda

MOURNING SHORE

For some reason
I come into the day
a little sad.
I always have.
At night we drift
in black waters of
some foreign sea.
Elemental simplicity,
no structural demands,
no boundaries,
wetness binds the gases
and molecular integrity
is easy to maintain.
The moon is our pilot
on that journey
dark and deep
and of such beauty
rough earth words
could never tell
of our collective sleep.
On sand hot white
I crack
and suck the air
in crude exchange.
The ends of hands,
of tongue, of feet,
begin the definition,

the solitude
of finite form,
the sickness of gravity.

SOLIDITY

From salty water,
wordless we come in,
wrapped in white cotton
by the hands of others.
Horizontal, heavy headed,
all mouth and tongue,
unaware that we begin
or that we end
searching with eyes that look
but do not see
for interpreters
of our infancy,
to give meaning where
there is no meaning
beyond pain and need,
and dependency.

Slowly we come into our words,
words that yield boundaries:
The carapace of self,
the mystery of other,
the tyranny of corners,
and edges of things.
Vertical, head erect,
we shed white cotton and
the hands of others,
and construct a world of words,
words that make water
turn to ice.

And though we think
that what we name
stands still,
it does not.
Solidity is a cheap
word trick.
What is named is really
just slow water.

Wordless, we go out,
wrapped in white cotton,
by the hands of others.
This time, there is a text,
the text of memory,
to yield an interpretation
of our senility.

Old words, our old words,
lying around in random patterns,
on the sand,
words of laughter,
thrown out at the sea,
on some nameless day
of sun and dogs and levity.
Or whispers dropped softly
in the dark
at the bottom of sea pools,
left along the beach,
when the tide ran out,
and the moon
cast its cool light
on our discovery:
The transiency of sun,
of surf,
and our solidity.
    / / /

Those who wrap white cotton,
be wise about those words.
The detritus of expression.
Solid waste.
The meaning they bear belongs
to those who do the interpretation,
not to the author of the text
who floats out to sea,
silent, free
in saline liquidity.

MISTAKES ABOUT WATER

That dark night
I was pulled out to sea,
it was just a mistake
about water.
They called it the East River,
which led me to believe
I could dance on its shores
with impunity.

But when I lost my footing,
I tasted salt,
and felt the power
of the moon
and quickly apprehended:
They were wrong.
It was a tidal estuary
and no place to dance
at all.
It was just a mistake
about water.

/ / /

Beckoned by those
who saw me fall,
and rescued my identity
when they could not
rescue me,
you arrived:
The members of my deathwatch.
One by one,
in solemn procession,
you descended
that dangerous
brown bank
to witness my departure,
to attend,
to stay with me.
I would not
be alone in my
going out to sea.

Your presence
so startled me,
those sad eyes,
and outstretched hands,
those words of sorrow
and supplication,
my body found
the will to swim
toward beauty,
and love,
and terror
on the shore.

Even though
the decision
was unilateral,
made without consultation,

I do not begrudge
my body's domination.
It cannot help itself;
it is just a poor
living thing.

But someday,
I will make another mistake
about water.
And when you arrive,
one by one,
in solemn procession,
the members of my deathwatch:
Do not make a mistake
about water.
Let me go,
for I have seen the green glory
of the sea,
and known the freedom
of not being me.

Notes to Text

Chapter 1

1 *Journey to the Forgotten River* (PBS television broadcast, Mar. 14, 1990).

2 Ibid.

3 Ramesh Bedi, *Elephant: Lord of the Jungle* 19 (1969).

4 Ibid., 62.

5 Ibid., 64.

6 Dereck Joubert, "Eyewitness to an Elephant Wake," 179 *National Geographic,* May 1991, 39, 40.

7 L. Harrison Matthews, in *The Natural History of the Whale* (1978), writes, "The order Cetacea is divided into three suborders: the Archaeocetic, all of which are extinct and known only from fossil remains; the Odontoceti or toothed whales, containing the majority of the living species forming the order; and the Mysticeti, the whalebone or baleen whales" (28).

"Most of the members of the Odontoceti are comparatively small porpoises and dolphins, though some, such as the Beaked whales and the Killer whale, reach a length of 30 feet and one, the Sperm whale, reaches 60 feet or more. . . . While the number of species of whalebone whales, the Mysticeti, is small, each animal is enormous individually. The Mysticeti include such mammoths as the Humpback whale, the Blue whale and the Fin whale. The Blue whale can measure one hundred feet or more" (43ff).

8 See generally Melba C. Caldwell and David K. Caldwell, *Epimeletic (Care-giving) Behavior in Cetacea, in Whales, Dolphins, and Porpoises* 755 (Kenneth S. Norris ed., 1966), discussing research involving odontocetes.

9 Richard Carrington, *Elephants* 83 (1958), quoting David E. Blunt, *Elephant* 97–98 (1933).

10 Matthews, *Natural History of the Whale,* 172.

11 Ibid., 173.

12 While land mammals, particularly other gregarious species like the elephant, may exhibit the other two kinds of epimeletic behaviors, only cetaceans can exhibit "supporting behaviors" because they alone live in an aquatic environment and must surface at short intervals

to breathe. Not only will the "aunts" help the mother push the newborn toward the surface, but they will also help keep other whales in the group away from the new mother and baby. With Bottlenosed Dolphins, the "aunt" is often the only other dolphin that the mother will allow near the calf. Naturalists have also observed female odontocetes assisting with the delivery of the calf. W. Nigel Bonner, *Whales* 173–174 (1980).

13 The stimulus of seeing an object behave abnormally (for a dolphin or a whale) may cause the instinctive reaction of pushing the object toward the surface. Matthews, in *The Natural History of the Whale,* points out that "There are no grounds, however, for imputing any use of intelligence in such acts, nor even for supposing that the animals know what they are doing"(173).

14 Christine M. Johnson and Kenneth S. Norris, in "Delphinid Social Organization and Social Behavior," define reciprocal altruism as "the sociobiological model for a system in which an individual performs an altruistic act for another, nonrelated individual. Such an 'altruistic act' is one that engenders a cost to the altruist. The compensating benefit for this act is delayed, and contingent upon the cooperation of others." In *Dolphin Cognition and Behavior: A Comparative Approach* 332, 342 (Ronald J. Schusterman et al., eds., 1986).

15 Peter G. H. Evans, *The Natural History of Whales and Dolphins* 203 (1987).

16 As one researcher warned, however, "we are still far from understanding the full content of vocalizations by any species." Ibid., 204.

17 "'Comity,' in the legal sense, is neither a matter of absolute obligation, on the one hand, nor of mere courtesy and good will, upon the other. But it is the recognition which one nation allows within its territory to the legislative, executive or judicial acts of another nation, having due regard both to international duty and convenience, and to the rights of its own citizens or of other persons who are under the protection of its laws." Hilton v. Guyot, 159 U.S. 113, 163 (1895).

18 *Webster's Ninth New Collegiate Dictionary* 328 (1991).

19 Gustave Flaubert, *Madame Bovary* (1857) (Paul De Man trans., 1965), 236.

20 Jacob Bigelow, *On Self-Limited Diseases* (1836), quoted in *Medical America In The Nineteenth Century* 103 (Gert H. Brieger ed., 1972).

21 Ibid., 105–106.

22 Anointing of the Sick, 1 *New Catholic Encyclopedia* 568–75 (1967).

23 Webb Garrison, *Strange Facts About Death* 99 (1978).

24 Ibid., 103.

25 "Macht doch den Fensterladen in Schlafgemach auf, damit mehr Licht herein komme." Ibid., 102.

26 Ibid., 99.

27 Ibid., 100.

28 Ibid., 102.

29 Cultural patterns vary greatly regarding pregnancy, labor, delivery, and the postpartum period. In almost all cultures, however, others attend to and assist the mother during labor and delivery. One anthropological study found that in the great majority of cultures—fifty-

eight out of sixty—older women actually assisted the mother during childbirth. Other cultures allowed the husband, and occasionally the father-in-law, to be present for the birth. Mike Samuels, M.D. and Nancy Samuels, *The Well Pregnancy Book* 15–16 (1986).

Anyone interested in the experience and institution of motherhood should read Adrienne Rich's *Of Woman Born*. In particular, her chapter entitled, "Alienated Labor" is relevant to the birth-watch. For me, the most memorable birth-watches in literature occur in Sigrid Undset's novel, *Kristin Lavransdatter*.

30 David Sudnow, *Passing On: The Social Organization of Dying* 64 (1967).

31 Ibid., 65.

32 Other factors have undoubtedly contributed to the disappearance of the deathwatch. One author suggested that improved obstetric and pediatric care has cut down dramatically on the types of death that most commonly occurred in the presence of the family. Furthermore, in today's society, the elderly live separated from their adult children. Thus, the most likely candidates for dying generally do so out of the sight of their children and grandchildren. Melvin Krant, M.D., *Dying and Dignity: The Meaning and Control of a Personal Death* 7 (1974).

33 Sudnow, *Passing On,* 85–86.

34 Ibid., 86.

35 Geoffrey Gorer, *Death, Grief, and Mourning,* 5 (1965).

36 Sudnow, *Passing On,* 48.

37 Ibid., 83.

38 Ibid., 83–84.

39 Thomas A. Raffin et al., *Intensive Care: Facing The Critical Choices* 14 (1989).

40 William A. Knaus, M.D., et al., "Prognosis in Acute Organ-System Failure" 202 *Annals of Surgery* 685, 685 (1985).

41 *In re* Quinlan, 348 A.2d 801, 806 (N.J. Super. Ct. Ch. Div. 1975), modified and remanded, 355 A.2d 647 (N.J.), cert. denied sub nom. Garger v. New Jersey, 429 U.S. 922 (1976) (hereinafter Quinlan I).

42 Ibid., 810.

43 Ibid., 812.

44 Ibid., 814.

45 Ibid., 815.

46 The lower court devoted fully one-third of its opinion to medical details about Karen Quinlan's body. Id. at 806–12. Later decisions about termination of life-support systems have winnowed the medical details down to a few terse paragraphs at the beginning of the opinion. See, e.g., Cruzan v. Harmon, 760 S.W. 2d 408, 411 (Mo. 1988) (en banc), *aff'd sub nom.* Cruzan v. Director, Mo. Dep't of Health, 110 S. Ct. 2841 (1990).

47 Joseph Quinlan et al., *Karen Ann: The Quinlans Tell Their Story* 214–15 (1977), quoting the trial court transcript.

48 The tight security cost the taxpayers of New Jersey an average of $4,199 a month. Ibid., 315–16.

49 Quinlan I, 348 A.2d at 807.

50 Quinlan et al., *The Quinlans Tell Their Story*, 208–214.

51 Ibid., 211.

52 Ibid.

53 *In re* Quinlan, 355 A.2d 647, 653 (N.J.), *cert. denied sub nom.* Garger v. New Jersey, 429 U.S. 922 (1976) (hereinafter Quinlan II).

54 Ibid.

55 Quinlan I, 348 A.2d at 813.

56 Since Quinlan II, many state courts have addressed the issue of removing life-sustaining treatment. See, e.g., Rasmussen v. Fleming, 741 P.2d 674 (Ariz. 1987) (en banc); *In re* Drabick, 245 Cal. Rptr. 840 (Cal. Ct. App. 1988), cert denied sub nom. Drabick v. Drabick, 488 U.S. 958 (1988); Lovato v. District Ct., 601 P. 2d 1072 (Colo. 1979) (en banc); McConnell v. Beverly Enters., 553 A.2d 596 (Conn. 1989); *In re* Severns, 425 A.2d 156 (Del. Ch. 1980); *In re* Browning, 568 So. 2d 4 (Fla. 1990); *In re* L.H.R., 321 S.E.2d 716 (Ga. 1984); *In re* Estate of Greenspan, 558 N.E.2d 1194 (Ill, 1990); Morgan v. Olds, 417 N.W.2d 232 (Iowa Ct. App. 1987); *In re* P.V.W., 424 So.2d 1015 (La.1982); *In re* Gardner, 534 A.2d 947 (Me. 1987); *In re* Riddlemoser, 564 A.2d 812 (Md. Ct. Spec. App. 1989); Brophy v. New England Sinai Hosp., 497 N.E.2d 626 (Mass. 1986); *In re* Torres, 357 N.W.2d 332 (Minn. 1984); Cruzan v. Harmon, 760 S.W.2d 408 (Mo. 1988) (en banc), *aff'd sub nom.* Cruzan v. Director, Mo. Dep't of Health, 110 S.Ct. 2841 (1990); McKay v. Bergstadt, 801 P.2d 617 (Nev.1990); *In re* Peter, 529 A.2d 419 (N.J. 1987); *In re* Westchester County Medical Ctr. ex rel. O'Connor, 531 N.E.2d 607 (N.Y.1988); Leach v. Akron Gen. Medical Ctr., 68 Ohio Misc. 1. (C.P. 1980); *In re* Estate of Dorone, 502 A.2d 1271 (Pa. Super. Ct. 1985), aff'd, 534 A.2d 452 (Pa. 1987); *In re* Jane Doe, 533 A.2d 523 (R.I. 1987); *In re* Grant, 747 P.2d 445 (Wash. 1987) (en banc), corrected, 757 P.2d 534 (Wash. 1988); *In re* L.W., 482 N.W.2d 60 (Wis. 1992) (en banc).

57 Cruzan v. Harmon, 760 S.W. 2d 408, 411 (Mo. 1988), (en banc) *aff'd sub nom.* Cruzan v. Director, Mo. Dep't of Health, 110 S.Ct. 2841 (1990).

58 Ibid.

59 Cruzan v. Director, Mo. Dep't of Health, 110 S.Ct. 2841 (1990).

60 Laurie Abraham, "Ethicists Try to Define Status of Vegetative Patients: Dead? Alive? Treatment Plans Hang on Decisions," *Am. Med. News*, Feb. 24, 1989, 3, 32.

61 Karen Quinlan's father, Joseph, started the lawsuit by seeking guardianship of the person and property of his daughter. Quinlan I, 348 A.2d 801, 806 (N.J. Super. Ct. Ch. Div. 1975), modified and remanded, 355 A.2d 647 (N.J.), cert. denied sub nom. Garger v. New Jersey, 429 U.S. 922 (1976). He amended the pleadings to seek a restraining order to prevent the Morris County prosecutor, the attending and treating physicians, and St. Clare's Hospital from interfering with the exercise of the authorization sought, and to enjoin the prosecutor from prosecuting for homicide when the authorization sought was affected. (Id.) At a pretrial conference, the attorney general intervened, the basis for his action being "the interest of the State in preservation of life, which has an undoubted constitutional

foundation." Quinlan II, 355 A.2d 647, 651–52 (N.J.), cert. denied sub nom. Garger v. New Jersey, 429 U.S. 922 (1976). In Cruzan v. Harmon, the confrontation between the family and the State of Missouri was more direct, due in part to the fact that Nancy Cruzan was a patient in a state hospital. 760 S.W.2d at 411. In addition, Cruzan v. Harmon was a product of Missouri law in which the legislature had set its mind to preserving human life, almost at any cost.

In the statute regarding living wills, it states that the statute does not "condone, authorize or approve mercy killing or euthanasia nor permit any affirmative or deliberate act or omission to shorten or end life." Mo. Ann. Stat. §459.055(5) (Vernon 1992). The Missouri Supreme Court found this legislation to be an "expression of the policy of this State with regard to the sanctity of life." Cruzan v. Harmon, 760 S.W.2d at 420.

Other states have developed a line of analysis for addressing these issues. In Superintendent of Belchertown State School v. Saikewicz, 370 N.E. 2d 417 (Mass. 1977), the Supreme Judicial Court of Massachusetts articulated a balancing test that has been cited in many other jurisdictions. The Saikewicz court invoked the following state interests: "(1) the preservation of life; (2) the protection of the interests of innocent third parties; (3) the prevention of suicide; and (4) maintaining the ethical integrity of the medical profession." (Id. at 425.) Against these interests the court balanced the individual's right to refuse life-prolonging medical treatment.

62 Autonomy basically means the right to be accorded the respect of others and to exercise free will in the sphere of personal action. Most of our notions of autonomy derive from Kantian philosophy. Kant based his theory on the rational being, or *vernunftwesen,* who exercised practical reason to legislate for himself according to his conception of law. Immanuel Kant, *Foundations of the Metaphysics of Morals* (1785).

In the context of health care, autonomy is the patient's right to make his own decisions regarding medical treatment. Tort law has developed two theories which seek to secure for the patient such self-determination. First, the law has concluded that a physician commits a battery when performing a medical procedure that goes beyond the scope of the patient's consent, thus becoming an intentional touching of a tortious nature. See, e.g. Schloendorff v. Society of N.Y. Hosp., 105 N.E. 92, 93 (N.Y. 1914). The second doctrine, informed consent, is based on negligence. The issue here is whether or not the physician made a full and complete disclosure to the patient of all the possible risks of a procedure or treatment so that the patient could make a truly informed decision. See Canterbury v. Spence, 464 F.2d 772, 786–92 (D.C. Cir. 1972), cert. denied, 409 U.S. 1064 (1972). Corollaries to this doctrine are the patient's right to refuse medical treatment based upon the information provided and the duty of the health-care providers to respect the patient's choice. Through these tort theories, courts have recognized that patients should be protected from unwanted bodily intrusions.

63 Generally courts apply one of two tests when making decisions regarding the termination of life-sustaining treatment for incompetent patients: substituted judgment or best interests. Stewart G. Pollock, "Life and Death Decisions: Who Makes Them and By What Stan-

dards?", 41 *Rutgers L. Rev.* 505, 525–30 (1989). For children, the parent or legal guardian gives informed consent for medical treatment, unless the parents' decision endangers the child. In that event, the courts will take over, invoking the doctrine of parens patriae. See, e.g., Newark v. Williams, 588 A.2d 1108 (Del. 1991); Favier v. Winick, 583 N.Y.S.2d 907 (N.Y. Sup. Ct. 1992). For a discussion of the evolution of the doctrine of parens patriae, see Neil H. Cogan, "Juvenile Law: Before and After the Entrance of Parens Patriae," 22 *S. C. L. Rev.* 147, 155–61 (1970); Laurence B. Custer, "The Origin of the Doctrine of Parens Patriae," 27 *Emory L. J.* 195 (1978). Courts tend to use the "best interests of the child" standard in making decisions for infants under their supervision, appointing a guardian who serves as an officer of the court. See, e.g., People ex rel. G.S., 820 P.2d 1178, 1180 (Colo. Ct. App. 1991); In re D.L., Jr., 589 N.E.2d 680, 684 (Ill. App. Ct. 1992).

64 Some courts have refused to find a constitutional right of privacy that includes the right to refuse medical treatment, relying instead exclusively on the common law rights to be protected from unwanted bodily intrusions. See, e.g., In re Conroy, 486 A.2d 1209, 1223 (N.J. 1985). In Cruzan v. Director Mo. Dep't of Health, the Supreme Court determined that the due process clause of the Fourteenth Amendment created a constitutionally protected liberty interest that embraced the right to refuse unwanted medical treatment. 110 S. Ct. 2841, 2858 (1990). Thus a competent person has "a constitutionally protected right to refuse hydration and nutrition" (Id. at 2852). Courts have extended these common law and constitutional rights of self-determination to incompetent patients. The problem has been how to exercise such rights since some form of surrogate decisionmaking must be invoked.

Chapter 2

1 Michael P. McQuillan, M.D., "Can People Who Are Unconscious or in the 'Vegetative State' Perceive Pain?" 6 *Issues L. & Med.* 373, 381–82 (1991).

2 Ronald E. Cranford, M.D., "The Persistent Vegetative State: The Medical Reality (Getting the Facts Straight)," Hastings Center Report 26 (Feb./Mar. 1988). See generally Francis J. Keefe and Laurence A. Bradley, "Behavioral and Psychological Approaches to the Assessment and Treatment of Chronic Pain," 6 *Gen. Hosp. Psychiatry* 49, 50 (1984), describing a system of assessing a patient's pain based upon five "pain behaviors": guarding, bracing, rubbing, grimacing and sighing; Daniel N. Robinson, Pain and Suffering: Psychobiological Principles, in 3 *Encyclopedia of Bioethics* 1177, 1180–81 (Warren T. Reich ed., 1978), discussing the differences between the issues of pain and suffering.

3 C. D. Rollins, Solipsism, in 7 *Encyclopedia of Philosophy* 487 (Paul Edwards ed., 1967).

4 Ibid., 490–91; see also John Wisdom, *Other Minds* (2d ed., 1965), considering, in a series of essays, whether we ever know what anyone else is thinking, feeling, or experiencing.

5 See Robert G. Bone, "Mapping the Boundaries of a Dispute: Conceptions of Ideal Lawsuit Structure From the Field Code to the Federal Rules," 89 *Colum. L. Rev.* 1 (1989), exploring

the normative values beneath the rhetoric of procedural reform and tracing the development of the rules that define the party structure of a lawsuit.

6 Lewis Carroll, *Alice's Adventures in Wonderland* (1865) (John Tenniel illus., 1929), 192, 194–95.

7 Amélie O. Rorty, "A Literary Postcript: Characters, Persons, Selves, Individuals," in *The Identities of Persons* 301, 309 (Amélie O. Rorty ed., 1976).

8 Defoe described the plague's disastrous effect on the birth-watch as well: "One of the most deplorable Cases in all the present Calamity was that of women with Child; who when they came to the Hour of their Sorrows, and their Pains came upon them, cou'd neither have help of one Kind or another; neither Midwife or Neighbouring Women to come near them." Daniel Defoe, *A Journal of the Plague Year* (1722) (Louis Landa ed., 1969),115–16.

9 Michael Gordon, Introduction to *The Nuclear Family in Crisis: The Search for an Alternative* (Michael Gordon ed., 1972),1–2. Sociological literature often uses these terms more loosely, however. For example, a nuclear family that happens to have other adult members residing with them (besides the mother and father, such as an unmarried sibling of one of the parents, or a widowed parent or grandparent), may be labeled an "extended family."

10 Many other commentators have argued that the family should decide whether to terminate life-support systems. See, e.g., Corrine Bayley, "Who Should Decide?," in *Legal and Ethical Aspects of Treating Critically and Terminally Ill Patients* 3, 9 (A. Edward Doudera and J. Douglas Peters eds., 1982), and Richard P. Byrne, "Deciding for the Legally Incompetent: A View From the Bench," in *Legal and Ethical Aspects* 25, 25; cf. Robert M. Veatch, "Limits of Guardian Treatment Refusal: A Reasonableness Standard," 9 *Am. J. L. & Med.* 427, 441–42 (1983), arguing that "bonded guardians," who may be family or close friends of the patient, should make decisions. See also Martha Minow, "The Role of Families in Medical Decisions," 1991 *Utah L. Rev.* 1, 13–14. See generally Lawrence Stone, *The Family, Sex and Marriage in England: 1500–1800* (1977), arguing that in earlier centuries the state did not perceive distinct boundaries between the family and society and intervened more directly in family life.

11 See, e.g., *In re* Storar, 420 N.E.2d 64 (N.Y.), *cert. denied sub nom.* Storar v. Storar, 454 U.S. 858 (1981) (local director of eighty-three-year-old incompetent patient's religious order applied to be appointed committee of his person and property, with authority to remove the respirator; the patient's ten nieces and nephews supported application).

12 *In re* Conroy, 486 A.2d 1209, 1223 (N.J. 1985) (stating that the court need not decide the constitutional issue because the common law right to self-determination encompasses the right to refuse medical treatment); *In re* Peter, 529 A.2d 419 (N.J. 1987) The patient had previously authorized consent to medical treatment; *In re* Browning, 568 So. 2d 4 (Fla. 1990).

13 *In re* Hier, 464 N.E.2d 959 (Mass. App. Ct. 1984) (incompetent ninety-two-year-old patient, in a psychiatric hospital for fifty-seven years, represented by court-appointed temporary guardian; no mention of any family members); *In re* Hamlin, 689 P.2d 1372 (Wash. 1983) (hospital and guardian petitioned to terminate life-support systems for patient, re-

tarded from birth, who had no relatives or close friends with whom medical staff could consult).

14 See, e.g., Rasmussen v. Fleming, 741 P.2d 674, 679 (Ariz. 1987) (en banc) (incompetent patient represented by public fiduciary; three siblings "did not take an active role in the determination of Rasmussen's treatment, they expressed a willingness to abide by the decision to place DNR and DNH orders on Rasmussen's medical chart"); Superintendent of Belchertown State Sch. v. Saikewicz, 370 N.E.2d 417, 420 (Mass. 1977) (superintendent of institution where mentally retarded sixty-seven-year-old patient had lived for almost fifty years petitioned for appointment of guardian ad litem with authority to make medical treatment decisions regarding his leukemia: "Two of his sisters, the only members of his family who could be located, were notified of his condition and of the hearing, but they preferred not to attend or otherwise become involved"); In re Torres, 357 N.W.2d 332, 335–37 (Minn. 1986) (incompetent patient represented by court-appointed conservator and court-appointed counsel; a first cousin testified he saw patient "at least once a week"); In re Ingram, 689 P.2d 1363 (Wash. 1984) (attorney for son of incompetent patient petitioned court for authorization to perform needed cancer surgery which patient opposed having).

15 Recently the Minnesota Court of Appeals granted guardianship of Sharon Kowalski to Karen Thompson. In re Kowalski, 478 N.W.2d 790, 797 (Minn. Ct. App. 1991). In 1990, "Mr. Kowalski resigned his guardianship, citing heart problems and weariness with the extended court proceedings." Tamar Lewin, "Disabled Woman's Care Given to Lesbian Partner," N.Y. Times, Dec. 18, 1991, A26. The trial court had granted guardianship to a "neutral" third person in an effort to allay hostilities between Kowalski's family and Thompson. 478 N.W.2d at 794. The Court of Appeals set aside the appointment, holding that the trial court abused its discretion in denying Thompson's petition for guardianship. Id. at 794–95.

16 Ibid., 863.

17 Ibid.

18 Ibid., 864.

19 Ibid., 797.

20 Elizabeth Bott, "Urban Families: Conjugal Roles and Social Networks," 8 Hum. Rel. 345, 347 n.3 (1955).

21 Ibid., 348.

22 See J. Clyde Mitchell, "The Concept and Use of Social Networks," in Social Networks in Urban Situations: Analyses of Personal Relationships in Central African Towns, 1 (J. Clyde Mitchell ed., 1969).

23 Another sociologist defined the "strength" of an interpersonal tie as a "combination of the amount of time, the emotional intensity, the intimacy (mutual confiding), and the reciprocal services which characterize the tie." Mark Granouetter, "The Strength of Weak Ties," 78 Am. J. Soc. 1360, 1361 (1973).

24 The Constitution limits federal courts to the adjudication of actual "cases or controversies." U.S. Const. art. III, §1. In order to raise a case or controversy, a litigant "must allege

personal injury fairly traceable to . . . allegedly unlawful conduct and likely to be redressed by the requested relief." Allen v. Wright, 468 U.S. 737, 751 (1984),citing Valley Forge Christian College v. Americans United for Separation of Church and State, Inc., 454 U.S. 464, 472 (1982). The injury must be "distinct and palpable." Warth v. Seldin, 422 U.S. 490, 501 (1975). It cannot be "'abstract' or 'conjectural' or 'hypothetical.'" Allen v. Wright, 468 U.S. at 741 (citations omitted).

Standing is the "doctrine most central" to enforcement of the case or controversy limitation. See Laurence H. Tribe, *American Constitutional Law* §§14, 107 (2d ed., 1988). "Whether a party has a sufficient stake in an otherwise justiciable controversy to obtain judicial resolution of that controversy has traditionally been referred to as the question of standing to sue." Sierra Club v. Morton, 405 U.S. 727, 731–32 (1972). Application of the doctrine centers primarily on the plaintiff and only peripherally on the issues she brings with her into court. Tribe, *Constitutional Law,* 107.

In Valley Forge Christian College, the Supreme Court examined the standing requirement and concluded that standing may be denied if a plaintiff fails to meet one of the following three requirements. First, the plaintiff must "rest his claim to relief on the legal rights or interests of third parties." 454 U.S. at 474. Second, the plaintiff must state "'abstract questions of wide public significance' which amount to 'generalized grievances,' pervasively shared and most appropriately addressed in the representative branches." Id. at 474–75 (citations omitted). Third, the plaintiff must present a claim falling within "'the zone of interests to be protected or regulated by the statute or constitutional guarantee in question.'" Id. at 475 (citation omitted). Arguably my friend's contention was that members of the deathwatch lacked standing to terminate life-support systems based on numbers two and three in the Valley Forge trio of standing sins.

This discussion is limited to problems of standing under the federal Constitution, though the termination of life support cases implicate both federal constitutional rights and common law rights of self-determination, and are most often pursued in state courts.

Obviously, the Constitution's standing requirement applies only to the federal courts. The doctrine does not obligate state courts to require, for example, an "injury in fact" before addressing federal claims. Tribe, *Constitutional Law,* §§3–15, 112–13. Nor does the federal doctrine of standing tell a state court whether a potential plaintiff has standing to participate in a state judicial proceeding. The principles embodied in the federal law of standing, however, are found in state constitutions, statutes, and rules of civil procedure as well. See generally 59 *Am. Jur.* 2d Parties Plaintiff §§19–40, 406–438 (1971),outlining and comparing state standing requirements. Given the generality of this discussion, I decided to limit it to the problems of standing under the federal Constitution and not to delve into the substantive laws regarding standing in any particular state.

See Henry P. Monaghan, "Third Party Standing," 84 *Colum. L. Rev.* 277, 279 (1984). The Yazoo doctrine is part and parcel of the law of standing. Standing, however, is only one of the many judicial inventions designed to avoid constitutional decisionmaking. Other doctrines also shut the door on potential constitutional questions: ripeness, mootness, political question, and exhaustion of remedies. See Tribe, *Constitutional Law,* §§3–10 to 3–13, 3–29. These doctrines reflect a strong ambivalence about the propriety of judicial review in a society based upon democratic principles. Henry P. Monaghan, "Constitutional Adjudication: The Who and When," 82 *Yale L. J.* 1363, 1366 (1973). For a classic articulation of the view that judicial intervention should occur only when absolutely necessary, and under carefully circumscribed conditions, see James B. Thayer, "The Origin and Scope of the American Doctrine of Constitutional Law," 7 *Harv. L. Rev.* 129 (1893). For further discussions about the utility of these "rules of avoidance," see Alexander M. Bickel, "The Least Dangerous Branch" (1962); Burton C. Bernard, "Avoidance of Constitutional Issues in the United States Supreme Court: Liberties of the First Amendment," 50 *Mich. L. Rev.* 261 (1951); Gerald Gunther, "The Subtle Voices of the 'Passive Virtues'—A Comment on Principle and Expediency in Judicial Review," 64 *Colum. L. Rev.* 1 (1964); Henry P. Monaghan, "Overbreath," 1981 *Sup. Ct. Rev.* 1.

25 Marbury v. Madison, 5 U.S. (1 Cranch) 137, 170 (1803).

26 See Note, "Complex Enforcement: Unconstitutional Prison Conditions," 94 *Harv. L. Rev.* 626 (1981), contrasting this older view of the judicial task, to adjudicate discretely a particular incident or practice, with a more modern view of the judicial task in complex litigation, to bring about systemic, structural reform of a social institution offensive to legal norms. See generally Monaghan, "Constitutional Adjudication," 1365–68, suggesting that constitutional adjudication evolved around and remains a system aimed at preventing injury to private interests; Cass R. Sunstein, "Judicial Relief and Public Tort Law," 92 *Yale L. J.* 749, 758 (1983) (book review): "most of our public law—both substantive and procedural—grows quite directly out of private law and corresponding efforts to treat the government as a defendant in a private lawsuit."

27 Spouses of the dying person brought the largest number of cases. Where the incompetent patient was an unmarried adult, the most common petitioners were the parents. See, e.g., Foody v. Manchester Hosp., 482 A.2d 713 (Conn. Super. Ct. 1984) (father of forty-two-year-old incompetent patient was conservator of the person; parents sought authorization to discontinue extraordinary means); In re Gardner, 534 A.2d 947 (Me. 1987) (mother and guardian ad litem sought declaratory judgment regarding removal of twenty-three-year-old incompetent son's feeding tube); Cruzan v. Harmon, 760 S.W.2d 408 (Mo. 1988) (en banc), aff'd sub nom. Cruzan v. Director, Mo. Dep't of Health, 110 S. Ct. 2841 (1990) (parents brought action as guardians to compel hospital to comply with their request to remove feeding tube from comatose daughter); Quinlan I, 348 A.2d 801 (N.J. Super. Ct. Ch. Div. 1975), modified and remanded, 355 A.2d 647 (N.J.), cert. denied sub nom. Garger v. New Jersey, 429 US. 922 (1976) (action by father to terminate life support for twenty-one-year-old daughter); In re Storar, 433 N.Y.S.2d 388 (N.Y. Sup. Ct.1980), rev'd, 420 N.E.2d 64 (N.Y.), cert. denied sub nom. Storar v. Storar, 454 U.S. 858 (1981) (seventy-seven-year-old mother petitioned for order terminating transfusions for mentally retarded adult son with leukemia).

In cases of incompetent minor patients, the petitioner was almost invariably a parent.

See, e.g., *In re* Barry, 445 So. 2d 363 (Fla. Dist. Ct. App. 1984) (parents of brain-damaged ten-month-old baby petitioned for approval to terminate life-support system); *In re* L.H.R., 321 S.E.2d 716 (Ga. 1984) (court enjoined hospital from interfering with parents' and guardian ad litem's wishes to have brain-damaged newborn's life-support systems removed).

In some instances, a sibling or adult child served as petitioner. See, e.g., *In re* Drabick, 245 Cal. Rptr. 840 (Cal. Ct. App.), cert. denied sub nom. Drabick v. Drabick, 488 US. 958 (1988) (brother of incompetent forty-four-year-old patient was conservator of the person and sought approval for removal of feeding tube).

28 In a five-to-four decision, the United States Supreme Court upheld the Supreme Court of Missouri. Cruzan v. Director, Mo. Dep't of Health, 110 S.Ct. 2841 (1990). A state may apply a clear and convincing evidence standard in proceedings where a guardian seeks to discontinue nutrition and hydration of a person in a persistent vegetative state. Id. at 2854.

Chapter 3

1 *Black's Law Dictionary* 488 (3d ed., 1951).

2 Ad Hoc Committee of the Harvard Medical School to Examine the Definition of Brain Death, "A Definition of Irreversible Coma," 205 *JAMA* 337, 337–38 (1968).

3 Ibid., 337 (italics omitted).

4 *The Wizard of Oz* (Metro Goldwyn-Mayer, 1939).

5 Lawrence C. Becker, "Human Being: The Boundaries of the Concept," 4 *Phil. & Pub. Aff.* 344, 353 (1975).

6 H. Tristram Engelhardt, "Medicine and the Concept of Person," in *Contemporary Issues in Bioethics* 94, 97 (Tom Beauchamp and LeRoy Waters eds., 1982).

7 Ibid., 98–99.

8 Robert M. Veatch, *Death, Dying and the Biological Revolution* 24 (1989).

9 Ibid., 29, 30.

10 See Veatch, *Death, Dying,* 27, arguing that the timing of traditional death behaviors should be the impetus that drives public debate about the definition of death. In the case of the Munchkins, such behavior involved singing "Ding, Dong, the Witch is Dead."

11 Physicians have proposed several other major sets of criteria to diagnose irreversible loss of brain function. For example, in 1971, the University of Minnesota Health Sciences Center published what have been called the "Minnesota Criteria." They differed from the Harvard Criteria in that they required neither a confirmatory EEG nor the absence of movement in response to painful stimuli. They specified a test for the presence of spontaneous respiration for a period of four minutes at a time, and required only the absence of brainstem reflexes. In addition, the tests needed to be repeated and remain unchanged only within twelve, not twenty-four hours. A. Mohandas and Shelly N. Chou, "Brain Death: A Clinical and Pathological Study," *J. Neurosurgery* 211, 212 (Aug. 1971). The Minnesota Medical As-

sociation adopted another set of criteria in 1976. See Ronald E. Cranford, "Minnesota Medical Association Criteria Brain Death: Concept and Criteria," 61 *Minn. Med.* 561, 562 (1978).

In 1977, a study organized by the National Institute of Neurological Diseases and Stroke (NINDS), headed by Earl Walker, published another set of brain-based criteria. In addition to the deep coma with cerebral unresponsivity and apnea, the Walker group required dilated pupils, absence of cephalic reflexis, and electrocerebral silence on an EEG. A. Earl Walker, M.D., et al., "An Appraisal of the Criteria of Cerebral Death: A Summary Statement," 237 *JAMA* 982, 982 (1977).

A President's Commission proposed a set of criteria that included deep coma, absence of brainstem reflexes, and apnea. Clinical indicators for the cessation of all brain functions had to be present for at least six hours. The Commission recommended confirmation by an EEG, and further testing for the absence of cerebral brain flow could also aid in diagnosis. President's Commission for the Study of Ethical Problems in Medicine, *Defining Death* 159–66 (1981). For an excellent history of the brain-based definition of death, see Veatch, *Death, Dying,* 15–58.

12 For another philosopher's discussion of what constitutes the significant properties of a person, see Joseph Fletcher, "Indicators of Humanhood," Hastings Center Report 1 (Nov. 1972). Some scholars also suggest that we not focus on consciousness, but rather on the capacity for social interaction. Rebecca Dresser, "Life, Death, and Incompetent Patients: Conceptual Infirmities and Hidden Values in the Law" 28 *Ariz. L. Rev.* 373 (1986); Kevin P. Quinn, "The Best Interests of Incompetent Patients: The Capacity for Interpersonal Relationship as a Standard for Decisionmaking," 76 *Cal. L. Rev.* 897 (1988). For a fascinating exploration of the impact of developments in artificial intelligence on our sense of what is human, see Steven Goldberg, "The Changing Face of Death: Computers, Consciousness and Nancy Cruzan," 43 *Stan. L. Rev.* 659 (1991).

13 Two philosophers have criticized Veatch, arguing against basing the definition of death on moral judgments They claim that personal identity should be critical in determining when a person is dead. Michael B. Green and Daniel Wikler, "Brain Death and Personal Identity," 9 *Phil. & Pub. Aff.* 105 passim (1980). Thus, "a given person ceases to exist with the destruction of whatever processes there are which normally underlie that person's psychological continuity and connectedness" (127). They characterize their argument as "ontological," not moral (106).

Many excellent articles urge some form of upper-brain criteria for death. See, e.g., David R. Smith, "Legal Recognition of Neocortical Death," 71 *Cornell L. Rev.* 850, 879 (1986) ("the inevitability of scientific progress suggests that the limits of present medical technology are no reason to avoid addressing the appropriateness of a neocortical death standard"); and Raymond Deverette, "Neocortical Death and Human Death," 18 *Law, Med. & Health Care* 96 (1990), supporting an integrated approach in which upper-brain death plays a key role in defining death.

14 The literature on the issue of defining death is extensive. For an excellent bibliography on

the legal definition of death see, Richard E. Leahy, *Legal Death: A Pathfinder to the Current State of the Law and Its Implications*, 9 *Legal Reference Services* Q. 73 (1989); see also Howard Brody, *Ethical Decisions in Medicine* (2d ed., 1981),including case studies in textbook format; Hans Jonas, *Philosophical Essays: From Ancient Creed to Technological Man* 132–40 (1974), explaining that for practical purposes brain death defines death, but for higher moral reasons a brain-dead person still enjoys sacred identity; Paul Ramsey, *The Patient as Person* (1970), providing a practical, wide-ranging discussion of death by a Christian ethicist; Joel Feinberg, "The Rights of Animals and Unborn Generations," in *Philosophy and Environmental Crisis* 43 (William Blackstone ed., 1974), ascribing rights to brain-dead individuals; John C. Hoffman "Clarifying the Debate on Death," 62 *Soundings* 430 (1979), proposing that the definition of death should be a primary, rather than secondary, moral consideration.

There is an interesting debate between D. Alan Shewmon and Robert L. Barry about whether neocortical death is consistent with the metaphysics of the rationality of the soul in Aquinas. Compare D. Alan Shewmon, "The Metaphysics of Brain Death, Persistent Vegetative State, and Dementia," 49 *Thomist* 24 (1985) and D. Alan Shewmon, "Ethics and Brain Death: A Response," 61 *New Scholasticism* 321 (1987), both of whom assert that the death of the brainstem substantially changes the metaphysics of life, with Robert L. Barry, "Ethics and Brain Death," 61 *New Scholasticism* 82 (1987), who argues that, brain-dead or not, human beings retain rational souls and moral rights.

For a thorough discussion of the redefinition debate, see Karen G. Gervais, *Redefining Death* 159–82 (1986). For an international perspective, see Christopher Pallis, "Brain Stem Death—The Evolution of a Concept," 55 *Medico-Legal J.* 84 (1987).

15 Not everyone agrees that finding a definition of death is a worthwhile endeavor. Roger B. Dworkin, in"Death in Context," argues that the effort expended on a search for a single definition of death is "wasted at best, counterproductive at worst," 48 *Ind. L. J.* 623, 628 (1973). The question of whether a death has occurred arises in a number of different contexts: When may an estate be probated? When does a life estate end? When is a victim of a crime dead? When can we stop medical treatment? Thus, "it would be odd indeed if all these different situations were susceptible to resolution by one definition of death" (631). "The simplest solution lies in recognizing that as there is no need to define death, so too there is no need for the law to use the term at all. . . . What is important . . . are the consequences, not the conclusory determination" (638). The law should only seek to describe the circumstances under which given consequences are to flow. For criticism of these views, see Alexander Capron, "The Purpose of Death: Reply to Professor Dworkin," 48 *Ind. L. J.* 640 (1973).

Another writer points out that even if we redefined death to include a persistent vegetative state, "it will be of no use in addressing the dilemmas of dying for patients in less fully debilitated conditions." Daniel Wikler, "Not Dead, Not Dying? Ethical Categories and Persistent Vegetative State," Hastings Center Report 41, 47 (Feb./Mar. 1988).

16 Robert Morison, "Death: Process or Event," 173 *Science* 694, 698 (1971).

Chapter 4

1 Plato, *Phaedo,* in *The Works of Plato* (Irwin Edman ed. and Benjamin Jowett trans., 1956), 186.

2 Aristotle, *De Anima* (John L. Ackrill ed. and David W. Hamlyn trans., 1968), 8–9.

3 One study suggests that most patients and family members (70 percent) who had experienced intensive care treatment were completely certain that they would do so again to prolong life for any period, including only one month. Marion Danis, M.D., et al., "Patients' and Families' Preferences for Medical Intensive Care," 260 *JAMA* 797, 800 (1988). Richard may therefore have been in the minority of patients who had spent time in an ICU.

4 At the time of Richard's illness, New York had no legislation recognizing advance directives for medical treatment. The New York Court of Appeals, however, had given effect to prior oral statements where there was uncontested evidence that the patient had indicated his views regarding the removal of life-support systems before becoming incompetent. *In re* Storar, 420 N. E.2d 64, 72 (N.Y.), cert. denied sub nom. Storar v. Storar, 454 U.S. 858 (1981). The court authorized the removal of a respirator based on this uncontested evidence and on the ground that the common law permitted a competent patient the right to decline medical treatment. *Id.* at 70, 72. Thus, at the time Richard requested the living will, there was no statutory authority for its recognition, although common law precedent gave effect to prior statements regarding intent. Since that time, New York has passed a statute providing for the appointment of a health care agent and proxy. N.Y. PUB. Health Law sects. 2980–94 (McKinney Supp. 1992).

5 Claude Levi-Strauss, *The Savage Mind* (1962) (Julian Pitt-Rivers and Ernest Gellner eds., 1966), 176 .

6 Geoffrey Gorer, "The Pornography of Death" (1955), reprinted in Gorer, *Death, Grief and Mourning,* 195.

7 There is considerable literature regarding DNRs. See, e.g., Mitchell T. Rabkin et al., "Orders Not to Resuscitate," 295 *New Eng. J. Med.* 364 (1976), discussing how the decision not to resuscitate is formulated and the need for stricter definitions of that process; Rabbi Levi Meier, "Code and No-Code: A Psychological Analysis and the Viewpoint of Jewish Laws," in *Legal and Ethical Aspects of Treating Critically and Terminally Ill Patients* (A. Edward Doudera and J. Douglas Peters eds., 1982), 90.

8 David Sudnow, *Passing On: The Social Organization of Dying* (1967), 44.

9 Richard A. Kalish, "Social Distance and the Dying," 2 *Community Mental Health J.* 152, 153 (1966).

10 David Zinman, "Heart Surgeons Rated," *Newsday* (Nassau and Suffolk County ed.), Dec. 18, 1991, 3.

11 Cruzan v. Harmon, 760 S.W.2d 408 (Mo. 1988) (en banc), *aff'd sub nom.* Cruzan v. Director, Mo. Dep't of Health, 110 S.Ct. 2841 (1990); *In re* Westchester County Medical Ctr. *ex rel.* O'Connor, 531 N.E.2d 607 (N.Y. 1988).

12 O'Connor, 531 N.E.2d at 609.

13 Id. at 610. In defending his court's decision in O'Connor, the former Chief Judge Wachtler distinguished the case from the later United States Supreme Court decision, Cruzan v. Director, Mo. Dep't of Health, on the basis that Nancy Cruzan was in a persistent vegetative state and Mary O'Connor was not. The O'Connor decision was not, he protested, an earlier version of Cruzan because "Mary O'Connor was not a Nancy Cruzan." Thus, according to Wachtler, the Court of Appeals of New York has not yet confronted how or whether to terminate life-support systems from someone in a persistent vegetative state who had not left clear and convincing evidence of his intent. Sol Wachtler, "A Judge's Perspective: The New York Rulings," 19 *Law, Med. & Health Care* 60, 62 (1991).

14 Ibid., 611, quoting Lampasso's testimony about a conversation with O'Connor.

15 Ibid., quoting Lampasso's testimony.

16 Ibid., quoting Helen's testimony about a conversation with her mother.

17 Ibid., quoting Helen's testimony.

18 Ibid., quoting Joan's testimony.

19 Ibid., 612.

20 Ibid., 613.

21 Ibid., 615.

22 Cruzan v. Harmon, 760 S.W.2d 408, 433 (Mo. 1988) (en banc), *aff'd sub nom.* Cruzan v. Director, Mo. Dep't of Health, 110 S.Ct. 2841 (1990).

23 Frigaliment Importing Co. v. B.N.S. Int'l Sales Corp., 190 F.Supp. 116, 121 (S.D.N.Y. 1960); Jacob and Youngs, Inc. v. Kent, 129 N.E. 889, 890 (N.Y. 1921).

24 O'Connor, 531 N.E.2d at 622 (Simons, J. dissenting).

25 *In re* Conroy, 486 A.2d 1209, 1230 (N.J. 1985).

26 Steven H. Miles and Allison August, "Courts, Gender and 'The Right to Die'," 18 *Law, Med. & Health Care* 85 (1990). Much of the article is based on the theoretical work of Carol Gilligan. She argues that women have a different approach to moral decisionmaking than men. The male model tends to view the moral agent as an autonomous individuated bearer of "rights," whereas the female model views the moral agent as a member of a complex, interdependent community in which decisions have an impact not only on the individual, but also on relationships among other members of the intimate group. See generally Carol Gilligan, *In a Different Voice* (1982); Robin West, "Jurisprudence and Gender," 55 *U. Chi. L. Rev.* 1 (1988).

27 Cruzan v. Director, Mo. Dep't of Health, 110 S.Ct. 2841, 2869 (1990) (Brennan, J., dissenting).

28 Id. at 2876.

29 Id.

30 Id. at 2875.

31 Id. at 2878.

32 Id. at 2885 (Stevens J., dissenting), quoting Poe v. Ullman, 367 U.S. 497, 551 (1961) (Harlan, J., dissenting).

33 Id.

34 Id. at 2885–86.

35 Id. at 2886.

Chapter 5

1   Arnold Van Gennep, *The Rites of Passage* (1908) (Monika B. Vizedom and Gabrielle L. Caffee trans., 1960).

2   Ibid.

3   See generally Joel Brereton, Sacred Space, in 4 *Encyclopedia Of Religion* 526 (Mircea Eliade ed., 1989).

4   Van Gennep, *Rites of Passage,* 11.

5   Ibid., 164–65.

6   The Research and Design Institute (REDE) was located in Providence, Rhode Island. It consisted of a group of architects, designers, and social scientists who sought to create "superior configurations for institutional facilities." Ronald Beckman, "The Therapeutic Corridor," 45 *Hospitals* 1, 2 (1971). Because funding dried up, the firm is now defunct. Colin W. Fink is presently a partner with the firm, North Country Team, Inc., of Essex, New York. The hospital was South County Hospital in Wakefield, Rhode Island.

7   Ruth M. Fitzgibbons, "Open-Plan Community Clinic," *Interiors,* Dec. 1974, 72, 74. The medical jargon of the early 1970s referred to this as progressive patient care ("PPC").

8   Carleton Knight III, "Designing for the Health Care Process and Marketplace," *Architecture,* Jan. 1987, 49, 49, quoting Normal Cousins.

9   Michael Wagner, "Healing Revolution," *Interiors,* Dec. 1990, 96, 97. The interior designers of the Planetree Model Hospital Project were Victoria Fay and Associates and architects Kaplan, McLaughlin, and Diaz. The Planetree Project opened in 1985 in the Pacific Presbyterian Medical Center in San Francisco.

10 Gaston Bachelard, *The Poetics of Space* (1958) (Maria Jolas trans., 1964), 4, 5.

11 Kenneth P. Cohen, *Hospice: Prescription for Terminal Care* (1979), 13.

12 Ibid.

13 Paul M. Sachner, "Heroes in Our Own Backyard," *Architectural Rec.,* Nov. 1988, 82, 104.

14 Jack M Zimmerman, *Hospice: Complete Care for the Terminally Ill* (2d ed., 1986).

15 The National Hospice Organization's Standards of a Hospice Program of Care lists the "unit of care" as the "patient/family." Anne Munley, *The Hospice Alternative,* App. A (1983), 320.

16 Leonard Liegner, M.D., "St. Christopher's Hospice, 1974: Care of the Dying Patient," 234 *JAMA* 1047–48 (1975).

17 Lo-Yi Chan, "Hospice: A New Building Type to Comfort the Dying," *Am. Inst. Architects J.,* Dec. 1976, 42.

18 Ibid., 43.

19 Janet Plant, "Finding a Home for Hospice Care in the United States," *Hospitals*, July 1, 1977, 54, 57.

20 Margaret Sanders, "Hospitals: The Prognosis," *Construction Specifier,* Aug. 1991, 46, 52.

21 Mary Baker, "Hospice Contracts Seen Cutting Health Spending," *Cap. Dist. Bus. Rev.,* May 27, 1991, Sec. 1, 1.

Notes to Commentary

Chapter 1

1 Alasdair MacIntyre, *A Short History of Ethics* 135 (1966).

2 Margaret C. Tavolga, "Behavior of the Bottlenose Dolphin," in *Whales, Dolphins, and Porpoises* (Kenneth S. Norris ed., 1966).

3 Harry F. Harlow and Clara Mears, *The Human Model: Primate Perspectives* 1 (1979), quoted in E. W. Menzel, Jr., "How Can You Tell if an Animal Is Intelligent?," in *Dolphin Cognition and Behavior: A Comparative Approach* 167 (Ronald J. Schusterman et al., eds., 1986)

4 John La Puma, M.D., et al., "Talking to Comatose Patients," 45 *Archives of Neurology,* 20, 21 (1988).

5 Shulhan Arukh 335:1 (Chaim N. Denberg trans.) in *Jewish Reflections on Death* 15 (Jack Riemer ed., 1974).

6 Franz Kafka, *The Diaries of Franz Kafka, 1910–23* (Max Brod ed., 1964), 103–104.

7 Louis De Rouvroy Saint-Simon, *Memoires* 486 (1901), quoted in Philippe Aries, *The Hour of Our Death* (1981), 18–19.

8 Aries, *The Hour of Our Death,* 569.

9 Leo Tolstoy, "The Death of Ivan Ilyich" (1886), in *Great Short Works of Leo Tolstoy* (Louise Maude et al., trans., 1967), 247, 301–302.

10 Eric Rhode, "Death in Twentieth-Century Fiction," in *Man's Concern With Death* (Arnold Toynbee et al., eds., 1968), 160.

11 George Rosen, *The Structure of American Medical Practice, 1875–1941* (Charles E. Rosenberg ed., 1983), 2.

12 Ibid., quoting Thomas L. Nichols, *Forty Years of American Life* 226 (1937), 15.

13 Franz Kafka, "A Country Doctor" (1917), in *The Penguin Complete Short Stories of Franz Kafka* (Nahum N. Glatzer ed., 1983), 220, 224.

14 Rosen, "American Medical Practice," 3–4.

15 Webb Garrison, *Strange Facts About Death* 29 (1978).

16 *Death in Literature* 119 (Robert F. Weir ed., 1980).

17 Plato, *Phaedo,* in *The Works of Plato* 109 (Irwin Edman ed. and Benjamin Jowett trans., 1956).

18 John Gardner and John Maier, *Gilgamesh* 67 (1984).

19 Jacob Bigelow, "On Self-limited Diseases" (1836), quoted in *Medical America In The Nineteenth Century* (Gert H. Brieger ed., 1972).

20 "Anointing of the Sick," 1 *New Catholic Encyclopedia* 573 (1967).

21 Ibid.

22 *Jewish Reflections on Death* 16 (Jack Riemer ed., 1974).

23 Lewis Carroll, *Through the Looking Glass and What Alice Found There* (1897) (Octopus Books, 1981), 81–82.

24 Emily Dickinson, "Dying" (1896), in *Final Harvest: Emily Dickinson's Poems* (Thomas H. Johnson ed., 1961), 111–112.

25 Katherine A. Porter, "Pale Horse, Pale Rider" (*The Old Order: Stories of the South*, 1990), 141, 182.

26 Ibid., 199–200.

27 Ibid., 204–205.

28 Morris Adler, "We Do Not Stand Alone," in *Jewish Reflections on Death* (Jack Riemer ed., 1974), 164.

29 Grace Paley, "Fear," in *New and Collected Poems* (1992), 59.

30 *Fresh Air with Terry Gross,* National Public Radio, March 26, 1992.

31 Aries, *The Hour of Our Death,* 571.

32 Ibid., 569.

33 Barbara Pym, *Quartet In Autumn* (1977).

34 John Gunther, *Death Be Not Proud* (1949), 183–89.

35 David Sudnow, *Passing On: The Social Organization of Dying* (1967), 64.

36 Thomas A. Raffin et al., *Intensive Care: Facing The Critical Choices* (1989), 5.

37 Ibid.

38 Molly Haskell, *Love and Other Infectious Diseases: A Memoir* (1990), 149–59.

39 Jain Malkin, "Wayfinding: An Orientation System for Hospitals," *Progressive Architecture,* Nov. 1989, 107.

40 Haskell, *Love and Other Infectious Diseases,* 149–59.

41 Sudnow, *Passing On,* 72–73.

42 Paul Schilder, *The Image and Appearance of the Human Body* (1950), 255, n.1.

43 Maya Deren, *Divine Horsemen: The Living Gods of Haiti* (1953), 42, 43.

44 Schilder, *Image and Appearance of the Human Body,* 44.

45 Seymour Fisher, *Body Experience In Fantasy and Behavior* (1970), describing R. L. Masson, "An Investigation of the Relationship Between Body-image and Attitudes Expressed Toward Visibly Disabled Persons" (1963)(unpublished Ph.D. dissertation, University of Buffalo), 245–56.

46 Jane Van Lawick-Goodall, *In the Shadow of Man* (1971), 217.

47 *In re* Jobes, 529 A. 2d 434, 438 (N.J. 1987).

48   Washington v. Glucksberg, 1997 WL 348094 (U.S.).

49   Vacco v. Quill, 1997 WL 348037 (U.S.).

50   Ibid., 15.

Chapter 2

1   *Compact Edition of the Oxford English Dictionary* (1971), 2054, 491.

2   Owen Fiss, *The Supreme Court 1978 Term,* "Foreword: The Forms of Justice," 93 *Harv. L. Rev.* 1, 13 (1979).

3   Restatement (Second) of Torts §826, §828 (1979).

4   Michael P. McQuillan, M.D., "Can People Who are Unconscious or in the 'Vegetative State' Perceive Pain?" 6 *Issues L. & Med.* 373, 377, 383 (1991).

5   Joseph Quinlan et al., *Karen Ann: The Quinlans Tell Their Story,* citing the trial transcript, 208–224.

6   Quinlan I, 348 A.2d 801, 819 (N.J. Super. Ct. Ch. Div. 1975), modified and remanded, 355 A.2d 647 (N.J.), cert. denied sub nom. Garger v. New Jersey, 429 U.S. 922 (1976).

7   Superintendent of Belchertown State Sch. v. Saikewicz, 370 N. E.2d 417, 428 (Mass. 1977).

8   A. A. Milne, *The House at Pooh Corner* (Ernest H. Shepard illus., 1961), 97–103.

9   George Berkeley, *Three Dialogues between Hylas and Philonous* (1713) (Colin M. Turbayne ed., 1954), 22, 42. For a good explanation of Berkeley's theories, see H. B. Acton, "George Berkeley," in 1 *Encyclopedia of Philosophy* 295 (Paul Edwards ed., 1967); Colin M. Turbayne, Introduction to *Three Dialogues Between Hylas and Philonous.*

10   George H. Mead, *Mind, Self and Society* (Charles W. Morris ed., 1934), 140.

11   *Random House Dictionary of the English Language* 229 (2d ed., 1987); William and Mary Morris, *Harper Dictionary of Contemporary Usage* 574 (2d ed., 1985); *Webster's Third New International Dictionary of the English Language* 1331 (1986).

12   Patricia Williams, *The Alchemy of Race and Rights* (1991), 207–208.

13   Ray Bradbury, "The Other Me," in *Zen in the Art of Writing: Essays on Creativity* (1989), 140–41.

14   Arnold Toynbee, Epilogue to *Man's Concern With Death* (Arnold Toynbee et al., eds., 1968), 257, 267, 270.

15   Cicely Saunders, "Watch With Me," 61 *Nursing Times* 1615, 1617 (1965).

16   Toynbee, *Man's Concern With Death,* 145, 148.

17   Elie Wiesel, "The Death of My Father" in *Legends Of Our Time* (1968), 1, 2.

18   Johannes Nohl, *The Black Death: A Chronicle of the Plague Compiled from Contemporary Sources* (1924) (C. H. Clarke trans., 1961), 73. See generally Philip Ziegler, *The Black Death* (1969) which synthesizes contemporary accounts of medieval plagues and the analyses of modern scholars to present the origins, spread, and social and economic impact of the plagues in Western Europe.

19 Elizabeth Bott, "Urban Families: Conjugal Roles and Social Networks," 8 *Hum. Rel.* 345, 347 n.3 (1955).

20 Peter Linebaugh, "The Tyburn Riot Against the Surgeons," in Douglas Hay et al., *Albion's Fatal Tree* (1975), 65, 67. See also Michel Foucault, *Discipline and Punish* (Alan Sheridan trans., 1977), 32–69.

21 W. Eugene Smith and Aileen Smith, *Minamata* (1975).

22 Kathryn M. Hunter, "Limiting Treatment in a Social Vacuum: A Greek Chorus for William T.," 145 *Arch. Internal Med.* 716, 719 (1985).

23 John Stuart Mill, *On Liberty* (1859) (David Spitz ed., 1975), 11, 14.

24 Carl E. Schneider, "Moral Discourse and the Transformation of American Family Law," 83 *Mich. L. Rev.* 1803, 1840 (1985).

25 Griswold v. Connecticut, 381 U.S. 479, 486 (1965) (finding that privacy rights in the marriage relationship are "older than the Bill of Rights").

26 Roe v. Wade, 410 U.S. 113, 152–53 (1973), citing, respectively, Loving v. Virginia, 388 U.S. 1, 12 (1967); Skinner v. Oklahoma, 316 U.S. 535, 541–42 (1967); Eisenstadt v. Baird, 405 U.S. 438, 453–54 (1972); Pierce v. Society of Sisters, 286 U.S. 510, 535 (1925); Meyer v. Nebraska, 262 U.S. 390, 399 (1923); see also Planned Parenthood of Cent. Mo. v. Danforth, 428 U.S. 52, 69 (1976), holding that "the State may not constitutionally require the consent of the spouse … as a condition for abortion during the first 12 weeks of pregnancy." The law still uses a "rights approach" in these cases, however, regarding the family as a collection of individuals. See Robert A. Burt, "The Constitution of the Family," 1979 *Sup. Ct. Rev.* 329, 331, characterizing the Court's role with respect to the family as "addressing conflicting claims of individual and community, of liberty and authority."

27 Walter O. Weyrauch, "The Family as a Small Group," in *Group Dynamic Law: Exposition and Practice* 153, 154 (David A. Funk ed., 1988).

28 Lee E. Teitelbaum, "Moral Discourse and Family Law," 84 *Mich. L. Rev.* 430, 435 (1985).

29 Neil J. Smelser, *Social Change in the Industrial Revolution: An Application of Theory to the British Cotton Industry* 183 (1959). There have been many excellent recent contributions to the history of families and family law. See, e.g., Michael Grossberg, *Governing the Hearth: Law and the Family in Nineteenth Century America* (1985); Martha Minow, "Forming Underneath Everything that Grows: Toward a History of Family Law," 1985 *Wis. L. Rev.* 819; Lee E. Teitelbaum, "Family History and Family Law," 1985 *Wis. L. Rev.* 1135.

30 Lee E. Teitlebaum, "Moral Discourse and Family Law," 84 *Mich. L. Rev.* 430, 436 (1985).

31 George P. Murdock, *Social Structure* 2–3 (1949).

32 Melford E. Spiro, *Is the Family Universal–The Israel Case*, 56 *Am. Anthropologist* 839 (1954) reprinted in *Nuclear Family in Crisis* 81, 89.

33 Melford E. Spiro, *Addendum*, 1958, in *A Modern Introduction to the Family* (Norman Bell and Ezra Vogel eds., 1968), reprinted in *Nuclear Family in Crisis* 89, 92.

34 Bowers v. Hardwick, 478 U.S. 186, 190 (1986).

35 Laurence H. Tribe, *American Constitutional Law* §15–21, 1422 (2d ed., 1988), quoting Bowers (citations omitted).

36   Braschi v. Stahl Assocs., 543 N. E.2d 49, N.Y. 1989, quoting 9 NYCRR 2204.6(d).

37   Ibid., 50.

38   Ibid., 55.

39   Ibid., 53.

40   Natalia Ginzburg, *Family Sayings* (1963) (D. M. Low trans., 1984), 23–24.

41   Or. Rev. Stat. §109.119(4)(1991). The Oregon statute is modeled on the concept of the "psychological parent." Nancy D. Polikoff, "This Child Does Have Two Mothers: Redefining Parenthood to Meet the Needs of Children in Lesbian-Mother and Other Nontraditional Families," 78 *Geo. L. J.* 459, 487 n. 131 (1990). Polikoff suggests expanding the definition of parenthood to include anyone who performs "parenting functions" and whom the child views as a parent (490–91). Consideration of those parents' "actions and intent … in creating additional parental relationships" would protect the autonomy of the child's legal parents (491); see also Katharine T. Bartlett, "Rethinking Parenthood as an Exclusive Status: The Need for Legal Alternatives When the Promise of the Nuclear Family Has Failed," 70 *Va. L. Rev.* 879 (1984), describing parental rights and responsibilities and proposing an alternative functional test for identifying the "psychological parent".

42   Moore v. City of East Cleveland, 431 U.S. 494, 503–504 (1977) (Powell J.).

43   Village of Belle Terre v. Boraas, 416 U.S. 1 (1974) (no family privacy rights infringed by a local zoning ordinance that excluded households consisting of unrelated persons from living in the village).

44   Smith v. Organization of Foster Families for Equality and Reform (OFFER), 431 U.S. 816 (1977).

45   U.S. Const. Art. III, §§1–2.

46   Judiciary Act of 1789, authorizing Supreme Court review of certain state court constitutional determinations and establishing lower federal courts. Judiciary Act, ch. 20, §13, 1 Stat. 73, 80–81 (1789). For an account of this Act, see Felix Frankfurter and James M. Landis, *The Business of the Supreme Court* 15–25 (1928).

47   Herbert B. Newberg, *On Class Actions* 8 (2d ed., 1985).

48   Fed. R. Civ. P. 23.

49   See, e.g., Minn. R. Civ. P. 23.01.

50   Jack H. Friedenthal et al., *Civil Procedure* 725–26 (1985).

51   Fiss compared a model of adjudication described as "structural reform" to the more traditional "model" lawsuit. Owen Fiss, "The Supreme Court 1978 Term, Foreword: The Forms of Justice," 93 *Harv. L. Rev.* 1, 17–28 (1979). This latter form of lawsuit, which he calls the "dispute resolution model" is "triadic and highly individualistic" (17). Such a lawsuit focuses on some incident of wrongdoing.

Conversely, the "structural reform" suit dwells not on a singular incident of wrongdoing, "but rather upon the conditions of social life and role that large scale organizations play in determining those conditions" (18). The wronged party in a structural reform lawsuit is a group, not an individual. Sometimes the group is defined by institutional affiliation: the inmates of X prison, or recipients of welfare. Professor Fiss suggests two main features of the group. First, it must exist "independently of the lawsuit." Second, the group is more than "simply an aggregation or collection of identifiable individuals." For example, it is not necessary to know the names of prison inmates. Future inmates, not yet identifiable, may be members of the group in the sense that they can be harmed once they become inmates of the institution. The plaintiff in a structural reform lawsuit is not a victim, but a spokesperson for the group (19).

Other scholars have recognized that judicial decisions not only resolve disputes, but also give meaning to our public values. See, e.g., Guido Calabresi, *The Costs of Accidents* (1970), examining the social policies of justice, loss-spreading, and deterrence in a fault-based insurance system; Richard A. Posner, "A Theory of Negligence," 1 *J. Legal Stud.* 29 (1972), asserting that liability for negligence, a judicial creation, brings about an efficient level of safe behavior because rational maximizers will take precautions to avoid mishap only to the extent the cost of avoidance is less than the cost of accident.

52 Stephen C. Yeazell, *From Medieval Group Litigation to the Modern Class Action* 85-96, citing Susan Reynold, *Kingdoms and Communities in Western Europe 900-1300* (1984).

53 Dillon v. Legg, 441 P. 2d 912, 922 (1968).

54 Amaya v. Home Ice, Fuel & Supply Co., 379 P.2d 513, 525 (Cal. 1963), *overruled by* Dillon v. Legg, 441 P.2d 912 (Cal. 1968).

55 William L. Prosser, *Handbook of the Law of Torts* §34, 213-15 (1st ed., 1941).

56 See generally John L. Diamond, "Dillon v. Legg Revisited: Toward a Unified Theory of Compensating Bystanders and Relatives for Intangible Injuries," 35 *Hastings L. J.* 477 (1984),compiling California cases following *Dillon*, suggesting that mechanical application of the "zone of physical danger" rule results in inequitable denial of meritorious claims, and arguing for a unified compensation theory awarding out-of-pocket expenses to all foreseeable plaintiffs.

57 Dillon v. Legg, 441 P. 2d 912, 915 (Cal. 1968).

58 Thing v. LaChusa, 771 P.2d 814 (1989). To support such a claim, the plaintiff must prove three things: a close relationship between the plaintiff and victim; the plaintiff's presence at the scene of the injury-producing event and contemporaneous awareness that the victim was injured; and a resulting serious emotional distress—"a reaction beyond that which would be anticipated in a disinterested witness and which is not an abnormal response to the circumstances." Ibid., 829. See generally Peter A. Bell, "The Bell Tolls: Toward Full Tort Recovery for Psychic Injury," 36 *U. Fla. L. Rev.* 333 (1984), proposing a "full recovery" rule compensating anyone for damages arising from the negligent infliction of emotional distress, to induce caution in would-be tort feasors, to make the largest number of victims whole, and eliminate the potential for exclusion of seriously injured plaintiffs' claims by arbitrary judicial rules; Virginia E. Nolan and Edmund Ursin, "Negligent Infliction of Emotional Distress: Coherence Emerging from Chaos," 33 *Hastings L. J.* 583 (1982), compiling California cases, suggesting that the aftermath of Dillon has been marred by judicial interposition of arbitrary rules as barriers to recovery, and offering the concepts of foreseeability and seriousness of emotional injury as a construct for resolving future cases; Richard N. Pearson, "Liability to Bystanders

for Negligently Inflicted Emotional Harm: A Comment on the Nature of Arbitrary Rules," 34 *U. Fla. L. Rev.* 477 (1982), arguing for a reinstatement of the "zone of danger" rule on the theory that it will most frequently allow recovery by the class of plaintiffs contemplated by the rule.

59 W. Page Keeton et al., *Prosser and Keeton on The Law of Torts* §56 at 374 (5th ed., 1984).

60 Ibid., 375 (citations omitted); see also *Restatement (Second) of Torts* §314 (1965): "The fact that the actor realizes or should realize that action on his part is necessary for another's aid or protection does not of itself impose upon him a duty to take such action." For an early discussion of the failure to impose a duty to rescue, see Francis H. Bohlen, "The Moral Duty to Each Other," Parts I and II, 56 *U. Pa. L. Rev.* 217, 316 (1908). For a more modern treatment of the duty to rescue, including an "economic model of rescue," see William M. Landes and Richard A. Posner, "Salvors, Finders, Good Samaritans, and Other Rescuers: An Economic Study of Law and Altruism," 7 *J. Leg. Stud.* 83 (1978).

61 Wayne R. LaFave, *Criminal Law* §3.3 (2d ed., 1986).

62 See John P. Dawson, Negotiorum Gestio, "The Altruistic Intermeddler," 74 *Harv. L. Rev.* 1073, 1101 (1961); Joel Feinberg, "The Moral and Legal Responsibility of the Bad Samaritan," *Crim. J. Ethics*, Winter/Spring 1984, 56, 68, arguing in favor of imposing more positive duties of assistance on bystanders in cases of "sudden and anticipated peril to others that require immediate attention, and are such that a bystander can either make an 'easy rescue' himself or else sound the alarm to notify those whose job it is to make difficult rescues".

63 Dan B. Dobbs, *Handbook on the Law of Remedies* §4.1 at 222 (1973).

64 Ibid., §3.9, at 204.

65 Ibid., §12.2, at 795–96.

66 Ibid., § 2.10, at 105.

67 Barbara G. Walker, *The Woman's Encyclopedia of Myths and Secrets* 168 (1983).

68 Jeremy Bentham, "A Fragment on Government" (1776), in 1 *Works of Jeremy Bentham* 221, 235 n.s (John Bowring ed., Edinburgh, 1843).

69 Jeremy Bentham, "Elements Of Packing as Applied to Juries" (1821), in 5 *Works of Jeremy Bentham*, 61, 92.

70 Jeremy Bentham, Preface intended for the Second Edition of a Fragment on Government (1822), in *A Comment on the Commentaries and a Fragment on Government* 502, 511 (James H. Burns and H. L. A Hart eds., 1977)

71 Roscoe Pound, *Spurious Interpretation*, 7 *Colum.L.Rev.* 379, 382 (1907). See also Lon Fuller, *Legal Fictions* (1967) and John C. Gray, *The Nature and Source of the Law* 30–7 (1921), which both criticize the use of pretense in judicial decision making. For a later twentieth-century discussion on legal fictions, see Avi Soifer, *Reviewing Legal Fictions* 20 *Ga.L.Rev.* 821 (1986).

72 Cruzan v. Harmon, 760 S. W.2d 408, 424–26 (Mo. 1988) (en banc), aff'd sub nom. Cruzan v. Director, Mo. Dep't of Health, 110 S. Ct. 2841 (1990).

73 Ibid., 411.

74 Ibid., 424–26.

75 Cruzan v. Director, Mo. Dep't. of Health, 110 S. Ct. 2841 (1990).

76 Tamar Lewin, "Nancy Cruzan Dies, Outlived by Debate Over Right to Die," *N.Y. Times,* Dec. 27, 1990, A1.

77 Amartya K. Sen and Bernard Williams, Introduction to *Utilitarianism and Beyond* 1, 3–4 (Amartya K. Sen and Bernard Williams eds., 1982).

78 John LaPuma, M.D., and Edward F. Lawlor, Ph.D., "Quality-Adjusted Life-Years: Ethical Implications for Physicians and Policymakers" 263 *JAMA* 2917, 2917 (1990).

79 Ibid.

80 John L. Mackie, *Ethics: Inventing Right and Wrong* 125 (1977).

81 J. J. C. Smart, *Utilitarianism,* in 8 *Encyclopedia of Philosophy* 206 (Paul Edwards ed., 1967.)

82 Ibid.

83 Sen and Williams, Introduction to *Utilitarianism and Beyond.*

84 Jeremy Bentham, *An Introduction to the Principles of Morals and Legislation* 2 (2d ed., 1823).

85 Mary Warnock, Introduction to John Stuart Mill, *Utilitarianism, On Liberty, Essay on Bentham* 1, 9 n.1 (Mary Warnock ed., 1962).

86 Amartya K. Sen, "Utilitarianism and Welfarism," 9 *J. Phil.* 463 (1979), quoted in J. A. Mirrlees, "The Economic Uses of Utilitarianism," in Sen and Williams, *Utilitarianism and Beyond,* 63, 64.

87 Lejeune v. Rayne Branch Hosp., 556 So. 2d 559 (La. 1990).

88 *In re* Spring, 405 N. E. 2d 115 (Mass. 1980). Lee J. Dunn and Nancy E. Ator, Vox Clamantis in Deserto, "Do You Really Mean What You Say in Spring," in *Legal and Ethical Aspects of Treating Critically and Terminally Ill Patients* 177–78 (A. Edward Doudera and J. Douglas Peters eds., 1982); see also Peter M. Horstman, "Protective Services for the Elderly: The Limits of Parens Patriae," 40 *MO. L. Rev.* 212 (1975), arguing for the introduction of full adversary proceedings before appointing guardians for the elderly; S. Van McCrary and Terry A. Walman, "Procedural Paternalism in Competency Determination," 18 *Law, Med. & Health Care* 108 (1990), concluding that full procedural protections—including the right to confront witnesses, an appropriate standard of proof, consideration of alternative actions, and an objective and impartial review board—are necessary to safeguard the interests of the alleged incompetent in guardianship proceedings. For a discussion of efforts by states to revise their guardianship statutes, see Penelope A. Hommell et al., "Trends in Guardianship Reform: Implications for the Medical and Legal Professions" 18 *Law, Med. & Health Care* 213 (1990).

89 Washington v. Glucksberg, 1997 WL348094, 17 (U.S.).

90 "In the 11 years from 1976 to 1987, spending for medical care exceeded inflation by almost 80%. In 1987, national health expenditures were $0.5 trillion, 11.1% of the gross national product. Spending for federal Medicare and Medicaid programs has grown from $70 billion in 1982 to $111 billion in 1987. Many factors contribute to rising health care costs: inflation of hospital and health care provider costs, the emergence of new diseases and disorders, and the development of new diagnostic and therapeutic modalities." Edward E. Schneider, M.D., and Jack M. Guralnick, Ph.D., "The Aging of America: Impact on Health Care Costs," 263

JAMA 2335, 2336 (1990). Joseph Richman, "Sanctioned Assisting Suicide: Impact on Family Relations," 3 *Issues L. & Med.* 53, 131 (1987).

91 Ibid.

92 Schneider and Guralnick, "Aging of America," 2337.

93 Phillippa Foot, "Euthanasia," 7 *Phil. & Pub. Aff.* 85 (1977).

94 *In re* President and Directors of Georgetown College 311 F.2d 1000 (D. C. Cir. 1963).

95 Ibid., 1006–07.

96 Guido Calabresi, *Ideals, Beliefs, Attitudes, and the Law* 83 (1985).

Chapter 3

1 John W. Levy, "Differential Perceptual Capacities in Major and Minor Hemispheres," 61 *Proc. Nat'l. Acad. Sci.* 1151 (1968).

2 Roger W. Sperry, "Lateral Specialization of Cerebral Function in the Surgically Separated Hemispheres," in *The Psychophysiology of Thinking* 209 (Frank J. McGuigan and R. A. Schoonover eds., 1973).

3 Raymond J. Deverette, "Neocortical Death and Human Death," 18 *Law, Med. & Health Care* 96, 103 n.13 (1990). For another work discussing the significance of metaphor in our discourse about illness, see Susan Sontag, *Illness as Metaphor* (1977).

Chapter 4

1 Alfred J. Ayer, *Language, Truth and Logic* 33 (1952).

2 Ibid., 45.

3 Thomas Nagel, "Death," in *Mortal Questions* 1, 3 (1979).

4 Reynolds v. United States, 98 U.S. 145, 161, 166 (1878).

5 Joan M. Gibson and Robert L. Schwartz, "Physicians and Lawyers: Science, Art, and Conflict," 6 *Am. J. L. & Med.* 173, 178 (1980).

6 Plato, *Phaedo*, in *The Works of Plato* 120 (Irwin Edman ed. and Benjamin Jowett trans., 1956).

7 Ibid.

8 Plato, *Alcibiades*, reprinted in *Body, Mind and Death* 36–37 (Anthony Flew ed., 1964).

9 *Phaedo*, 141.

10 Ibid.

11 *Phaedo*, 177.

12 John Milton, "Comus" (1634), in *The Poems of John Milton* 168, 199–200 (John Carey and Alastair Fowler eds., 1966).

13 Ninian Smart, "Death and the Decline of Religion in Western Society," in *Man's Concern with Death*, 138, 140 (Arnold Toynbee et al., eds., 1968).

14 Ibid., 139.

15 Aristotle, *De Anima* 8–9 (John L. Ackrill ed. and David W. Hamlyn trans., 1968).

16 David W. Hamlyn, Introduction to *De Anima*, x, xi. This account of Aristotle's beliefs regarding the immortality of the soul is unavoidably simplistic. True, Aristotle concluded "the soul does not exist without a body and yet is not itself a kind of body. For it is not a body, but something which belongs to a body, and for this reason exists in a body" *(De Anima,* 14). Other passages in *De Anima*, however, suggest that personal immortality exists in some fashion due to the "eternal" nature of the active intellect. In discussing the active and passive intellect, Aristotle referred to the active intellect as "immortal and eternal." Hamlyn suggested that the text of this passage may be corrupt *(De Anima,* translator's notes, 141). Taking the "least extravagant" interpretation, "Aristotle provides no grounds here for any kind of belief in personal immortality" (142). Not all scholars agree, however, and there have been many conflicting interpretations of this passage. Even with these multiple interpretations of Aristotle, "it is illuminating to regard Aristotle as the archetypal protagonist of the alternative and opposite view of the nature of man, even though he was neither so consistent nor so wholehearted a monist as Plato was dualist" (Flew, Introduction to *Body, Mind and Death,* 1, 9).

17 *De Anima,* 9.

18 Ibid., 10.

19 Rene Descartes, *Discourse on Method* (1637) (Elizabeth S. Haldane and G. R. T. Ross trans., 1931), quoted in *Body, Mind and Death,* 129.

20 Flew, Introduction to *Body, Mind and Death,* 24.

21 Gilbert Ryle, *The Concept of Mind* 15–16 (1949).

22 Ninian Smart, "Attitudes Towards Death in Eastern Religions," in *Man's Concern with Death,* 95, 96.

23 Ibid., 97.

24 Ghassan Kanafani, "The Death of Bed Number 12," reprinted in *Modern Arabic Short Stories,* 28, 29 (Denys Johnson-Davies ed. and trans., 1976).

25 Sigmund Freud, "Thoughts for Times of War and Death" (1915), in *Standard Edition of the Complete Psychological Works* 273, 298 (James Strachey et al., eds. and trans., 1957). For a study of Western attitudes toward death, see Ernest Becker, *The Denial of Death,* ix (1973).

26 In some states, the requirements for valid living wills, including sample forms, can be found in what are called "Natural Death Acts." California enacted the first such statute in 1976. Cal. Health and Safety Code §§7185–7194.5 (West Supp. 1992). An alternative to natural death acts is the durable power of attorney statute. With a power of attorney, the patient appoints an agent to act on his behalf. This agent can make medical decisions for the incompetent patient, including the decision to terminate life-support systems. A majority of states now have some form of "living will" legislation, "right to die" legislation, "natural death acts," or "durable power of attorney" statutes. See Judith Areen, "Advance Directives Under State Law and Judicial Decisions," 19 *Law, Med. & Health Care* 91 (1991).

27 Paul Schilder, *The Image and Appearance of the Human Body* 205 (1950).

28 Jessie Taft, *Otto Rank* 175 (1958), quoting a letter from Otto Rank to Jessie Taft, Feb. 8, 1933.

29 Ernest Becker, *The Denial of Death*, ix (1973).

30 Ibid., 17, quoting Gregory Zilboorg, *Fear of Death*, 12 *Psychoanalytic Q.* 468–71 (1943).

31 Alfred R. Radcliffe-Brown, *Structure and Function in Primitive Society* 133 (1952).

32 Joseph Epstein, "But I Generalize," in *The Middle of My Tether: Familiar Essays*, 189, 199 (1983).

33 Radcliffe-Brown, *Structure and Function*, 135.

34 Ibid., 148; see also Mary Douglas, *Purity and Danger: An Analysis of Concepts of Pollution and Taboo* 140–58 (1966), discussing primitive sexual rituals and their role in maintaining social structures.

35 Ibid., 183, 191–200.

36 Sigmund Freud, *Totem and Taboo* (1913), 51–74 (James Strachey trans., 1950). For another discussion of "tabooed words," see Sir James George Frazier, *The New Golden Bough* 107–12 (Theodor H. Gaster ed., 1961).

37 Mary O'Brien, *The Politics of Reproduction* 156 (1983).

38 Virginia Held, "Birth and Death," reprinted in *Feminism and Political Theory* 87, 95 (Cass R. Sunstein ed., 1990).

39 Geoffrey Gorer, "The Pornography of Death" (1955), reprinted in Geoffrey Gorer, *Death, Grief and Mourning*, App. 4, 195 (1965).

40 Ibid., 195, 196, 199.

41 Thomas Mann, *The Magic Mountain* (1924), 291–92 (H. T. Lowe-Porter trans., 1951).

42 See John Stuart Mill, *On Liberty* (1859), reprinted in *Utilitarianism, On Liberty, Essay on Bentham*, 126, 205–208. For a discussion of the taboos existing in the practice of law, see Walter O. Weyrauch, *The Personality of Lawyers: A Comparative Study of Subjective Factors in Law, Based on Interviews with German Lawyers* 140–43 (1964).

43 Radcliffe-Brown, *Structure and Function*, 133–41.

44 *Handbook on Irish Genealogy* 11 (1978).

45 Rosamunde Pilcher, "September" (1990), quoting Henry Scott Holland (1847–1918). I am grateful for the assistance of Rosamunde Pilcher in identifying the author of this beautiful passage.

46 *The Catholic Encyclopedia* 154 (Robert C. Broderick ed., 1976), citing Matthew 27:50, Acts 7:59, and Colossians 2:20, 3:1–11.

47 Tom L. Beauchamp and James F. Childress, *Principles of Biomedical Ethics* 126–27 (2d ed.,1983). See also John J. Paris, "Terminating Treatment for Newborns: A Theological Perspective" 10 *Law, Med. & Health Care* 120 (1982), criticizing the widespread belief that life and technology are the ultimate values, without regard to medical prognosis or cost of medical treatment; J. Stuart Showalter, "Determining Death: The Legal and Theological Aspects of Brain-Related Criteria," 27 *Cath. Law.* 112, 114–16 (1982), explaining the Catholic view that death is not final, and therefore all possible means do not have to be used to keep a person alive.

48 Gerald Kelly, *Medico-Moral Problems*, quoted in Paul Ramsey, *The Patient as Person* 122 (1970).

49 Judith Areen et al., *Law, Science and Medicine* 111 (1984), quoting "The Prolongation of Life," 4 *The Pope Speaks* 393, 397 (1958).

50 Ibid.

51 E.g., Ronald Sullivan, "State Says Hospital to Revive a Dying Patient," *N.Y. Times*, Nov. 20, 1984, B6.

52 See, e.g., Robert Kastenbaum and Ruth Aisenberg, *The Psychology of Death* 55–64, 44 (1972).

53 Jacques Choron, *Modern Man and Mortality* 70–83 (1964).

54 Ian S. Madfes, "Death Anxiety and Related Characteristics Among Hospice and Nonhospice Nurses" 18 (1990) (unpublished Ph.D. dissertation, California School of Professional Psychology, Berkeley/Alameda).

55 Herman Feifel et al., "Physicians Consider Death," 2 *Am. Psychol. Ass'n. Proc.* 201, 201–202 (1967).

56 Joyce B. Cochrane, "Death Anxiety, Disclosure Behaviors, and Attitudes of Oncologists Towards Terminal Care" 19 (1987) (Unpublished Ed.D. dissertation, Temple University). For a summary of the various studies done on avoidance behavior by medical professionals about terminal care, see Harriet Goodman, "Death Work: Staff Perspectives on the Care of Terminally Ill Patients in an Acute Care Hospital" 15–19 (1990) (Unpublished Ph.D. dissertation, City University of New York).

57 David Sudnow, *Passing On: The Social Organization of Dying* 74 (1967).

58 Irvin D. Yalom, M.D. and Carlos Greaves, M.D., "Group Therapy with the Terminally Ill," 134 *Am. J. Psychiatry* 396, 398 (1977).

59 Seymour Fisher, *Body Experience in Fantasy and Behavior* 114 (1970).

60 Edith Jacobson, "Depersonalization," 1959 *J. Am. Psychoanalytic Ass'n.* 581–83.

61 Erik H. Erikson, "Ego Development and Historical Change," in *Identity and the Life Cycle* 18, 49 (1 *Psych. Issues* 1959).

62 Brian Clark, *Whose Life Is it Anyway?* 91 (1978).

63 John Hinton, "The Dying and the Doctor," in *Man's Concern with Death* 30, 37 (Arnold Toynbee et al, eds., 1968).

64 Leonard Liegner, M.D., "St. Christopher's Hospice, 1974: Care of the Dying Patient" 234 *JAMA* 1048, 1048 (1975).

65 Melvin J. Krant, M.D., *Dying and Dignity: The Meaning and Control of a Personal Death* 13 (1974).

66 Donald Oken, M.D., "What to Tell Cancer Patients: A Study of Medical Attitudes," 175 *JAMA* 1120, 1122 (1961).

67 Dennis H. Novak, M.D., et al., "Changes in Physicians' Attitudes Towards Telling the Cancer Patient," 241 *JAMA* 897, 898 (1979). But see Alan Meisel and Loren H. Roth, "Toward an Informed Discussion of Informed Consent: A Review and Critique of the Empirical Studies," 25 *Ariz. L. Rev.* 265 (1983), criticizing the reliance placed on these studies.

68 Jay Katz, *The Silent World of Doctor and Patient* 85–103 (1984). For another plea for a conversation between doctor and patient, and in particular for the patient to take the initiative, see Michael R. Flick, "The Due Process of Dying," 79 *Cal. L. Rev.* 1121, 1162–63 (1991).

69 Diane L. Redleaf et al., Note, "The California Natural Death Act: An Empirical Study of Physicians' Practices" 31 *Stan. L. Rev.* 913, 917 (1979).

70 Flick, "Due Process," 1166 n.165.

71 Wallace I. Sampson, M.D., "Dying at Home" 238 *JAMA* 2405, 2406 (1977).

72 G. E. Burch, M.D., "Of the Family of the Sick" 92 *Am. Heart J.* 405, 405 (1976).

73 Washington v. Glucksberg, 1997 WL 3480894 (U.S.); Vacco v. Quill, 1997 WL 348037 (U.S.).

Chapter 5

1 Roy Rappaport, *Ecology, Meaning and Religion* 206 (1979).

2 Edmund R. Leach, *Ritual*, in 13 *International Encyclopedia of the Social Sciences* 520, 524 (David L. Sills ed., 1968).

3 Evan M. Zuesse, *Ritual*, in 12 *Encyclopedia of Religion* 405 (Mircea Eliade ed., 1989). These very broad definitions eliminate the religious component of ritual.

4 Victor W. Turner, *From Ritual to Theatre* 79 (1982).

5 Zuesse, 12 *Encyclopedia of Religion*, 405.

6 Sally Falk Moore and Barbara G. Myerhoff, Introduction to *Secular Ritual* 3, 9 (Sally Falk Moore and Barbara G. Myerhoff eds., 1977).

7 Mircea Eliade, *Patterns in Comparative Religion* (1948), 370–71 (Rosemary Sheed trans., 1958).

8 Ibid., 396–98.

9 Joel Brereton, *Sacred Space*, in 4 *Encyclopedia of Religion*, 526, 526.

10 Ibid., 528–29. See generally Eliade, *Patterns in Comparative Religion*, 367–87, and *The Sacred and the Profane: The Nature of Religion*, 20–67 (Willard R. Trask, trans., 1959), setting the agenda for recent scholarship on sacred spaces.

   Since so many rituals in the deathwatch go beyond just communication with divinity, I will use the term "ritual space" from here on, except when directly referring to van Gennep's theory.

11 Victor W. Turner, *The Ritual Process* 95 (1969).

12 Walter O. Weyrauch, "The Family as a Small Group," in *Group Dynamic Law: Exposition and Practice* 166 (David A. Funk ed., 1988).

13 Joachim Wach, *Sociology of Religion* 66, 67 (1944).

14 5 *Encyclopedia Judaica* 1426 (1972).

15 For the laws and customs regarding the treatment of the sick, dying, and the dead, see *Code of Jewish Law*, §§192–94 (Rabbi Solomon Ganzfried ed. and Hyman E. Goldin trans., 1991).

For a general discussion of the Talmudic sources and various codes of Jewish law on the modern treatment of the *goses* and related ethical issues, see Fred Rosner, *Modern Medicine and Jewish Ethics* 197–203 (1986); see also *Jewish Bioethics* 266–316 (Fred Rosner and J. David Bleich eds., 1979), confronting ethical issues surrounding death and dying; *Jewish Medical Law* 148–54 (Avraham Steinberg, M.D., ed. and David B. Simons, M.D., trans., 1989), outlining Jewish ethical codes and principles concerning medical care, the treatment of the dying, and procedures after a patient's death.

I am grateful to my friend and colleague, Jeffrey I. Roth, for his assistance in the research on Jewish law.

16 Sally Falk Moore, *Law as Process: An Anthropological Approach* 40–41 (1978).

17 Rosemary J. McKeighen, "A Study of Expectancy and Family Grief Reactions" 21 (1967) (unpublished M. S. thesis, University of California, Los Angeles).

18 Ibid., 75, 77.

19 See generally Louise Harmon and Deborah Waire Post, *Cultivating Intelligence: Law, Power and the Politics of Teaching* (1996). While Deborah has given me many insights, and we do swim together, she is emphatically not the woman in the pool. Actually, the woman in the pool is a composite of several friends with whom I share ideas, including the more lawyerly portions of myself. This confession is dedicated to my husband, Daniel P. Jordan Jr., who has a historian's respect for the truth. He would also like me to confess that I have never taught Civil Procedure, but I refuse to on the grounds that it is never advisable to do everything your spouse wants.

20 Suzanne K. Langer, *Feeling and Form*, 92–93 (1953).

21 Ibid., 96.

22 Letter from Colin Fink, partner, North Country Team, Inc., to Louise Harmon, Associate Professor, Jacob D. Fuchsberg Law Center, Touro College, May 9, 1992 (on file with *Minnesota Law Review*).

23 Lynn Nesmith, "Designing for 'Special Populations,'" *Architecture*, Jan. 1987, 62.

24 Karin Tetlow, "Healthy Color," *Interiors*, Dec. 1989, 94.

25 Ibid.

26 Joseph A. Koncelik, *Designing the Open Nursing Home*, citing Leon A. Pastalan, "Privacy Preferences Among Relocated Institutionalized Elderly," in EDRA5 (Environmental Research Ass'n, Inc., ed., 1974), 14 (1976).

27 Michael Crosbie, "Reassuring Setting for High-Tech Medicine," *Architecture*, Jan. 1987, 43.

28 "Wythenshawe Hospital Maternity Unit," *Architects' J.*, March 30, 1966, reprinted in *British Hospital and Health-Care Buildings* 192, 199 (Peter Stone ed., 1980).

29 "Paisley and Stirling Maternity Units," *Architects' J.*, Nov. 4, 1970, reprinted in *British Hospital and Health-Care Buildings*, 205, 212.

30 Judith Davidsen, "Birthing Center," *Interior Design*, Nov. 1990, 190, 192. See also Margaret F. Gaskie, "Making Special Care Special," *Architectural Rec.*, June 1990, 98, 98–101, describing another birthing center design in Miami.

31 Karin Tetlow, "Design Heals," *Interiors*, Dec. 1990, 61, 62, 64.

32 Roger S. Ulrich, "View Through a Window May Influence Recovery from Surgery" 224 *Science* 420 (1989).

33 Ibid.

34 Margaret Sanders, "Hospitals: The Prognosis," *Construction Specifier,* Aug. 1991, 46, 52.

35 Wallace Shawn and Andre Gregory, *My Dinner with Andre* , 61–62 (1981).

36 Kent C. Bloomer and Charles W. Moore, *Body, Memory and Architecture* 45–49 (1977).

37 Christian Norberg-Schultz, *Existence, Space and Architecture* 86, 88 (1971).

38 Bloomer and Moore, *Body, Memory and Architecture,* 47.

39 Charles Boyce, *Dictionary of Furniture* 26 (1985).

40 Joseph Aronson, *The Encyclopedia of Furniture* 37–43 (3d ed., 1965).

41 Laszlo Aranyi and Larry L. Goldman, *Design of Long-Term Care Facilities* 24, 20 (1980).

42 Norberg-Schultz, *Existence, Space and Architecture,* 31–32.

43 Ibid., 32.

44 Kenneth P. Cohen, *Hospice: Prescription for Terminal Care* 13 (1979).

45 Ibid., 14–15.

46 Ibid., 17–18, 19.

47 Ruth Huber and John W. Gibson, "New Evidence for Anticipatory Grief," 6 *Hospice J.* 49, 55, 65 (1990). See also Linda L. Steele, "The Death Surround: Factors Influencing the Grief Experience of Survivors," 17 *Oncology Nursing J.* 235 (1990), finding that survivors of terminally ill people who had participated in a hospice program prior to the death showed "decreased feelings of guilt, dependency, loss of control, despair, numbness, shock and disbelief."

48 David K. Reynolds, Ph.D., and Richard A. Kalish, Ph.D., "The Social Ecology of Dying: Observations of Wards for the Terminally Ill," 25 *Hosp. & Community Psychiatry* 147, 148 (1974).

49 Dr. Timothy E. Quill, "Risk Taking by Physicians in Legally Gray Areas," 57 *Albany L.Rev.* 693, 699 (1994).

50 Ibid., 700.

51 Morris D. Kerstein, M.D., "Caring for the Terminally Ill: A Hospice," 129 *Am. J. Psychiatry* 237–238 (1972) (letter to the editor).

52 Henry S. Perkins, M.D., and Albert R. Jonsen, M.D., "Dying Right in Theory and Practice: What Do We Really Know of Terminal Care?" 145 *Arch. Internal Med.* 1460, 1460–63 (1985).

53 Ibid., 1462.

54 Monica Geran, "Hospice for Children," *Interior Design,* Feb. 1986, 192, 194.

55 *Architectural Rec.,* June 1986, 116, reviewing Janet R. Carpman et al., "Design that Cares: Planning Health Facilities for Patients and Visitors" (1986).

56 Ibid.

57 Robert J. Miller, "Hospice Care as an Alternative to Euthanasia," 20 *Law, Med. and Health Care* 127, 132 (1992).

58 "On Death and Dying: The Final Hurry," 32 *The Economist,* Mar. 22, 1997.

59 David S. Gochman and Gordon S. Bonham, "The Social Structure of the Hospice Decision," 6 *Hospice J.* 15, 30, 32 (1990).

60 Muriel Dobbin, "Government Acts to Curb Procedures at Life's End: 'Palliative Care' Code Aims at Treatment for Terminally Ill Patients," *Rocky Mountain News,* April 13, 1997, 46a.

61 Ibid.

62 Jacqueline Shaheen, "New Jersey Q & A: Making the Decision for Hospice Care," *N.Y. Times,* Mar. 24, 1991, Sec. 12, 3.

63 Ann Armstrong-Dailey, "Children's Hospice Care," 16 *Pediatric Nursing* 337, 339 (1990).

64 Ibid.

65 "On Death and Dying," *The Economist,* Mar. 22, 1997, 32.

66 Congressional conferees and administration negotiators on a health care bill have accepted a House redefinition of the Medicare hospice benefit as two ninety-day periods, followed by an unlimited number of sixty-day periods, each of which must be certified by a physician. "Perspectives: Caution Mixes with Courage in Sweeping Health Care Bill," in *Faulkner & Gray's Medicine & Health,* Aug. 4, 1997, no. 31, vol. 51.

67 Janet Plant, "Finding a Home for Hospice Care in the United States," *Hospitals,* July 1, 1997, 58–61.

68 Marjorie C. Dobratz, "Hospice Nursing: Present Perspective and Future Directives" 13 *Cancer Nursing* 116 (1990).

69 Michael Kearney, "Hospice Medicine," in *Ideas in Health Care* 15, 28 (D. Seedhouse and A. Cribb eds., 1989).

70 Press Release, Office of Public Affairs, M.D. Anderson Cancer Center, University of Texas, Oct. 12, 1990.

71 Medicare Catastrophic Coverage Repeal Act of 1989, Pub. L. No. 101–234, §101(b)(2), 103 Stat. 1979, 1980 (1989).

72 Mary Baker, "Hospice Contracts Seen Cutting Health Spending," *Cap. Dist. Bus. Rev.,* May 27, 1991, §1, at 1.

73 Ibid.

74 William G. Bartholome, "Physician-Assisted Suicide, Hospice, and Rituals of Withdrawal," 24 *Journal of Law, Medicine & Ethics* 233, 235–36 (1996).

Acknowledgments

I COULD never have written this book without the valuable assistance of a lot of people. There was a core of excellent and faithful research assistants who helped out with this version of the book. I am particularly indebted to Tiombe Tallie-Russell, Daphna Zekaria, and Allan Chambers. I would also like to thank the staff of the Touro Law Library for their courteous, competent, and dogged pursuit of arcane materials.

I benefited greatly from skillful editing, first by Elizabeth Cumming of the *Minnesota Law Review,* and then later by my friend, Charles Wheeler, and by Susan Meigs for Beacon Press. Deborah Chasman at Beacon had the vision to see the original work in a new and different way; she is the one who imagined the metamorphosis. Amelia Wilson helped me take apart the old and put together the new, and I could have done neither without her.

I am grateful to the *Minnesota Law Review,* and in particular to its editor-in-chief, J. Jeffery Oxley, for publishing *Fragments* in its first incarnation, and for granting me permission to transform the original law review article into a book. The poem "The Other Me," by Ray Bradbury, is reprinted by permission from Don Congdon Associates, Inc., copyright © 1990 by Ray Bradbury Enterprises. The poem "Fear," by Grace Paley, from her *New and Collected Poems* (1992) is reprinted with permission from her publisher, Tilbury House. The photograph of Edvard Munch's painting "Death in the Sick-Room" was taken by J. Lathion copyright © Nasjonalgalleriet, Oslo, and is reproduced with their permission and that of the Munch Museum, copyright © The Munch-Ellingsen Group, Artists Rights Society, New York.

Finally, my thanks to my family—to my sister, Mimi, and my brother, John, and to our beloved mother, Cosme, for sharing our father's deathwatch. And, of course, all my gratitude to my husband, Dan, and our children, Nan, Kate, and Jo. I do nothing in life without their love and support.

Index